CREATIVE meetings BIBLE LESSONS, & WORSHIP IDEAS

THE ideas LIBRARY

FOR YOUTH GROUPS

THE IDEAS LIBRARY

CREATIVE
meetings
BIBLE LESSONS,
& WORSHIP
IDEAS

FOR YOUTH GROUPS

THE ideas LIBRARY

Youth Specialties

ZondervanPublishingHouse
Grand Rapids, Michigan
A Division of HarperCollinsPublishers

Project editor: Vicki Newby
Cover design: Curt Sell
Interior design: Curt Sell and PAZ Design Group
Art director: Mark Rayburn

Printed in the United States of America

03 04 05 06 /VG/ 14 13 12 11 10

CONTENTS

Looking for a meeting about a specific topic? Locate the topic you want to cover in your lesson, then choose an idea. (Worship ideas are not indexed here, since their topics are sufficiently clear on page 6 where they're listed.)

Here's where you can glance down the list of Bible books (listed in Bible order, Genesis to Revelation), locate the chapter and verse you want to teach on, then read where to find an idea in this book for that Bible passage.

Some ideas are based on only a verse or two; others are based on entire chapters. For example, the lesson "Esther and the King" deals with the entire book of Esther, while Exodus 20 is the subject of "Signposts to Life."

So what Bible lesson did you create that caught your group off guard—and got them thinking hard about Scripture, themselves, and God?

Are your kids still talking that creative meeting last month? Youth Specialties pays $40 (and in some cases, more) for unpublished, field-tested ideas that have worked for you.

You've probably been in youth work long enough to realize that sanitary, theoretical, tidy ideas aren't what in-the-trenches youth workers are looking for. They want—you want—imagination and take-'em-by-surprise novelty in meetings, arties, and other events. Ideas that have been tested and tempered and improved in the very real, very adolescent world you work in.

So what do you do now?
• Sit down at your computer, get your killer meeting or Bible lesson out of your head and onto your hard drive, then e-mail it to Ideas@YouthSpecialties.com. Or print it off and fax it to 619-440-0582 (Attn: Ideas).
• If you need to include diagrams, photos, art, or samples that help explain your idea, stick it all in an envelope and mail it to our street address: Ideas, 300 S. Pierce St., El Cajon, CA 92020.
• Be sure to include your name, your addresses, phone numbers, and e-mail address.
• Let us have a few months to give your idea a thumbs up or down*, and a little longer for your money.

*Hey, no offense intended if your idea isn't accepted. It's just that our fussy Ideas Library editor has these *really* meticulous standards. If the meeting, Bible lesson, or worship idea isn't creative, original, and delightfully instructive, she'll reject it (reluctantly, though, because she has a tender heart). Sorry. But we figure you deserve only the best ideas.

BIBLE STUDY
METHODS

In this section aren't lessons per se, but rather methods, techniques, and approaches for teaching any Bible lesson, whether topical and scriptural. They can also be adapted to fit just about any group—even groups of kids who aren't familiar with the Bible

ABC BIBLE STUDY

Here's a creative way to get kids more actively involved in Bible study. Give them a passage of Scripture (several verses or an entire chapter if you are working your way through a book of the Bible) and have them locate the items listed on the handout on page 16. Have the kids share their answers with each other, discuss, and close with conversational prayer. *Marsha Dealey*

8-STEP BIBLE STUDY

These eight steps can help young people to have more effective personal Bible studies, or they can be used to give direction to group Bible studies as well. Have the kids break into small groups of three or four and work through an assigned passage of Scripture, using the steps below. Then have the small groups each share highlights of their Bible study with the entire group at the close of the meeting period. *Bob Gleason*

1. Before beginning your study, pray: "Father, reveal some new truth to me in this study. Speak to me as you have never spoken before..."

2. Read the assigned passage through at least five times, in as many different versions and translations as you have.
3. What do you consider the two most important lessons of the passage?
4. What did God say to you personally, that you needed most to hear? Write it down and share it with someone.
5. What new truth, if any, did you discover from this passage of Scripture?
6. What does this text teach about Jesus?
7. Were there any difficulties in understanding any portion of the text? If so, how did you resolve it?
8. What change, if any, do you intend to make in your life or your thinking as a result of this study?

QUESTIONS AND INSPIRATIONS

Here is a simple but effective method of Bible study that works very well with junior high and high school young people. The time allotted for this method can be adjusted to your particular time frame. In general, however, you should allow 10 to 15 minutes reading time for each chapter or section you are studying. Ask the young people to read the assigned passages and write out at least one question and one thing they learned or were inspired

ABC Bible Study

Locate the following in today's passage of Scripture:

The theme of the passage. _____

The BEST verse. _____

The most CHALLENGING verse. _____

The most DIFFICULT verse to do or understand. _____

The most ENCOURAGING verse. _____

Your FAVORITE verse. _____

A GIFT from God. _____

The most HELPFUL verse. _____

The most INFORMATIVE verse. _____

ABC Bible Study

Locate the following in today's passage of Scripture:

The theme of the passage. _____

The BEST verse. _____

The most CHALLENGING verse. _____

The most DIFFICULT verse to do or understand. _____

The most ENCOURAGING verse. _____

Your FAVORITE verse. _____

A GIFT from God. _____

The most HELPFUL verse. _____

The most INFORMATIVE verse. _____

by. After this has been completed, break into small groups of at least five (if you have a small youth group of less than 10, then keep everyone together) and spend whatever time it takes sharing each one's questions and inspirations.

The main benefit of this simple system is that in the sharing process the group teaches itself. The leader takes a very low profile as a facilitator and becomes the speaker/teacher only when the group has no explanation of someone's question. Many times one person's inspiration is directly related to someone else's question. *Vic Varkonyi*

HUMAN SLIDE SHOW

Here's a nifty way to present a Bible passage or story. Break your group into different groups and give each one a Scripture passage. Each group is to pretend it is presenting a slide show of the passage given. The story is divided into different slides to illustrate the story. Each slide will have the members of the group in a still-life pose to depict each scene. As one person in the group narrates, the group poses in each slide at the appropriate time in the story. A parable can be broken into four to eight slides. This idea not only teaches a Bible story, but it's loads of fun. If you have a devotion planned, the Human Slide Show is an excellent method of presenting the Scripture passages you will use. *Milton Horn*

SENSE SCRIPTURES

To add a new dimension to your next Bible study or lesson, begin by reading the passage to the group. Then explain that you are going to read it again while students close their eyes and tell you what they sense from the story or situation. In other words you want them to put themselves into the actual scene being described. Then they are to tell you what they see, hear, smell, taste, and feel. With the active imaginations that most students have, the results should be exciting.

For example, when Jesus calmed the storm in Matthew 8, responses might sound like this:

See—dark clouds, lightning, big waves, seagulls
Hear—thunder, splashing, men hollering, boat creaking
Taste—water, salt, cottonmouth (fear), lunch coming up
Feel—seasick, the boat rocking, the humidity, the cold
Smell—rain, salt, wet people who smell bad anyway, fish

In the "feel" section, consider emotions as well—fear, anger (because Jesus was sleeping), confusion, frustration, etc. This approach can help young people relate to Scripture in a fresh and intimate way. *John Collins*

BIBLICAL 60 MINUTES

One of the longest-running TV shows is the news program, "60 Minutes." It usually features quality investigative reporting along with some exciting drama as well. Why not use the format of that program as a Bible study exercise?

Divide the group into smaller units and have them do some investigative reporting (study) of a biblical text and then present their findings as if it were a "60 Minutes" program. The following example covers the events of Pentecost as described in the second chapter of Acts. Each group could take one section, act out the events, select a reporter who describes the action, and so forth. Let the group's creativity run wild. *Bruce Schlenke*

60 Minutes: Pentecost—What Really Happened
The Event (Acts 2:1-4)
Interviews with the Witnesses (Acts 2:5-13)
Peter's News Conference (Acts 2:14-41)
Follow-up Report (Acts 2:42-47)
Letterbag (Responses to the Story)

CAR-AZY BIBLE STUDY

This idea will animate even the most indifferent of youth group members during your next Bible study. Conduct it in cars. That's right, automobiles (four-door models, preferably). Divide the kids up four to a car, supply them with Bibles and discussion questions (or whatever regular lesson you use), and brief them with the prime rule for this study: The person in the driver's seat is the only one who may talk. If kids have questions they want to ask, they must wait until their turns in the driver's seat.

Tell kids that every three or four minutes you'll blow your whistle (or honk your horn), at which signal everyone is to rotate clockwise within their own cars—and the discussion continues with a new leader. When students have rotated through every seat in their car, the next whistle rotates them out of their original car into the driver's seat of another car—and so on. If this gets boring after awhile, blow the whistle two or three times in succession—and people will move around to different cars quickly!

Discussions are bound to be more lively, and you can control how fast or how slow you want the study to progress. You can do the same thing indoors or outdoors with chairs, but it's just plain more fun in the church parking lot or in the driveway of a group member's house. *Michael W. Capps*

SPONSOR STATIONS

For a change of pace in your youth meetings, divide a scriptural passage or theme into as many parts as you have adult sponsors. If 1 Corinthians 13 was on your teaching schedule, then you would assign two of love's characteristics (patience, kindness, does not envy, etc.) to each of seven or so sponsors, with the instructions to prepare a creative 10-to-15-minute presentation that they will give several times during the meeting. As the evening begins, divide the students into however many teaching stations there are, and explain to them how to rotate from one station to another every 10 or 15 minutes.

Here's one way a sponsor can creatively approach "Love does not keep account of wrongs," for example. As a new group of students arrives at her station, the sponsor asks group members to sit in a circle—then jumps all over a couple of kids who are slow to obey her. She pulls out a notebook in feigned fury, scribbles down their names and misdemeanors, and lets them know in no uncertain terms that she will never forget this. While she's at it she reads previous offenses of kids in that particular group—offenses, she points out coldly, that she'll never forget. A scriptural analysis of her behavior and brief student discussion can follow. *Randy Hausler*

CHEAT SHEETS

Want your students to take time during the coming week reviewing the lesson you just delivered? Promise a quiz next week over the same material, with tantalizing rewards for high scores—and then give them legitimate crib sheets to study from. You may even want to give them copies of the actual quizzes. Add Scripture references to the questions to allow them to find the answers for themselves in the Scripture. In short, do anything you can to help them do well on the upcoming quiz.

On Q day, however, they can't use notes during the quiz. *Len Cuthbert*

FOLD-A-LESSON BIBLE STUDIES

To make the most of kids' fascination with the unpredictable and unconventional, prepare this lesson aid. On a large sheet of newsprint, list the concepts from your lesson in the order you'll present them.

Take the Beatitudes, for instance (Matt. 5:3-12). Each verse has two parts—"blessed" and "for theirs is"—for a total of nine of each. Using two sheets of newsprint, create five long rectangles by folding the paper from the bottom to the top in segments of about two inches. Unfold the sheet, then in the top

rectangle write the lesson's title ("The Beatitudes"). In the next four rectangles on the sheet, write the verses' "blessed" on the left half and their corresponding results next to them in the right half. On the second sheet, follow this pattern for the last five verses. Use lots of colors in writing up verses in the sections. Then refold the sheets and secure each one with a paper clip to keep it from unfolding.

When you're ready to teach, tape the folded and paper-clipped sheet to the wall. As you teach the lesson, simply remove the paper clip and unfold each section as you're ready to expound on it. Some kids may wish to follow along in their Bibles, but the fold-a-lesson helps the resistant see and hear the Word. *Mark Simone*

QUICK-DRAW BIBLE BASICS

If you teach junior high Sunday school, you know you can no longer count on your students knowing basic Bible stories. To quickly ground the novice in who's who in the Bible while keeping more knowledgeable students motivated, try this quick-draw game.

Assign one or two chapters for the kids to read as homework (creation story, early life of Samuel, excerpts from the life of Christ, and so on). The next Sunday play a modified version of Pictionary, using the words from the assigned reading as the source of the drawing clues.

With the story of Joseph, for example, assign Genesis 37 and 39 to read. Write out the following clues for the artists: "He made a richly ornamental robe for him" (37:3), "...binding sheaves of grain in the field" (37:7), "Throw him in the cistern here in the desert" (37:22).

Tell the kids before they start how long they have to draw and how accurate the guess has to be. If the group is willing to slow the pace of the game, ask those drawing to explain the situation around what they drew. *Joyce Vermeer*

BIBLE STUDY CARDS

When your group tends to respond with word-for-word answers out of the Bible, try using this idea in a game fashion.

Before the meeting begins develop your Bible study questions so that the answers are one word or short phrases. When you are ready to start the lesson, give each person a stack of 3x5 cards and a pen. After reading the passage ask the group your first question. Each person must find the answer in the passage and then write it in his own words on a card. When everyone has finished, each student shows his answer. Duplicate or very similar answers are canceled out and only those with original or unique (and correct) answers score a point. *Len Cuthbert*

PERSONALIZED PASSAGES

A great way to get kids more involved in Bible passages is to personalize them. Prepare questions ahead of time, such as the ones below, that each person must answer either by writing them out individually (like a quiz) or by sharing in small groups. The following is a sample from Proverbs, chapter 10:

(10:13) My friends think I'm a good listener because...
(10:14) I get into trouble when I talk too much about...
(10:15) One good thing about having lots of money is...
(10:15) One good thing about having very little money is...
(10:16) If someone gave me $100, I would...

(10:16) If I had $10 to spend at the shopping center, I would...
(10:19) I feel I have important things to say about...
(10:20) People don't listen when I...
(10:23) I think it's real fun to...
(10:23) Something that some people consider fun but I don't is...
(10:24) I am afraid of...
(10:24) My greatest hope is that...

By using questions like these, you'll find people responding to verses which might otherwise have held no meaning for them. Base the questions on modern translations for added meaning (those above are from the *Living Bible*). *Bob Steir*

POOR MAN'S HOLY LAND TOUR

You can have a "Poor Man's Holy Land Tour" by taking kids on a tour of places within walking or riding distance inside your city. This includes taking them to the tallest building and having a Bible study there about Satan's temptation for Jesus to jump from the high mountain. It also includes a trip to an overgrown old cemetery where you can study about the man from Gadara. The options are endless: a city jail, a motel bedroom (David's sin), Jewish Synagogue, mountainside (for Sermon on the Mount), garden (for Garden of Gethsemane), upstairs room in some home (for the last supper), old boiler room (for the story of the Jewish children in the fiery furnace), on the roadside (for the story of the good Samaritan or Paul's conversion experience), a lakefront or a wilderness area (depending on where you live). The possibilities are endless and the impression made in the study usually beats most other audio visual techniques combined. *Marion D. Aldridge*

PICTURE PAGES

This activity will help kids remember more Scripture by drawing them a picture. The biblical languages, especially Greek, are remarkably picturesque. Even stick drawings, not to mention more sophisticated cartoons, can implant ideas in a young person's mind better than anything you might say.

Buy yourself a large sketchbook, or use a pad made from end rolls of newsprint. Study the passage in a few commentaries and word-study books in order to get a feel for the biblical truth; then start drawing.

Using Colossians 2:6-7, for example, you might have six drawings—the word received (a person receiving a diploma), walk (a person walking), rooted (a tree), building up (a house under construction), strengthening (an athlete lifting weights), overflowing (a broken toilet). Write the key words at the bottom of each page and have the group call out suggestions for pictures to be drawn. If you have artistic kids in the group, let them create the drawings. The group will have fun with this, and they'll get a firmer grasp on the meaning of the passages you're studying. *Greg Fiebig*

Do It!

For an occasional change of pace during Scripture readings, cue your group to listen carefully to what is read—and then do it. If you're reading Psalm 95:6, for example ("Let us kneel before the Lord our Maker"), then kids get off their chairs and kneel. Isaiah 40 offers several opportunities: "wait for the Lord" (tap their fingers, sigh, look at their watches), "gain new strength" (flex muscles, do push-ups), "mount up with wings like eagles" (flap arms), "run," and "walk."

And make sure there's a water fountain down the hall when you read what Jesus said in John 4 about drinking of living water. *Michael Frisbie*

Phone Phrenzie

Students not paying attention to devotionals and other talks during your weekly meetings? Motivate your kids to listen with a contest that has a clandestine feel to it.

First create a sheet like the sample. Amend it to fit your own group.

You may want to delegate the job of game controller to an eager and fair-minded volunteer, since the job requires dedication. Number several envelopes one through however many kids you suspect will play, and—for your private purposes— cross-reference each number with the student who will receive that envelope. Stuff each envelope with a copy of the above instructions and, on a second sheet, write a code name for that student. You'll also need to prepare a phone line to an answering machine.

Following the devotional or lesson, compile (or get from the speaker) five questions that test the kids' ability to listen for details in the talk. When

the kids start calling on Monday, they hear the first question, then give their code name and the answer to that question. At the end of the day, you (or the game controller) tabulate the results, eliminating those who replied with incorrect answers. When students call on Tuesday, they hear a second question, and so on.

The winner is the caller who answers all five questions correctly. Keep the tapes to avoid misunderstandings. Break ties creatively—make the winner the one who calls earliest on the final day, for example. Each Sunday award the prize for the previous week's contest either just before or after the talk or lesson. *Richard Dunn*

PHONE PHRENZIE

So you've signed up to play Karl's Phone-Five-Replies! All right, then—get ready. Here are the instructions:

1. On Sunday morning sign up and pay close attention to Pastor Karl.
2. Phone the KPFR headquarters every day this week, Monday-Friday, 9 AM till 9 PM, to hear and then answer the daily question.
3. Answer with your code name first, then your answer. (On the other sheet in this envelope is your code name. Do not show it to anyone!)
4. Either respond immediately (you have only 20 seconds to complete your answer) or hang up and call back. Only one answer per code name will be accepted.
5. If you make one mistake, you are disqualified for the remainder of the week.

The KPFR number is:
358-9741

CRYPTOQUIP

Communicating Scripture to young people is often very difficult. Getting them to memorize it is next to impossible. But "cryptoquipping" them with it is the ultimate.

Cryptoquipping is a way to help young and old alike learn and memorize Scripture truths and promises. A quip can be used to introduce retreat topics, Bible studies, or Sunday school lessons. Here's how it works:

> WIL AMTY WT ORM
> BWIY ECI YR YCWY
> ORM, YNCWY YOCE DI
> YVC TWEC BWO.
> W-A

This cryptoquip is a simple substitution cipher in which each letter stands for another. If you find that Y equals T, it will be that way throughout the puzzle. The solution is accomplished by trial and error. Short words can give you clues for locating the vowels. The age of your group will determine the number of "equal-to" clues that you give away.

Try the above example; then make up cryptoquips for your own verse. Be sure to double-check your letters for accuracy, because the kids will never let you forget it if you're wrong. By the way, this quip is found in Luke 6:31 (NAS). *William T. Bell*

BODY LANGUAGE BIBLE MEMORIZATION

Creating actions to represent key words and phrases of memory verses promotes retention and provides a platform for repetition.

Break a verse down into phrases or select prominent words and disperse them to individuals or small groups, either orally or on cards prepared beforehand. Give the students an opportunity to create an action to illustrate their portions of the verse. When they have done so, recite the verse with all the groups demonstrating their parts as you proceed through it. You can also have the whole group get involved in doing all the actions. Repetition will help everyone memorize the verse thoroughly.

Here are some variations:
• Have each small group develop all the actions for the verse. They should practice several times so they know the verse and actions well enough to present their version to the rest of the group. All groups make presentations.
• Select individuals to come to the front. Have them demonstrate an action that immediately comes to mind when you give them the words of the verse. You can have the group of selected people teach the actions to the rest of the group.
• Develop actions to the verse yourself and have the group follow your lead. *Len Cuthbert*

Four   God   sew   loved...

CREATIVE
BIBLE LESSONS

More than 70 very different, very fun, and very solid Bible-teaching ideas, from "Noah and the Ark I.Q. Test" (page 43) in the Old Testament to "Mary and Martha Malpractice" (page 67) in the New.

A FAITH PHYSICAL

Pass out the checklist on page 26 from the book of James to your youth group. This would be excellent following a lesson on faith and works or on the book of James.

In the column "Especially when..." kids should indicate exactly when they get angry, critical, jealous, etc. In this way, they can start recognizing those people and those situations that are particularly hard to handle and they can begin asking God for help in dealing with them. After completing the "physical" discuss each item separately. *Bobby Shows*

UNITY

This is an attempt to simulate unity and its meaning within your group. To begin, read Ephesians 4:1-16 on "the unity of the body of Christ," and discuss what unity really means. What is Paul trying to say? How would we as a group illustrate Paul's description of unity?

At this point bring out enough Legos so that every member of the group has plenty to work with. There must be plenty of space for people to work. (The best way is in a large carpeted room where everyone can sit on the floor.) If this is not possible, then put four people to a large table.

Now explain that each person should for five minutes, in silence, think of himself. Who am I, what do I believe in, what do I want to be, etc.

At the end of five minutes, allow each member five minutes more, in silence, to build who they think they are out of Legos. At the end of this five-minute period, have each individual, again in silence, find a partner and for 10 minutes (five minutes apiece) attempt in silence to put their two objects together. They can only nod their heads yes or no as an indicator to the other. At the end of this 10-minute period, allow another 10-minute period in which the players explain verbally what their objects stand for and why they would or would not allow certain parts of their object to be connected with their partner.

At the end of this 10-minute period, the two people should now seek out two others and, in silence, attempt to put their objects together for 10 minutes. At the end of this 10-minute silent period, allow the members of the four to explain their objects to the others and why they did or did not connect their objects at a certain part. Give each

A Faith Physical

Problem	A lot	Sometimes	Hardly ever	Especially when...
1. Anger James 1:20				
2. Sharp Tongue James 1:26				
3. Showing Favoritism James 2:1				
4. Critical James 3:1				
5. Bragging James 3:13				
6. Being Phony James 3:14				
7. Jealousy James 3:16				
8. Fighting James 4:1				
9. Want Only Things That Give Pleasure James 4:3				
10. Loving the World James 4:4				
11. Pride James 4:6				
12. Not Sorry for Wrongs James 4:9				
13. Knowing Right, But Not Doing It. James 4:17				
14. Griping James 5:9				

person enough time to explain the object. Now let the four find four more people and repeat the process until all objects are united into one object and all have had an opportunity to explain what their object stands for. Now read Ephesians 4:1-16 once more, and everyone ought to be able to see unity in diversity as Paul has explained it. *Edward E. Lopeman*

BODY LIFE

Have everyone form a circle or a line. If in a circle, they should be facing inward. Give each person a three-foot piece of string. Ask each person to tie one end around his own left hand and the other around the right hand of the person standing on his left. After everyone does this, everyone will be tied together. You could also use tape, and have the kids tape their wrists together. Then give the group a project which requires cooperation and time. One example is to walk into the dining room, sit down around a table, pour a drink into glasses for each person, pass out cookies, say grace, eat and drink, walk to the kitchen, and each person wash his own cup and plate.

After this experience, cut the string (or tape), form a circle on the floor or around a table, and discuss what feelings were experienced during the experiment and why. Ask them what they thought the purpose was, and then how this related to being in the body of Christ. What problems, joys, or principles surfaced during the experiment? You might close by reading Romans 12 or 1 Corinthians 12. *William C. Moore*

AN EXERCISE IN HUMILITY

First read aloud John 13:1-18, then ask the following questions:
• Why was it significant that Jesus washed the disciples' feet?
• Why did people wash each other's feet?
• Why was it a custom in those days?
• How would it feel to have Christ wash our feet?

After a short discussion using questions similar to those above, divide into groups of four or five. Have one person from each group fill a dishpan or shallow tub with water about two inches deep. Take turns washing each other's feet. Dry with paper towels. The entire washing should be done without talking, trying to convey the love Christ showed his disciples. Five minutes later, when all are finished, discuss again the passage in John, this time asking, "How did you feel?" Reactions will be varied, but intensely personal. Sum up the discussion with the thought that Christ is in each of us and symbolically we can wash each other's feet in our everyday actions. *Ralph Watkins*

FAMILY AFFAIR

Prior to reading the story of the prodigal son, assign by card a character (father, younger son, eldest son) to each person in the group. After hearing the story, divide into three groups—all the fathers in one group, younger sons in another, and eldest sons in another. The discussion that follows should strengthen them in their roles, talking over their feelings so they are prepared to meet with their families.

Each card contains a number at the bottom that indicates that person's family assignment. After the discussion groups, each family (father and two sons with the same number on the bottom of their card) meets to role-play the night after the feast at supper with the father, prodigal, and eldest son around the table. Each person responds as his or her "role" determines. After the family discussion, meet together with the whole group and discuss what happened. *Kenneth J. Mitchell*

CUPCAKE

This is a simple object lesson best suited for younger kids. Have two volunteers come forward and give each kid a chocolate cupcake. They are to eat some of the cupcake and describe it—good, bad, delicious, so-so. Hopefully, they will consider the cupcakes to be very good. Explain that the cupcakes are going to represent life.

Next place all the ingredients that went into the cupcakes in several small containers on a table. Have the volunteers taste each and describe how they taste to the group. Some will be bad, some good. Explain that these ingredients represent all the things that happen to us during our lifetime. Our lives are made up of both good things and bad things that happen to us; we can rely on the promise that "All things work together for good to them that love God" (Rom. 8:28). Without the bad-tasting ingredients, the cupcakes just wouldn't have turned out. Other Scriptures that can be used in this lesson are Ephesians 5:20 and Proverbs 3:5. *Marcella Stockin*

27

FRUIT PICKING

This small group experience is based on Galatians 5:22-23, where the "fruit of the spirit" are listed. If you have a large group, divide it into smaller groups. It works best with groups that have had plenty of time to get to know each other. There should be less than eight in each group so that no one will be left out.

Pass out the list that on page 29 to each person and following a brief lesson on the meaning of each of the nine "fruit," have the kids refer to their lists. Ask everyone to jot down the name of a person in the group who most exhibits a particular fruit in his life, next to the fruit on his list. For example, you might put Joe's name next to "peace" because he rarely causes division in the group, or next to "joy" because he is so happy. Instruct kids that they may put more than one name next to a fruit on their list.

When all have completed writing in names on their list, then ask one person to sit silently while the others share where they jotted down her name and why. When everyone is through, ask this person to share which of the fruit he feels the least of in her life and why. Go around the group until everyone has had a chance to do this.

LETTER TO AMOS

Use the handout on page 30 when studying the Old Testament book of Amos. Discuss the arguments presented. Some suggested questions for discussion:
• Evaluate the merchant's arguments in light of justice. At what points do they convince or fail to convince you?
• Suppose this letter were written today—how would you react? Where do the rights of the individual stop? Can justice be administered without striking a balance between individual rights and rights of the community?
Homer Erekson

MELODY IN S

A fun version of an old story is on page 31. Use it when you want to discuss love or the story of the prodigal son. *George E. Gaffga*

MOLD ME

Give each person a lump of clay or Play-Doh and have each one mold it into "an image of her own life." This can be abstract or an actual likeness. Allow each person to share and explain her sculpture with the rest of the group.

Next, study 2 Timothy 2:20-21 and have them shape their clay into a type of "vessel" that they wanted to be. Again, these can be shared and explained by each person. Following an act of dedication in which each person asks to be "filled" and "used" by God, the vessels can be allowed to harden and put on display. The song "Spirit of the Living God" is an appropriate song of dedication. *Jack Keyte*

MOMENT OF DISILLUSIONMENT

This is a Bible study and role-play on John 13:1-14:11. Read the passage aloud in groups of 12. Assign the following parts to be read by members of your group:

Jesus	Judas Iscariot
Peter	Disciple whom Jesus loved
Thomas	Philip

A narrator should read all of the parts which are not directly attributed to a person. After reading the passage once, reread the passage playing the same roles. Perhaps you will want to arrange yourselves in a manner similar to the way in which the disciples must have been seated.

After the second reading, discuss the following questions:
• If you had been Peter, how would you have acted when Jesus tried to wash your feet? Why? How did Peter act? How should he have acted?
• Why did Jesus wash the disciples' feet? How can leaders in our group "wash" others' feet?
• Why did the disciples not understand what Jesus meant when he spoke to Judas Iscariot? (13:26-28)
• Why did Jesus tell his disciples not to be troubled? (14:1)
• If two of the spiritual leaders of this youth group suddenly "wiped out" in their Christian lives, how would you react? *Mark Senter*

FRUIT PICKING

Love_____
Joy _____
Peace _____
Patience_____
Kindness _____
Goodness _____
Fidelity _____
Gentleness_____
Self-control _____

Love_____
Joy _____
Peace _____
Patience_____
Kindness _____
Goodness _____
Fidelity _____
Gentleness_____
Self-control _____

Love_____
Joy _____
Peace _____
Patience_____
Kindness _____
Goodness _____
Fidelity _____
Gentleness_____
Self-control _____

Love_____
Joy _____
Peace _____
Patience_____
Kindness _____
Goodness _____
Fidelity _____
Gentleness_____
Self-control _____

Love_____
Joy _____
Peace _____
Patience_____
Kindness _____
Goodness _____
Fidelity _____
Gentleness_____
Self-control _____

Love_____
Joy _____
Peace _____
Patience_____
Kindness _____
Goodness _____
Fidelity _____
Gentleness_____
Self-control _____

Love_____
Joy _____
Peace _____
Patience_____
Kindness _____
Goodness _____
Fidelity _____
Gentleness_____
Self-control _____

Love_____
Joy _____
Peace _____
Patience_____
Kindness _____
Goodness _____
Fidelity _____
Gentleness_____
Self-control _____

Love_____
Joy _____
Peace _____
Patience_____
Kindness _____
Goodness _____
Fidelity _____
Gentleness_____
Self-control _____

Letter to Amos

Dear Mr. Amos,

Your intemperate criticisms of the merchants of Bethel show that you have little understanding of the operations of a modern business economy. You appear not to understand that a businessman is entitled to a profit. A cobbler sells shoes to make money, as much as he can. A banker lends money to get a return on his loan. These are not charitable enterprises. Without profits, a tradesman cannot stay in business.

Your slanders reveal also a lack of appreciation for the many contributions made to our land by the business community. Visitors to Israel are greatly impressed by the progress made in the past few decades. The beautiful public buildings and private homes are a proud monument. Increasing contacts with foreign lands add to the cultural opportunities open to our citizens. Our military strength makes us the envy of peoples already swallowed up by their enemies.

Despite the great gains during Jereboam II's reign, there is some poverty. That we admit. But is it just to blame us for the inability of some people to compete? You say that the peasants were cheated out of their lands. Not so! They sold their property. Or in some cases, it was sold for back taxes. Some peasants put up the land as collateral on a loan, then failed to meet the payments. No one was cheated. The transactions to which you refer were entirely legal. Had you taken the trouble to investigate the facts, your conclusions would have been more accurate.

The real reason for poverty is lack of initiative. People who get ahead in this world work hard, take risks, overcome obstacles. Dedication and determination are the keys to success. Opportunities don't knock; they are created by imagination and industry. Our success can be an inspiration to the poor. If we can make it, they can too. With the growth of business, Israel grows. More jobs, better pay and increased opportunity for everyone. The old saying contains more than a germ of truth: What's good for General Chariots is good for the country.

Yours for Israel,

I.M. Merchant

I.M. Merchant

Melody in S

Sure enough, the scholarly scribe stood up and slyly said to the Savior, "Sir, surely you surmise that I seek a sustained subscription to a solid life beyond the solid shale sepulcher. So what steps shall I secure for such a subsistence?"

The Savior said, "What saith the statutes?" The stupid scribe responded, "It says, 'Serve, Sigh for, and Sway with your Savior with all your substance, soul, spirit, and strength. And sway with the sire who settles by your side as you sway with yourself'."

"Sure," said the Savior, "Stay so and you shall survive." So, the silly scribe, seeking to save his skin, said, "Sir, I solicit you to set before me my sidekick." The Savior sent home his statement by citing a sample:

A sorry sap was sauntering slowly side to side when suddenly six serious assassins set themselves to smash that silly sap. Stripped, stunned and shaken, he stumbled and sank to the solid slate of the sidewalk. After seemingly several seconds slipped by, a slothful sort of celibate saw the simple soul seething on the sidewalk; so he stopped and then simply strolled by. Soon a selfish shepherd who subsited on a small salary stalled a second and left the sorry simpleton stranded. Suddenly, a stalwart Samaritan slid straightaway to the subdued subject who was stunned. Seeing the seriousness of the situation, he restored the strength of that sorry soul and sitting him in the saddle of his staunch stallion, surveyed him safely to some septic sanitarium where he secured some serious substantial sleep for the standed sojourner.

"So," said the Savior, "Seeing such circumstances, who seems to be the sympathetic saint in such a situation?"

"Surely, the Samaritan," stammered the scribe.

"Superb," said the Savior, "So must you shape yourself."

PARABLE

This is an excellent way to get young people involved in the parables of Jesus. Divide into small discussion groups and give each group a parable from the Scriptures. Then have the groups work on the following questions concerning their parable:
• What do you feel was the meaning of the parable in Jesus' time?
• How does it speak to us now?
• What do you find most profound in its message?
• Prepare a short modern skit of how you think this parable would have happened today.

The groups should be allowed enough time to work through each question and prepare their skit. Then the entire group meets together and each small group presents its skit and shares its thoughts on the parable that it worked on. The discussion/preparation period and the presentation of the skits can be done in two different meetings, over a period of two days, or two weeks if desired. Either way, the experience can be very rewarding. *Randall Foos*

STRING STORIES

Here's a way to make the stories and parables from the Bible take on a new, fresh meaning and to allow all the members of the group to participate. Form a circle and supply each person with paper, string, and a pen. Have each drop the string onto the paper and trace its outline. Now, have each individual draw from his string design a creature, person, animal—any living thing. Divide the kids into small groups of three or four, and give them the assignment of utilizing all of their group pictures in portraying a story or parable from the Bible. For variation, have them make up any story, but conclude with a lesson learned from the Scriptures. *Gary Liddle*

THE THANKFUL LEPER

Use the exercise on page 33 as a way to point kids toward recognizing the need for expressing thanks to God, rather than constantly bombarding him with requests. Give each person a copy of Luke 17:11-19, the account of Jesus healing the 10 lepers. A modern translation of the passage is most effective for the purpose. Then give each student The Thankful Leper worksheet.

After completing this assignment, divide the kids into small groups to share their answers and explain the meanings of the cards they made. Close the meeting with prayer, emphasizing thanksgiving. *Ron Carlson*

CREATION MEDITATION

Meditation is difficult for all of us and this one is excellent for those who are new at it. Ask the kids to sit on the floor in a circle with legs crossed. Place a cup of soil and a cup of water before each participant. Ask them to note where the water and the soil have been placed and then have them close their eyes and relax. Explain that you will be reading selected verses from Genesis and that you want them to use their imaginations in giving God thanks for his creation. Read the verses and comments on page 34.

Each section should be read slowly, and quietly, with pauses after each question. The questions listed are rhetorical and should not be answered. The entire meditation may be adapted to your own geographical area. *Douglas Iben*

CREATIVE TEACHING WITH THE PSALMS

The Psalms can be effectively used for teaching the concepts of prayer and petition, praise and thanksgiving. They are also helpful in communicating to a group the grappling of individuals and the community of the faithful with the emotions of grief, despair, sorrow, love, hate, joy, and excitement.

Below are outlines for lessons on two types of psalms.

I. Complaint Psalms
  A. Information
    1. Intention of complaints: to petition God to change or alleviate the situation.
    2. Examples of the two types:
    Individual—Psalm 5, 6, 13, 22, 28, 38, 43, 54, 61
    Community—Psalm 44, 74, 80, 83, 94
    3. Historical situations of the complaint: 1 Samuel 7, Jeremiah 14:1-9, 17-22.
    4. Situations of the complainers: illness, defeat, persecution, oppression, discouragement, physical needs (childbearing, rain, food, etc.), sin.
    5. Constituent parts of all complaints:

The Thankful Lepper

Carefully read the account of Jesus healing the 10 lepers. As you read it, attempt to identify with the feelings of the lepers who did not return to Christ, with the leper who returned to express thanks, and with the feelings of Christ in this situation. Then answer the following questions:

1. How do you think Christ felt when only one individual out of 10 returned to give thanks?

2. Describe what you think the grateful leper must have felt and thought during his healing encounter with Christ.

3. What excuses can you think of for the nine healed lepers who did not return to give thanks to Christ?

Now attempt to apply this passage of Scripture to your life by reacting to the following:

1. With whom in this story do you most identify, the nine who did not return or the one who came back?

2. What excuses do you usually think of for not thanking Christ for what he has done in your life?

3. What was the last thing Christ did for you or provided for you that you wish to thank him for?

4. Using the paper and colors provided for you, construct a colorful thank-you card addressed to Christ. The outside of the card should express through symbolic colors and expressive symbols the event or object for which you are thankful. In the inside of the card, write a short letter, poem, or prayer that expresses your thankfulness.

Creation Meditation

Read Genesis 1:1, 3 and say: "Thank God for light. What if you lived in darkness? Picture the face of someone that you dearly love—a friend, a parent, a boyfriend or girlfriend. Now let that face melt away into darkness. What if you lived in darkness? Thank God for light!" (Keep your eyes closed.)

Read Genesis 1:6 and say: "Do you take water for granted? What if we should run out of it? Taste a few drops. Keep it in your mouth. Appreciate it for a moment. All of life depends on it. Thank God for water."

Read Genesis 1:9 and say: "Do you take soil for granted? Reach out now and touch it. Rub it between your fingers. Smell it. What if we should pollute all of it? Could we exist? Thank God for soil!"

Read Genesis 1:14 and say: "What if the seasons never changed? What if it were always winter? Picture your yard at home with no flowers, no leaves on the trees, no green bushes—not just for a few months out of the year, but for the whole year long. Thank God for the seasons."

Say: "Lie back now and completely relax while we continue to thank God for his creation." (It is good to change positions for the sake of comfort and relaxation.)

Read Genesis 1:20 and say: "Thank God for birds. They teach us to soar. Picture yourself as a gliding seagull. You are flying over the ocean. You approach the shoreline and see the water lapping the shore. Now fly away and see whatever you want to see. Right now, in your imagination. Fly as high or as far as you would like. Come back to land now. You are again walking upon the shore. Thank God for birds."

Read Genesis 1:24 and say: "Now picture yourself as some kind of animal. Any kind. What kind of animal are you? Where do you live? What is it like there today? What are you doing? Thank God for animals."

Read Genesis 1:26-27 and say: "Thank God for you. Do you appreciate yourself? Keep your eyes closed. Run your hand through your hair. Is it fine or coarse? Now touch your ear. Run your finger along its edge. Feel its shape. Now without opening your eyes, put your hand in front of your face. Try to remember what it looks like. Try to picture how many lines run across your palm. Try to feel how the veins run across the backside of your hand. Now open your eyes and look closely at your hand, and thank God for you.

"Let's pray. Dear God, we thank you for all your creation. Help us never to take it for granted. In Jesus' name. Amen."

(a)invocation, (b) complaint, (c) prayer for change. In some psalms there are two additional parts: (d) motivation for God to help, and (e) assurance of God's hearing.

6. An Example: Psalm 22
   a. Invocation (My God, my God)...22:1a
   b. Complaint (I cry...you do not answer)...1b-2
   c. Motivation (Our fathers trusted you)...3-5
   d. Complaint (Scorned by men)...6-8
   e. Motivation (You have been my God)...9-10
   f. Supplication (Be not far from me)...11
   g. Complaint (Many bulls encompass me)...12-18
   h. Supplication (Be not far off)...19-21
   i. Assurance of hearing and praise (He has heard, when he cried)...22-31

B. Group Activity
   1. Have the group go over the parts of a complaint psalm; then have them divide the different parts of a particular psalm into its invocation, complaint, and supplication (and motivation and assurance of hearing if applicable).
   2. Have them identify the different emotions and attitudes (despair, anger, sorrow, fear, dread, disgust, etc.) and why the writer had reason to feel this way. Have them examine what the writer wanted God to do about his situation.
   3. Have the group as a whole or in small groups share experiences in which they have had similar feelings and attitudes. Ask them how they responded to the situation, e.g., praying, asking for advice from friends, self-pity, etc.
   4. Have each person in the group take 10 to 15 minutes to write a psalm of his own, and then share some of them with the whole group. It can be either a complaint of the community, i.e. one that affects your whole group, or Christians as a whole, or an individual complaint.

II. Psalms of Praise
   A. Information
      1. Intention of a hymn of praise: to praise God for who he is and what he has done; and to call others to praise him.
      2. Examples: Psalm 19:1-6, 29, 30, 33, 47, 48, 65, 66, 92, 93, 95, 96, 97, 98, 100, 111, 113, 145-150.
      3. Situations of the writers: Experience of deliverance from sickness, distress; thankfulness for God's helping the needy, for the gift of children, for the righteous, for his love, for his justice and mercy; and praise for creation, ad infinitum.
      4. There is no specific form or any particular arrangement of the content in a psalm of praise.
   B. Group Activity
      1. Have the group identify the different moods of the psalm—joy, praise, relief, thanks, etc.—and the reasons the writer felt this way.
      2. Have the group as a whole or in small groups share times when they have been thankful or wanted to praise God. Ask them to share what they did about it, e.g. shouted, prayed, told a friend, etc.
      3. Have each one in the group write their own psalm of praise, and then read some of them to the whole group.

Remind the group that the criteria of a complaint or praise psalm is not first and foremost that it be wonderful poetry, but that it first of all is addressed to God from the heart, and not contrived. The results of really putting some thought into this are quite rewarding, and the group can come to some insights about the Psalms, themselves, and each other. *K.C. Hanson*

ENGLISH TEST

A fun way to show kids how we often make judgments too hastily is by using the test on page 39. Pass out copies and have each person make the corrections as instructed. Most will blow it every time. When they are finished, follow up with a discussion on Matthew 7:1-6.

Here is the way the paragraph should look when it is corrected. *Ron Malin*

He is a young man, yet experienced. In vice and wickedness, he is never found. In opposing the works of iniquity, he takes delight. In the downfall of his neighbors, he never rejoices. In the prosperity of his fellow creatures, he is always ready to assist. In destroying the peace of society, he takes no pleasure. In serving the Lord, he is uncommonly diligent. In sowing discord among his friends and acquaintances, he takes no pride. In laboring to promote the cause of Christianity, he has not been negligent. In endeavoring to tear down the church, he makes no effort. To subdue his evil passions, he strives hard. To build up Satan's kingdom, he lends no aid. To the support of the gospel among heathen, he contributes largely. To the devil he will never go. To heaven he must go, where he will receive his just reward.

ESTHER AND THE KING

The Old Testament book of Esther is one of the most fascinating stories of the Bible and is an excellent book for group study and discussion.

Have the group read through the entire book in one sitting. This normally takes about 20 minutes (if you read from a modern translation). Then discuss the following questions:

1. Esther never mentions the name of God. In spite of this, can you find evidence of God in Esther? (Have the group take a chapter at a time and point out places where they find God, such as verses 4:14 or 6:1-2. There are many more.)
2. Discuss the advice that was given to various people in the story. (Such as 1:16, 3:8, 4:13, 5:14, etc.) Which was good advice, which was bad? Who gives you advice?
3. Order the main characters in the story from best to worst. Who was the best person, who was the worst? (Give reasons why.) The main characters (in alphabetical order) are:
a. Ahasuerus, the King
b. Esther
c. Haman
d. Memucan (1:16)
e. Mordecai
f. Vashti, the Queen
g. Zeresh, Haman's wife
4. If you could write a moral to the story, what would it be?

Of course, there are other excellent questions that will come up in the study of Esther, but these will help toward good discussion.

Esther can also be written as a play and acted out for the church very effectively. The story contains interesting dialogue and characters, a good plot, suspense, and a bit of irony. Most of all it will help young people gain more insight into and appreciation for the Old Testament.

GUEST SPEAKER FROM THE EARLY DAYS

This role play is an effective way to help youth explore the personalities and feelings of biblical characters who often seem unreal. Combined with a Bible study, it can add depth to the learning experience.

A biblical character is selected and someone in the group (perhaps the youth director) first researches that character and then assumes the identity of that character in a speech to the entire group. For example, he could become Peter, and try to relate to the group his reactions and feelings when:
• Andrew first introduced him to Jesus.
• Jesus stepped into his boat and addressed the crowd.
• Peter walked on the water.
• Peter confessed Christ as Lord and then immediately rebuked him for speaking of his death.
• Peter refused (at first) to have his feet washed by Jesus.
• The events of Maundy Thursday unfolded.
• Peter denied Christ.
• Christ spoke to Peter on the beach after his resurrection.

Following the speech, the group can question Peter about the things he said, and Peter can respond as he feels the real Peter would have. For further discussion the group can then be divided into smaller groups and discuss related questions such as these:
• If you were one of the other disciples, how would you feel about Christ spending so much time with Peter?
• If someone did to you what Peter did to Christ, how would you feel?
• What do the words of Christ to Peter on the beach after his resurrection tell you about Christ's love for Peter?
• When have you ever felt like Peter in any of these situations?

This same approach can be used with any of a number of personalities from the Bible. It is guaranteed to get your group thinking in new ways about the pioneers of our faith. *Arlin Migliazzo*

ENGLISH TEST

Mark this paragraph into sentences using capitals at the beginning, periods at the end of sentences, and commas, etc. where needed. Once begun, DO NOT GO BACK and try to correct.

He is a young man yet experienced in vice and wickedness he is never found in opposing the works of iniquity he takes delight in the downfall of his neighbors he never rejoices in the prosperity of his fellow creatures he is always ready to assist in destroying the peace of society he takes no pleasure in serving the Lord he is uncommonly diligent in sowing discord among his friends and acquaintances he takes no pride in laboring to promote the cause of Christianity he has not been negligent in endeavoring to tear down the church he makes no effort to subdue his evil passions he strives hard to build up Satan's kingdom he lends no aid to the support of the gospel among heathen he contributes largely to the devil he will never go to heaven he must go where he will receive his just reward.

ENGLISH TEST

Mark this paragraph into sentences using capitals at the beginning, periods at the end of sentences, and commas, etc. where needed. Once begun, DO NOT GO BACK and try to correct.

He is a young man yet experienced in vice and wickedness he is never found in opposing the works of iniquity he takes delight in the downfall of his neighbors he never rejoices in the prosperity of his fellow creatures he is always ready to assist in destroying the peace of society he takes no pleasure in serving the Lord he is uncommonly diligent in sowing discord among his friends and acquaintances he takes no pride in laboring to promote the cause of Christianity he has not been negligent in endeavoring to tear down the church he makes no effort to subdue his evil passions he strives hard to build up Satan's kingdom he lends no aid to the support of the gospel among heathen he contributes largely to the devil he will never go to heaven he must go where he will receive his just reward.

IMAGE OF CHRIST

Here's a short lesson on the person of Jesus Christ. Divide the group into small groups and give each group one of the Scripture references below to discuss. Then have each group come up with the scriptural "image of Christ" that was in their selection. Have one person in each group share their findings. *Eleanor Hoffmann*

Scripture:
1. Philippians 2:5-11
2. Matthew 25:34-40
3. Isaiah 42:1-9
4. John 10:11-16
5. John 6:44-51
6. Luke 4:38-44
7. Matthew 16:16

Image:
1. Lord and Servant
2. Kind and Friend
3. Suffering Servant
4. Shepherd
5. Teacher and bringer of life
6. Compassionate
7. Peter's confession

THE LOST COIN

Hide a silver dollar (or half dollar) somewhere in the room and announce that whoever finds it can keep it. After the coin is found, gather the group together and discuss the parable of the lost coin found in Luke 15. Ask the one who found the coin what he or she plans to do with it. From this a parallel can be drawn between how the coin is to be used and how God wants to use us, rather than simply putting us on the shelf. This illustration works best with junior high and younger. *Rich Young*

PAUL'S LETTER TO THE AMERICANS

This is an activity that causes both the kids and leader to reflect on their present lives and help them get a feeling for Paul's letters to the churches.

Have the kids write a letter to themselves from "Paul" praising and admonishing themselves on their lifestyle (it's important to praise as well as admonish). Give them about 20 minutes then break into small groups and have them share their letters.

Another adaptation is to use a specific passage (Eph. 6:10-24 for example) and rewrite it to themselves. Or have small groups compose a letter to the whole youth group, evaluating what the youth group is or is not doing. *Kris Yotter*

PERSONALIZED PSALMS

This is a great method of worship or meditation that is very effective. Sit down with The Psalms—many of which lend themselves to this kind of creative meditation. Choose one and read through this psalm several times. Each time try to identify yourself with the feeling and emotions related in the psalm. Put yourself into it as much as you can. Begin feeling the mood of the psalm. As you begin feeling the emotion of the psalm, identify these emotions with some experiences, attitudes and circumstances of your own life. Then express yourself to the Lord by writing a psalm of your own using the original psalm as a pattern or guideline.

If your group really gets into this method, they might want to start their own notebook of personalized psalms. *Dwight Scott*

TRANSLATING THE LORD'S PRAYER

Whether your group is too familiar with the Lord's Prayer or completely unfamiliar with it, this is a great exercise that will not only familiarize them with the Lord's Prayer, but help them to understand some of its deepest meanings.
1. By using any one of numerous available sources (Concordance, Bible Dictionary, Good News for Modern Man Index), locate the two passages in the New Testament that contain the Lord's Prayer. Discuss the similarities and differences between Matthew's (Matt. 6:9-13) and Luke's (Luke 11:2-4) versions.
2. Distribute as many translations of the New Testament that you have available (New International Version, New American Standard, The Message, Phillips, New English). Have the young people read aloud from at least three different versions.
3. Have the students individually compose and write their own version of the Lord's Prayer using any or all the translations available. They may select the words and phrases of each verse they feel are most effective or meaningful.
4. After all have finished, have them share their Lord's Prayer translation with the others in the group.
5. By consensus or voting, compose a group translation of the Lord's Prayer that best conveys the group's understanding of the prayer.

The group translation could then be used in the regular worship service accompanied by a very meaningful explanation by the youths as to how and why they composed their prayer the way they did. *Kenneth Cramer*

21ST CENTURY

Future shock is something that affects all of us, and this discussion can help your kids start preparing for the future.

Begin with a devotional on Revelation 21:1-5. Talk about what God has planned for the future: a new heaven and a new earth; no more tears, no more death; no more grief, crying, or pain, etc. That's all great but what about the world we live in now? What is going to happen in the next few years?

Divide into groups and distribute the subject list on page 40. Have each group select areas of interest, then give them 45 minutes to illustrate, symbolize, or fantasize the world they would like to see in 20 years. Display all the posters at the end of the session and have each group talk about its poster. *Jimmie L. Hancock*

A VERY SPECIAL BIBLE READING

So often when one simply reads a Bible passage out loud, it loses the interest of many youths. If you have ever found this to be true, then the following personal approach can really help. Instead of expecting every word to mean something to every youth, assign a special verse or verses to specific youths for personal consideration. The following reading is an adaptation of 2 Timothy 2:1-18.

As I read God's word tonight, I ask that you not only give attention to the entire reading, but special attention to those verses I will give to you personally. I trust that they will be extra meaningful to you.

Our Lord in his Holy Word says, __Bob__ [insert name of youth and read to him or her], be strong with the strength Christ Jesus gives you. For you must teach others those things you and many others have heard me speak about. Teach these great truths to trustworthy men who will, in turn, pass them on to others.

__Judy__, take your share of suffering as a good soldier of Jesus Christ, just as I do, and as Christ's soldier do not let yourself become tied up in worldly affairs, for then you cannot satisfy the one who has enlisted you in his army.

And __Mark__, follow the Lord's rules for doing his work, just as an athlete either follows the rules or is disqualified and wins no prize.

__Kathy__, work hard like a farmer who gets paid well if he raises a large crop.

Let everyone here tonight think over these three illustrations, and may the Lord help you all to understand how they apply to you.

__Donny__, don't forget the wonderful fact that Jesus Christ was a man born into King David's family, and that he was God, as shown by the fact that he rose again from the dead. It is because I, Paul, have preached these great truths that I am in trouble here and have been put in jail like a criminal. But the Word of God is not chained, even though I am.

And __Tommy__, you too should be like the Apostle Paul, more than willing to suffer if that will bring salvation and eternal glory in Christ Jesus to those God has chosen.

__Karen__, be comforted by this truth, that when you suffer and die for Christ it only means that you will begin living with him in heaven.

And if you think that your present service for him is hard, __Mike__, just remember that someday you are going to sit with him and rule with him. But if you give up when you suffer, and turn against Christ, then he must turn against you.

Even when you are too weak to have any faith left, __Nate__, he remains faithful to you and will help you, for he cannot disown you who is part of himself, and he will always carry out his promise to you.

__Jenny__, remind your friends of these great facts, and command them in the name of the Lord not to argue over unimportant things. Such arguments are confusing and useless, and even harmful.

Work hard, __Ginger__, so God can say to you, "Well done!" Be a good workman, one who does not need to be ashamed when God examines your work. Know what his words say and mean.

__Jim__, steer clear of foolish discussions which lead people into the sin of anger with each other. Things will be said that will burn and hurt for a long time to come. Hymenaeus and Philetus, in their love of argument, are men like that. They have left the path of truth, preaching the lie that the resurrection of the dead has already occurred; and they have weakened the faith of some who believe them.

21st Century

Travel/Transportation
Government
Work
Recreation
Housing/Architecture
Entertainment
Personal Items
Church
Food
Clothes
Education
Environment
Household Gadgets
Social Relations
Economy (Money)

21st Century

Travel/Transportation
Government
Work
Recreation
Housing/Architecture
Entertainment
Personal Items
Church
Food
Clothes
Education
Environment
Household Gadgets
Social Relations
Economy (Money)

21st Century

Travel/Transportation
Government
Work
Recreation
Housing/Architecture
Entertainment
Personal Items
Church
Food
Clothes
Education
Environment
Household Gadgets
Social Relations
Economy (Money)

21st Century

Travel/Transportation
Government
Work
Recreation
Housing/Architecture
Entertainment
Personal Items
Church
Food
Clothes
Education
Environment
Household Gadgets
Social Relations
Economy (Money)

But _Darrell_ , God's truth stands firm like a g reat rock, and nothing can shake it. It is a foundation stone with these words written on it for you, _Marci_ , "The Lord knows those who are really his," and "A person who calls himself a Christian should not be doing things that are wrong."

The above consisted only of 2 Timothy 2:1-18. If more students are involved, 2 Timothy chapters 2 through 4 and 1 Timothy 4:7-5:2 lend themselves well for personal adaptation. *Timothy Quill*

HYPOS VS. CHUNS

Here's a creative approach to an understanding of Matthew 6:1-18. In this passage Jesus makes a very clear distinction between the behavior of the hypocrites (Hypos) and the behavior of the Christians (Chuns). There are three basic categories referred to:
1. Acts of righteousness (vv. 1-4)
2. Prayer (vv. 5-15)
3. Fasting (vv. 16-18)

Divide your youth group into the Hypos and the Chuns. Then have each group give an example of each of the categories listed above. You can approach this from a couple of different directions. One approach would be to have the Hypos give an illustration of how they would behave according to category one. You would then have the Chuns use the same illustration only changing it to fit their identity. Another approach would be to have each group come up with its own illustration of each category and compare notes after all are finished. *Tom Bougher*

LAZARUS REVISITED

Have the group read through John 11. Then either individually or in small groups have the kids decide on the person they would like to raise from the dead, if they could. It could be anyone from Adam to someone who died that day. After they have selected a person, have them discuss why they chose the person they did. You could then discuss what you would do if this person was raised from the dead. *John Shedwick*

NOAH WAY

Here's a fun version of the story of Noah that you might want to use next time you are studying that portion of the Old Testament. Believe it or not, it does have some discussion possibilities as well as a few laughs. *Derek McAleen*

THE LORD IS MY SKI BOAT

Putting a biblical passage into contemporary imagery will often help young people understand more clearly the applications of that passage. Try dividing your youth into small groups and, after reading through the 23rd Psalm, have the groups each decide on a metaphor and rewrite the 23rd Psalm using this metaphor. You can also give the young people a list of metaphors ahead of time and have them form groups around the ones they like. Some options could be: The Lord is my dirt bike. The Lord is my skateboard. The Lord is my math teacher, etc. Here is a sample Psalm 23 rewrite done by a group of junior high young people:

The Lord is my ski boat,

That is just what I've always wanted.

He makes me ski on blue water;

He leads me along quiet seas.

He gives back my zeal for life

He guided me behind the wake,

For my well-being's sake.

Even though I come to choppy waters,

I show no fear, for someone is watching.

Your life jacket and boots, they comfort me.

You let me jump the wake before my critics and I do not fall.

My skills are mounting.

Certainly exciting and successful times will follow me all the days of my life,

And I will dwell in the skiers hall of fame forever.

You may not end up with the greatest theology in the world, but the kids will probably have a lot better grasp of a particular Bible verse than they did before they started. *Mark Rozelle*

Noah Way

And the Lord said unto Noah: "Where is the ark which I commanded thee to build?"

And Noah said unto the Lord: "Verily, I have had three carpenters ill. The gopher-wood supplier hath let me down—yea, even though the gopher-wood hath been on order for nigh upon 12 months. What can I do, O Lord?"

And God said unto Noah: "I want that ark finished even after seven days and seven nights."

And Noah said: "It will be so."

And it was not so. And the Lord said unto Noah: "What seemeth to be the trouble this time?"

And Noah said unto the Lord: "Mine subcontractor hath gone bankrupt. The pitch which thou commandest me to put on the outside and on the inside of the ark hath not arrived. The plumber hath gone on strike. Shem, my son who helpeth me on the ark side of the business, hath formed a pop group with his brothers Ham and Japheth. Lord, I am undone."

And the Lord grew angry and said: "And what about the animals, the male and the female of every sort that I ordered to come unto thee to keep their seed alive upon the face of the earth?"

And Noah said: "They have been delivered unto the wrong address but should arriveth on Friday."

And the Lord said: "How about the unicorns, and the fowls of the air by sevens?"

And Noah wrung his hands and wept, saying: "Lord, unicorns are a discontinued line; thou canst not get them for love nor money. And fowls of the air are sold only in half-dozens. Lord, Lord, Thou knowest how it is."

And the Lord in his wisdom said: "Noah, my son, I knowest. Why else dost thou think I have caused a flood to descend upon the earth?"

COUNTING THE COSTS

Load your kids up and drive to the nearest building in the community that was started and never completed. If possible, tour the building grounds and the inside. Ask the group to share possible reasons why the building was never completed. Conclude this part by asking, "What do you think of the contractors?" or "What do the people passing by in this community think?"

Then read Luke 14:25-30. Discuss how it relates to the unfinished building. Talk about commitment and how to avoid starting something that you can't complete, or not finishing something that you have started. Discussion can also center around what it means to be disciples and what costs there are to be a disciple of Jesus Christ. *Doug Newhouse*

IMAGES OF THE CHURCH

The New Testament uses quite a few metaphors to describe the function of the church in the world. These metaphors help us understand not only who we are as the church, but what our relationship should be to Christ and to each other.

You might want to begin with a study of each of these word pictures of the church, and then have the students rank them from most important to least important, or from best to worst. Of course, the idea is not necessarily to imply that any of the metaphors are unimportant or more important than others, but simply to generate discussion on the subject. You might have the students think of some additional metaphors, borrowing from modern-day culture to create their own images on the church.

Here is a list of metaphors used in the New Testament:

- **Bride.** We are the bride; Christ is the bridegroom. (2 Cor. 11:2, Eph. 5:25, Rom. 7:4, Rev. 19:7)
- **Branches.** Jesus said that he was the vine, and that we are the branches. (John 15:1-8)
- **Flock.** Jesus said that we were sheep and that he is the Good Shepherd. (John 10:11-15, Matt.10:16)
- **Kingdom.** Jesus was called the Mighty King, the King of Kings, and we are brought into his kingdom. (Col. 1:13)
- **Family.** We are the sons and daughters of God, brothers of Christ, brothers and sisters to each other, joint heirs with Christ, the household of God. (Heb. 2:10-11, Gal. 4:1-7)
- **Building.** We are temples of the Holy Spirit, a building not made with hands. (2 Cor. 5, Eph. 2:19-22)
- **Body.** We are all part of the body of Christ, each person being a different part of the body. (1 Cor. 12, Eph. 4)
- **Salt.** We are the salt of the earth. (Matt. 5:13)
- **Light.** We are the light of the world. (Matt. 5:14)
- **Fishermen.** Jesus called us to be fishers of men. (Matt. 4:19)
- **Soldiers.** Fighting against "principalities and powers," wearing the full armor of God. (Eph. 6:10-17, 1 Thess. 5:8)

J.W. Arroz

LIGHTS OF THE ROUND TABLE

This idea will create a little extra interest in becoming part of a small discipleship or Bible study group. The group is called "The Lights of the Round Table," playing on the idea that we are "lights" to the world. The theme is carried out by having the meetings in the evening, around a round table, with candlelight to study by.

The round table top can be cut from two full size sheets of plywood. Each sheet makes up half of the table. When the two sides are placed together, you've got a table that can seat 12 comfortably. If the group is larger than 12, make two tables. The table tops can be placed on top of a regular square or rectangular table. A king-sized sheet can be laid over the table, or you can paint the plywood. Provide a candle for each place at the table, and you've got an intimate setting with few distractions.

For some reason, it's a lot easier to get youth to become one of the "Lights of the Round Table" than it is to get them out for a regular Bible study. If you make it a special kind of thing, more exclusive than ordinary meetings, and ask for a specific commitment of time, students tend to respond. If you hold these meetings on a week night, keep them short enough that they don't infringe on study time. *Dennis R. McDonough*

NOAH AND THE ARK I.Q. TEST

On page 45 you will find a fun little quiz that will generate new interest in the old familiar story of Noah and the Ark. Most people assume they know everything about the facts of the story, but this test may prove otherwise. *Charles Wiltrout*

Here are the answers:

1. c (Gen. 6:11-13)
2. b (Gen. 6:9, 7:1)
3. c (Gen. 9:20)
4. d (Gen. 6:17)
5. d (Gen. 6:3, 7:6)
6. a (Gen. 6:10)
7. d (Gen. 5:32)
8. b (Gen. 6:15)
9. c
10. a (Gen. 6:16)
11. b (Gen. 6:16)
12. b (Gen. 7:7)
13. b (Gen. 7:2-3)
14. d (Gen. 7:6)
15. d (Gen. 7:11)
16. a (Gen. 7:11, 8:14)
17. b (Gen. 8:6-10)
18. b (Gen. 8:8-9)
19. d (Gen. 8:12)
20. a
21. e (Gen. 9:20-21)
22. d (Gen. 9:8-16)
23. b (It was Mt. Ararat, not Mt. Sinai)

STONE REMINDER

Following a study of John 8:1-11 concerning the woman taken in adultery, give each person in the group a small stone to take home. Discuss the sin of gossip and the warnings from Scripture about cutting people down. We often do it only to make ourselves look good, which is basically the same reason people were so anxious to stone the woman in the Bible story. Ask the students to take the stone home and place it by their telephone. When they're tempted to gossip and attack someone verbally, they might be reminded by the stone to ask themselves, "Am I without sin? Do I qualify to take this stone and throw it at this person?" Many times a visual reminder such as this can be very effective in changing behavior patterns. *Jim Allard*

AFTER THE WELL

For an interesting approach to a study of John 4 (the Woman at the Well), have kids role play the situation after the story ends in Scripture. Someone should play the part of the woman as she confronts the man she has been living with. The scene can open up with the man asking "What took you so long? I thought you were just going up to the well for a bucket of water..."

From there the dialogue can go in any direction. Each character should respond as they think the actual characters might have responded then, or as they (the kids) might have responded had they been in the same position.

Follow up with a discussion of what happened.
Gail Moody

APATHY PARTY

This object lesson is worth a million laughs and deals with a problem that Christ addressed in his letters to the seven churches in Revelation (Rev. 3:14-19).

Announce ahead of time that you are going to have an apathy party and that everyone is to come dressed in the most bland and boring clothing they can dig up. Have them wear what they would wear if they just didn't care.

As kids arrive have sponsors greet them at the door and hand out a list of rules for the party (see page 48). Each sponsor is to have several paper bags large enough to cover the heads of anyone who laughs or gets excited or shows any enthusiasm whatsoever.

The following games may be played at this party:
- **Monotone readings.** Provide books of prose, poetry, phone books, and dictionaries so that each person can read a selection from one using a monotone, emotionless voice. The driest, most boring reading will be declared the winner.
- **Costume contest.** Judges declare the winner wearing the most blah clothes.
- **Deadpan face staring.** Have an elimination contest. Have kids pair up and try to outstare their partner. The winner is the one who stares the longest without laughing or looking away or closing her eyes (blinking is permitted). Each contestant may say things to get the other one to laugh but must not act or sound enthusiastic herself.
- **Balancing-air-on-a-spoon relay.** Tell teams that you were going to have them balance raw eggs on spoons for a relay but that you weren't in the mood to go to the store. So they can balance air on their spoons instead. The first player on each team walks to a mark and back while balancing air on a spoon. (Right!) Upon that player's return the next player heads to the mark and back. Sponsors have the right to indiscriminately make runners start over if they deem that runners have dropped the air from their spoons. (Not fair!)

Noah and the Ark
I.Q. TEST

1. Why did God decide to destroy all living things with the flood?
   a. Because Israel was disobedient.
   b. Because the Romans were corrupt and needed to be punished.
   c. Because everyone was wicked and evil.
   d. Because he knew it was the only way to get rid of disco dancing and junk food.

2. Why did God pick Noah to survive the flood?
   a. Noah was the only guy around who knew how to build an ark.
   b. Noah was the only guy around who loved God and would obey him.
   c. Noah won the trip in a sweepstakes.
   d. Noah begged God to save himself and his family.

3. What was Noah's profession?
   a. Animal expert
   b. Boat builder
   c. Farmer
   d. Temple priest

4. How did Noah find out about the coming flood?
   a. He read about it in the Bible.
   b. He had a dream about it.
   c. He was notified by a prophet.
   d. God told him.

5. How long did Noah have to build the ark and get ready for the flood after he found out about it?
   a. 40 days
   b. One year
   c. Three years
   d. 120 years

6. What were the names of Noah's three sons?
   a. Ham, Shem, and Japheth
   b. Ham, Sam, and Jeff
   c. Ham, Turkey, on Rye
   d. Huey, Dewey, and Louie

7. How old was Noah when his three sons were born?
   a. In his 20's
   b. In his 30's
   c. About 60 years old
   d. About 500 years old

8. How big was the ark?
   a. 50 cubits high, 30 cubits wide, and 300 cubits long
   b. 300 cubits long, 30 cubits high, and 50 cubits wide
   c. 300 cubits wide, 50 cubits long, and 30 cubits high
   d. About the size of the Queen Mary

9. How long is a cubit?
   a. About the same as three schmuckos
   b. About 2.5 meters
   c. About the length of one's forearm
   d. About a yard (three feet)

10. How many doors did the ark have?
    a. One
    b. Two (One on the side, and one on top)
    c. Just the one on the captain's quarters
    d. Who knows?

11. How many floors did the ark have?
    a. One
    b. Three
    c. It was a ranch style, split-level ark
    d. Who knows?

12. How many people did Noah take
    on the ark with him?
    a. 3
    b. 7
    c. 11
    d. 13

13. True or False: Noah took only two of
    each species with him on the ark?
    a. True
    b. False

14. How old was Noah when the
    flood came?
    a. 35
    b. 50
    c. 120
    d. 600

15. Where did the flood waters come from?
    a. A broken pipe
    b. From the sky
    c. From inside the earth
    d. Both b and c

16. How long did the flood last?
    a. A little over a year
    b. 40 days and 40 nights
    c. About three months
    d. Who knows?

17. What bird did Noah send out first
    to see if there was dry land?
    a. A pigeon
    b. A raven
    c. A chicken
    d. A sparrow
    e. None of the above

18. What did the dove return with the
    first time Noah sent it out?
    a. A pepperoni pizza
    b. Nothing
    c. An olive leaf
    d. An olive branch
    e. An olive pit

19. What did the dove return with the
    last time Noah sent it out?
    a. Olive Oyl
    b. A message of peace
    c. Nothing
    d. It did not return

20. Where is the story of Noah in the Bible?
    a. The book of Genesis
    b. The book of Exodus
    c. The book of Noah
    d. The book of Moses

21. After the flood was over, what
    did Noah do?
    a. He continued his righteous life, never
       sinning again.
    b. He planted a vineyard.
    c. He got drunk.
    d. He opened a boat store.
    e. Both b and c

22. God sent a rainbow as a way of
    saying to Noah:
    a. "There's a pot of gold at the end of
       every rainbow."
    b. "Somewhere over the rainbow."
    c. "Every cloud has a silver lining."
    d. "You don't have to worry about floods
       anymore, Noah."
    e. "Don't forget what happened Noah.
       Next time it will be worse!"

23. True or False: Recent scientific
    expeditions have found remains of
    the ark on Mt. Sinai.
    a. True
    b. False
    c. Maybe

The first team to complete the relay gets disqualified for trying too hard, and the last place team gets disqualified for trying to lose.

• **Book-balancing relay.** This is another team relay like "Balancing Air" but kids must balance a book as they walk to the mark and back. However, they may hold the book however they want to because after all it doesn't matter anyway and besides that...who cares?

Sponsors may then announce that all further games have been canceled because by now everyone is thoroughly bored and utterly apathetic. Sponsors may commend those in the group who gave exceptionally fine demonstrations of apathy and boredom. Those who refused to participate in the games are to receive highest praise for their apathy and lack of cooperation. In order to really get into the feel of the lukewarmness of it all, the proper refreshments would include the following:

• Flat, lukewarm soda in small cups or, better yet, lukewarm tap water. (The sponsors may explain that they just didn't have the energy to get anything better.)

• Small pieces of cold frozen pizza.

• Small cups of melted ice cream.

Follow the refreshment time with a discussion on Revelation 3:14-19 about the consequences of being lukewarm or apathetic. Allow the kids to share their reactions to the party and the refreshments. This might be a good way to creatively shock a lukewarm youth group out of its doldrums. You might wrap up with some good refreshments and a little enthusiasm. *Ed Skidmore*

CLUES TO HAPPINESS

What are some of the clues to real happiness? Jesus spoke on the subject in his opening pronouncements in the Sermon on the Mount (Matt. 5:1-12). The word happy could easily substitute where the word blessed is found in many translations. As a way of helping the young people to think about this passage from Matthew before they study it, give each of them a sheet of paper. Ask them to list all of the things that make them happy, contented, or leave them feeling good. Then, compare their lists with the list of Beatitudes found in Matthew 5. There will probably be a great difference between the two. Yet, the sharing can prove to be fruitful as you can help the group begin to discover what it means to be poor in spirit, to be meek, merciful, pure in heart, peacemakers, etc. In short, the group can uncover some new light on the meaning of happiness. *Vernon Edington*

FAMILY CHAPTER

This is a study of 1 Thessalonians 2. It calls attention to the family titles used by Paul in this chapter:

Brothers—verses 1, 9, 14, 17
Mother—verse 7
Father—verse 11

Study the chapter as a group, bringing in other Scripture that might be relevant. (For example, Acts 17 for info on Paul's ministry in Thessalonica; Jeremiah 31:1 and Ephesians 3:14-15 for other references to the family of God.) Then hand out the questions on page 47 for small groups or individuals to work on. Close with some sharing of insights and commitments. *Doug Newhouse*

FOOLISH FARMER

This idea deals with materialism and more specifically the parable of the foolish farmer (or the rich fool) in Luke 12:13-21. Divide the group into families of six to eight people and give them a copy of the Foolish Farmer instructions on page 50.

This will result in some heated discussion within each family. It will be interesting to see how the parable is interpreted and adapted to meet the needs of the group. Some will want to take the parable very literally and radically; others will see it as hyperbole or not applicable today.

After all the families have had sufficient time, have them come back together and share their results, along with the reasoning that went into their decisions.

To add an interesting twist to this exercise, give the above instructions to all of the family groups, but only give half of the groups the last line that asks them to read the Scripture. There should be a noticeable difference between the groups that use the Bible passage as a basis for their decisions and those that don't. This could lead to a related discussion on the importance of Scripture and how the Bible affects our day-to-day decision-making process. *Richard L. Starcher*

A GOD'S-EYE VIEW

Used in conjunction with Psalm 8, the narrative on page 52 dramatically illustrates the majesty of God's creation. It is also a good self-image booster as it reminds us of the significance we have in God's eyes.

Apathy Party

RULES

NOT ALLOWED:

Laughing (giggling, chuckling, etc.)

Crying

Smiling (grinning)

Frowning (scowling)

Loud voices (neither happy nor angry)

Fast movements

Bright eyes

Enthusiastic hand gestures

Applause

Interesting conversations

Exclamations ("Wow!", "Hey!" etc.)

ALLOWED:

Yawning

Bored looks (glazed eyes, rolling eyes, deadpan expression)

Slow movements

Tapping fingers

Twiddling thumbs

Monotone voice

Boring conversations

Staring into space...

** If you are caught performing any of the activities that are not allowed, you must put a sack over your head until you are able to control yourself and behave in a properly boring manner.
** Anyone who cannot get control of himself in a reasonable amount of time will have to go into the hall until he can return apathetically. Have a real ho-hum time…

Family Chapter

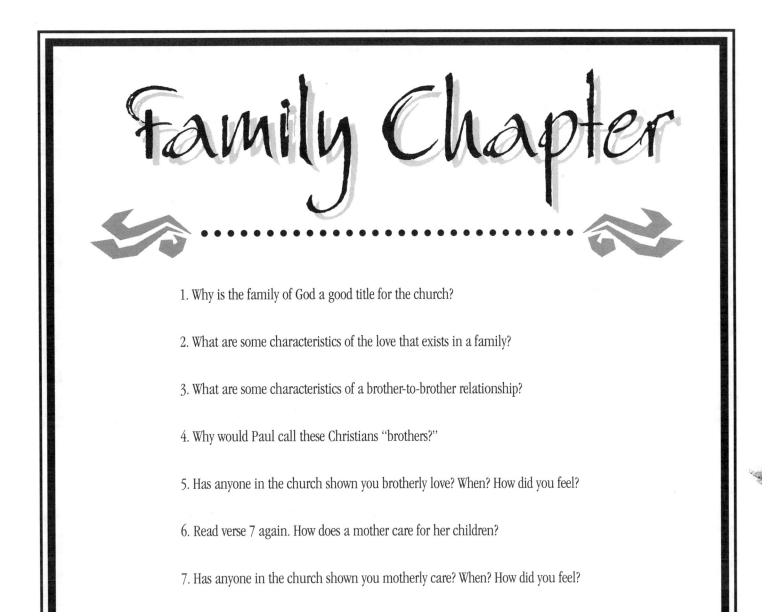

1. Why is the family of God a good title for the church?

2. What are some characteristics of the love that exists in a family?

3. What are some characteristics of a brother-to-brother relationship?

4. Why would Paul call these Christians "brothers?"

5. Has anyone in the church shown you brotherly love? When? How did you feel?

6. Read verse 7 again. How does a mother care for her children?

7. Has anyone in the church shown you motherly care? When? How did you feel?

8. Reread verse 11. How does a father deal with his children?

9. Has anyone in the church dealt with you in a fatherly way? When? How did you feel?

10. Why should the church provide all three of these relationships—brotherly love, motherly care, and fatherly correction?

11. Does your church have these relationships?

12. What can you do to improve these relationships in the church? In your youth group? With your sponsors?

Foolish Farmer

You are a family and must make a family decision. Everyone in the family must be in agreement; any one person may veto the decision of the group.

You have just received $100,000 from an unexpected source. You must now decide as a family how you will use that money. The only requirements are that you must explain specifically what you will do with the money and you must decide in the next 10 minutes.

Read Luke 12:13-21 before you begin your discussion.

Foolish Farmer

You are a family and must make a family decision. Everyone in the family must be in agreement; any one person may veto the decision of the group.

You have just received $100,000 from an unexpected source. You must now decide as a family how you will use that money. The only requirements are that you must explain specifically what you will do with the money and you must decide in the next 10 minutes.

Read Luke 12:13-21 before you begin your discussion.

After reading the narrative aloud to the group, you might want to have the kids read Psalm 8 in unison. With this as a background, you can then discuss the following questions or other questions of your choice:
• How does this psalm make you feel about God?
• How does this psalm make you feel about yourself?
• What does this psalm suggest a person's self-image should be? (Also see Matt. 10:29-31)
• What do you think it means when the psalmist says that God crowned human beings with love and honor?
• Why do you think God needed to create such a large universe? *Glenn Davis*

GRAB-BAG TALENTS

Here's a fun, creative, contemporary activity to use in conjunction with a study of the parable of the talents, found in the New Testament. That narrative, you will recall, involved a man who gave three people a similar amount of money (talents), instructing them to trade with the talents while he was away. Upon his return, he found that the three people had handled the talents in different ways. The first person had multiplied his original amount 10 times; the second man five times. The third man, however, buried his one-pound talent. The full story is told in Luke 19:11-27. (Note: While it is true that the talent in this story is money, the emphasis is not on the money, but on what is done with the gift. Don't allow the group to get hung up on the different meanings of "talent.")

Fill small paper or plastic bags with a variety of these items: paper clips, cotton swabs, tape, Popsicle sticks, rubber bands, toothpicks, straws—whatever you can find. Put a little of everything in each bag. Give each person a bag with these instructions: "See what you can do with what's inside." Don't say anything about the reason for this activity, don't mention the parable, give no other details at this point. Have some glue, paper, scissors, and other staple items available if needed.

Then watch what kids do. Some kids will get busy right away; others may give up immediately. Incidentally, tell kids it is okay to borrow or exchange items.

After 20 minutes or so, have kids display and explain their creations. Then read the parable of the talents and discuss these questions:
• What words or phrases do you recall from the parable we just read?

• Briefly retell the parable in your own words (get views from more than one person).
• What did you think when I handed you a bag filled with junk? Be honest.
• How is the bag-of-junk activity like the parable of the talents?
• How do you feel when you don't do your best or reach your potential? How do you feel when you do your best and reach your potential? *Robin Kreider*

ISAIAH'S PROPHECY

Often we fail to fully appreciate Jesus Christ's death for us. Perhaps we are too familiar with the details of the Crucifixion. Maybe the story has become so commonplace that we forget that it was our sins that led Jesus to the cross and a horribly painful death. In this study and sharing exercise, youth group members will look at the prediction of Jesus' death by Isaiah, and recognize that it was their sins that brought the prophecy's fulfillment. Read Isaiah 53. Read the entire chapter out loud, alternating verses. Then ask these questions:
• Who do you think Isaiah was talking about?
• What does Isaiah say that reminds you of Jesus? Then have kids write out their own paraphrases of a few of the more meaningful verses in the chapter. They are to insert Jesus' name in the paraphrase whenever there is a singular personal pronoun. When finished, let several volunteers read what they have written.

To complete the study, have kids reread verses 4-6 again, paraphrase them, and write their own name in place of each plural personal pronoun.

Then discuss these questions:
• Pretend you are the only person who has ever lived. Did Jesus have to die just for you? Why?
• What has Jesus' death done for you?
• What is your response to Jesus right now? *Doug Newhouse*

JUMBLED PROVERBS

Generate interest in the Book of Proverbs with this activity. Explain how the proverbs in chapters 10-21 are written in a parallel style. Two phrases are usually separated by the conjunctions "but," "and," or "than." When you are sure that kids understand the parallel style, have them try to match the appropriate clauses in the jumbled selection of parables on page 54.

A God's-Eye View

I want you to use your imagination. Imagine that I have a long sheet of paper that stretches all the way across the front of the room, out the door, outside the building, and continues until you can't see it anymore.

Now imagine that I take a pin and poke a tiny hole in the paper—that is the earth. All the cities, mountains, and oceans of our planet are represented by that speck.

About 5/8ths of an inch from the pinhole, make another pinhole—that's the moon.

Now imagine that 19 feet away, I draw a 2-inch circle that is the sun. Six hundred feet away, the length of two football fields, we come to Neptune.

After leaving the solar system, and our pinhole planets, we would have to travel along 1,000 miles of paper to come to the nearest star. That's roughly the distance between Chicago and Denver.

Distances in space are so vast they are measured in light years, the distance that light will travel in a year; light travels at over 186,000 miles per second. That's so fast that a bullet shot at that speed and circling the earth would hit you seven times before you fell to the ground, even if it took you one second to fall.

At the speed of light, you could travel from Los Angeles to New York in 1/60th of a second. You could reach the moon in less than 12 seconds, the sun in eight minutes, and cover the entire solar system in 11 hours.

But even at those speeds, it would take you 4.3 years to reach the nearest star. You would need 400 years to reach the North Star, and to cross just one galaxy, our own Milky Way, would take 120,000 years. And astronomers now estimate that there are over 100 million galaxies.

This exercise can be done individually, in small groups, or in a large group. There is only one rule: Kids cannot refer to the Bibles. The winner of the game is the group or individual with the most correctly matched proverbs.

Wrap things up with a discussion on the proverbs themselves. You will find that most of the proverbs in the Book of Proverbs and in other Old Testament books like Ecclesiastes contain definitions by implication. For example: "He who trusts in his own mind is a fool, but he who walks in wisdom will be delivered" (Proverbs 28:26). The definition: walking in wisdom is not trusting one's own mind.

This sort of thing can be done with all the proverbs. Find the truths that are there and then look for ways that they can be applied today. *Jerry Daniel*

A New Humanity

The declaration on page 55 can be used as an effective discussion starter. Give everyone a copy, discuss each paragraph one at a time, and try to arrive at a consensus on the three principles that are called for. The process should get everyone thinking, and should be an interesting exercise in communication and group problem-solving as well.

Conclude the exercise by looking at 2 Corinthians 5:17-20. Help the group to realize that as Christians we are in fact members of a new humanity —a community called out by Christ with a specific mission. This session can be followed up with a definite plan for implementing the principles and putting them into action in some concrete way. *Brad Davis*

Biblical Time Machine

The dilemmas people faced in the Bible can often seem remote to us today because they happened so long ago. This activity is aimed at making biblical dilemmas more immediate and understandable to contemporary young people.

Begin by selecting several passages of Scripture that describe people faced with a dilemma. Examples are when God spoke to Abraham about offering up Isaac, when Ruth had to decide whether to return to her people or to stay with Naomi, when Jesus is asked why he hasn't paid taxes, when the disciples realize that there is a crowd of over 5,000 people who are hungry and need to be fed, when the people of the Corinthian church are faced with a variety of leaders and are wondering who to follow.

Read one of these stories to the group. Ask kids to describe the main truth to be learned from the story. Have them then describe a modern context in which a similar type of dilemma might be found. Discuss how the truth learned from the Bible story might apply in this circumstance.

Ask the group to get in small groups of about six each. Give each group one of the biblical dilemmas you've selected or let groups pick their own. They should read the passage where the dilemma is found, discuss its main point and then recreate it within a modern context. They should find a modern situation that parallels the same circumstances.

Each group should act out its dilemma for the other groups. Encourage discussion on complexities of the issues presented in the dilemmas, the gray areas they open up, and the questions that evolve. Aim at leading the group to make some discoveries as to how it might begin to deal with dilemmas in a realistic manner. End the discussion by asking kids to think and share how the insight they have could, should, or will affect their lives. *Anna Citrino*

The Friend at Midnight

One of the lesser known of Jesus' parables is the story of the friend at midnight in Luke 11:5-8. But here's a way to teach it to young people that will make it unforgettable.

Have one volunteer be the person who went to bed early. Tell that person: "It is approaching midnight in Jerusalem, and you are sound asleep. You are sleeping in a big bed with the rest of your family. To get up out of bed would be a tremendous inconvenience and would wake everybody up. There is nothing in the world that would get you up out of bed at this time of night."

Have a second volunteer come forward and be the neighbor at the door. Tell that person: "It is midnight and some out-of-town guests have just arrived at your house. They are very hungry. But, alas, you don't have a thing in the refrigerator; nothing in the pantry. There are no stores open. It would be a terrible disgrace to send your guests to bed hungry. So, you go next door to your neighbor's house, try to wake him (or her) and borrow some food. You won't take no for an answer. You try to get food no matter what."

And to the first person again, you say: "Remember …you aren't getting out of bed for anything!"

Now challenge the two people to role-play the situation with gusto. Set a time limit or let it go on for

JUMBLED PROVERBS

11:22	Like a gold ring in a swine's snout,	but the mercy of the wicked is cruel.
12:10	A righteous man has regard for the life of his beast,	that one may avoid the snares of death.
12:11	He who tills his land will have plenty of bread,	than a fatted ox and hatred with it.
12:19	Truthful lips endure for ever,	but he who is kind to the needy honors him.
13:14	The teaching of the wise is a fountain of life,	not so the minds of fools.
13:24	He who spares the rod hates his son,	but a lying tongue is but for a moment.
14:1	Wisdom builds her house,	and a word in season, how good it is.
14:31	He who oppresses a poor man insults his Maker,	but he who follows worthless pursuits has no sense.
15:7	The lips of the wise spread knowledge,	is a beautiful woman without discretion.
15:17	Better is a dinner of herbs where love is,	but folly with her own hands tears it down.
15:23	To make an apt answer is a joy to a man,	but he who loves him is diligent to discipline him.

A New Humanity

WE who are gathered here together in the presence of each other, do hereby and forthwith solemnly covenant and agree wholeheartedly to the formation, preservation, and perpetuation of A NEW HUMANITY—the ordering and governance of which is entirely up to us.

ON this momentous and historic occasion, therefore, let us duly establish and confirm, once for all, the manner and means by which our NEW HUMANITY will forge a history of its own from within the womb of the prevailing social milieu.

IT is not ours to condemn that humanity which is old and passing away, but rather to affirm and commend that HUMANITY which is NEW and ours—and thereby promulgate a vital and viable alternative to the status quo.

THIS being the case; and we, being of one heart and one mind, do here and now lay down and inscribe, for posterity's sake, the following fundamental principles upon which our NEW HUMANITY is now and ever hereafter eternally founded.

PRINCIPLE ONE: _____

_____

PRINCIPLE TWO: _____

_____

PRINCIPLE THREE: _____

_____

**Agreed to and witnessed by:

as long as it is interesting. When the actors are finished, applaud them and then discuss what happened.

Ask kids to identify the lessons that are taught by this parable. Make sure that kids understand this was a lesson on prayer, taught by Jesus. His point was that we should pray with the kind of persistence that the neighbor in need had at midnight.

SCRIPTURE'S COMMON DENOMINATORS

The next time you are looking for a good way to get your kids into Scripture, divide everyone into groups of threes and give each group the following list. Kids must look up each set of verses and decide on a common theme found in each of them. Encourage them to try to write out themes in an active voice rather than a passive voice. For example: "God is merciful" (active) rather than "The mercy of God" (passive). Add other sets of verses as needed.

Also invite kids to explain which verse means the most to them and why. *Pat Andrews*

Here are the answers:

1. God is merciful
2. Peace between God and humanity
3. Christ is head of the Church
4. Form a God-conscience
5. Friendship
6. Have a visible faith
7. Do not return evil for evil
8. Anger
9. Forgive those who wrong you
10. Charity or love
11. We should imitate Christ
12. Don't be a bad example
13. Children and parents
14. Serve God
15. Have confidence in God
16. God is good and caring
17. Don't be a hypocrite
18. Be patient
19. Act on Word of God
20. Deny self
21. Avoid discord and arguing
22. Keep God's commandments
23. Choose friends well
24. Obey God
25. Persevere
26. Be wise

SIGNPOSTS TO LIFE

Here's a good way to use the 10 Commandments as a discussion starter. Read the following paraphrase of the commandments or make a signpost of each one to hang on the wall:

1. I shall be the only God you will have.
2. I am the only image you shall worship.
3. My name shall always be taken seriously.
4. You shall receive my day as a holy one.
5. You shall act responsibly toward your parents.
6. You shall respect the sacredness of life.
7. You shall respect the possessions of others.
8. You shall be loyal to your family.
9. You shall always tell the truth.
10. You will be content and satisfied with what I give you.

After discussing each of these, ask the following questions:

1. Do the 10 Commandments apply to us today?
2. What is a covenant?
3. What are some covenants we make today?
4. What is the basis of God's covenant with Israel?
5. Why did this fail with Israel in the Old Testament?
6. Did Jesus change the Law?
7. How are the 10 Commandments signposts for us?
8. How did Jesus express the essence of the Law?

Larry J. Michael

B.A.D. BIBLE STUDY

Here's a Bible study outline that's really B.A.D.! The initials stand for "Being and Doing," and it's a perfect way to generate interest in study in the book of James. If presented at a retreat, the theme can be carried a little further by dividing into teams with the names of "bad" people like "The Dalton Gang" or "The Al Capone Mob."

Here's a sample outline to follow for the study: (All Scripture references are in James unless otherwise noted.)

I. Dealing with B.A.D. Attitudes
   A. Anger (1:19-21)
   B. Hypocrisy (1:22-27)
   C. Prejudice (2:1-12)
   D. Pride (4:13-17)
II. B.A.D. Words
   A. Faith (2:14-26)

Scripture's Common Denominators

_____ 1. Matthew 9:13, Luke 6:36, 1 Timothy 1:12-13

_____ 2. Acts 10:36, Romans 5:1, Philippians 4:7

_____ 3. 1 Corinthians 12:27, Ephesians 1:22, Colossians 1:18

_____ 4. 2 Corinthians 1:12, 1 Timothy 1:19, 1 John 3:21

_____ 5. Proverbs 17:9, John 15:14, James 4:4

_____ 6. John 7:38, Romans 1:16 or 3:22, Galatians 3:8

_____ 7. 1 Corinthians 4:12, 1 Thessalonians 5:15, 1 Peter 3:9

_____ 8. Galatians 5:20, Titus 1:7, Matthew 5:22

_____ 9. Mark 11:25, Luke 6:32, Colossians 3:13

_____ 10. 1 Timothy 1:5, 1 Peter 4:8, 1 John 4:16

_____ 11. John 13:15, 1 Corinthians 15:49, Ephesians 5:1

_____ 12. Matthew 17:27, Romans 14:1-15, 2 Corinthians 6:3

_____ 13. Matthew 4:22, Mark 7:10, Ephesians 6:1-2

_____ 14. Philippians 3:13, Hebrews 12:28, Jude 1

_____ 15. John 16:33, 1 Timothy 6:17, 1 John 3:21

_____ 16. Luke 15:20-27, 2 Corinthians 1:3, Ephesians 2:4

_____ 17. Mark 7:6-7, Acts 5:1-11, 2 Timothy 3:5, 2 Timothy 3:5

_____ 18. 2 Thessalonians 1:4-7, 2 Peter 1:6, James 5:7

_____ 19. John 13:17, Hebrews 4:2, James 1:22-23

_____ 20. Matthew 5:29-30, Acts 5:1-11, Philippians 3:7

_____ 21. 2 Timothy 2:14-23, Titus 3:1-2, 9, James 4:1

_____ 22. John 15:10-12, James 2:10, 1 John 5:2-3

_____ 23. 2 Corinthians 6:14, 2 John 10; Revelation 18:4

_____ 24. John 2:7, Acts 4:19, Romans 16:19

_____ 25. 2 Thessalonians 3:13, 2 John 8, Jude 21

_____ 26. Romans 11:33, Colossians 2:3, James 3:15

B. Wisdom (3:13-18)

C. Obedience (4:1-12)

D. Patience (5:7-12)

E. Prayer (5:13-20)

III. B.A.D. People

    A. Abraham and Isaac (2:21-24; Gen. 12,15,21-22)

    B. Rahab (2:25; Josh. 2)

    C. Job (5:11, Job 1-2)

    D. Elijah 5:17; I Kings 17-18)

IV. B.A.D. Advice from the Book of James

    A. Chapter 1

      1. Greeting (1:1)

      2. Trials (1:2-18)

        a. The Purpose of Trials (1:2-12)

        b. The Pedigree of Trials (1:13-16)

        c. The Purpose of God (1:17-18)

      3. The Word (1:19-27)

    B. Chapter 2

      1. Partiality (2:1-13)

        a. The Command (2:1)

        b. The Conduct (2:2-3)

        c. The Consequences (2:4-13)

      2. Faith and Works (2:14-26)

        a. The Inquiry (2:14)

        b. The Illustration (2:15-27)

        c. The Indoctrination (2:18-26)

    C. Chapter 3

      1. Sins of the Tongue (3:1-12)

        a. Its Bridling (3:1-4)

        b. Its Boasting (3:5-12)

      2. True Wisdom (3:13-18)

    D. Chapter 4

      1. Worldliness (4:1-17)

        a. Its Cause (4:1-2)

        b. Its Consequences (4:3-6)

        c. Its Cure (4:7-10)

        d. Its Characteristics (4:11-17)

    E. Chapter 5

      1. Riches, Patience, and Swearing (5:1-12)

      2. Prayer (5:13-18)

      3. The Conversion of the Erring (5:19-20)

Tommy Baker

FOUR PICTURES OF UNITY

Every youth group struggles to maintain relationships characterized by harmony and mutual concern. It's all too easy for young people to pick at petty differences, and without warning those small problems can become devastating schisms within the group.

This Bible study is intended to help young people identify the aspects of living in God's family that are shared by all. By recognizing the kind of unity God desires for his people, they can take steps to restore that harmony and heal any breaks that may have occurred.

These four pictures identified by the Apostle Peter in 1 Peter 1:22-2:10 are outlined by Warren W. Wiersbe in his book, *Be Hopeful* (Victor, 1982). Use the following questions to talk with your group about the need for unity:

Children of the Same Family (1:22-2:3)

1. How did we become children in the same family?

2. What brought about our new birth?

3. How is the Word described? What do you think this means? How important is the Word to God's family?

4. According to Peter, how should "brothers" treat each other?

5. Can we disagree with each other and still have "sincere love" for each other?

6. How was the Word "preached" to you?

7. Describe how children in God's family are like "newborn babies." Do we ever leave this stage? How? Do some remain spiritual "babies?" Why? What's the result when babies won't grow up?

Stone in the Same Building (2:4-8)

1. What is Jesus called in this passage?

2. What are we called? What's the difference between Jesus and us in this building?

3. How was Jesus treated? What's the result? What does that say to us, who are part of the same building?

4. What are some characteristics of a stone? How do these apply to the Christian?

5. Why is it valuable to have different kinds of stone when you're building? How does this principle apply to our group?

Priests in the Same Temple (2:9)

1. What are the privileges of priests?

2. What are the responsibilities of priests?

3. How do other people view priests? Is this good or bad?

4. How should priests live in relation to other priests?

5. How should priests live in relation to other people?

Citizens of the Same Nation (2:9-10)

1. How are these citizens described?

2. What does "a people belonging to God" mean?

3. How does the ownership of something increase its value? Give some examples. Now apply that truth to the Christian who is "owned" by God.

4. Where should Christians find their source of self-worth? Where do we usually try to find it?

5. What "nation" are we a part of? Where is this nation located?

6. Read Philippians 3:20. What insight does this verse add to the words of Peter?

7. What is our responsibility to each other as citizens of God's nation? What happens when citizens fight each other?

8. What is our responsibility to other people?

Conclude your Bible study by reviewing the reasons Peter outlines for maintaining harmony and unity in your group. If time permits or need demands, briefly discuss any problems that have been dividing the group. Ask group members to resolve that they will make an effort to heal wounds and promote harmony. Ask for specific ways they can accomplish these goals. If group members can verbalize their decisions, encourage them to do so. Close your study with prayer. *Doug Newhouse*

MEASURING UP

Here's an exciting way to get your group to think about the almost-taboo subject of obedience to God and his will for them individually. Have a Measuring Up Party to which they must bring a ruler, yardstick, tape measure, or some other measuring instrument as their admission.

Meet at the local high school football stadium. Divide them into three groups, and have them mark off the measurements of the ark inside the stadium (450 feet long x 75 feet wide x 45 feet high). When they finish have them meet in the bleachers and point out to the others the area they measured (for example, show how high up the side of the bleachers equals 45 feet). Measuring height is easier if they measure a single brick or block in a nearby wall, divide 45 feet by that distance, and then count that many bricks or blocks up. For example, if the bricks are six inches (half a foot) high, divide 45 by .05, which equals 90. Count 90 bricks up for the correct height.

Next, lead them in a discussion of how difficult this task must have been for Noah to accomplish. Relate Noah's difficulty to their own responsibility for following God, but be sure to point out that Noah was chosen on the basis of his attitude (Gen. 6:9) rather than his ability to build big boats, of which there is no previous record. You may want to refer them as well to Noah's open sin in Genesis 9:20 to help them realize that he was not perfect, and that all of us can "measure up" to God's calling if we are only willing to be obedient. (You can also read the related passage of Heb. 11:7.) *William A. Gunter*

PARABLE OF THE SOWER

Here's a good way to help your junior highers understand the parable of the sower a little better. Using a plant starter box, fill each tray with one of the four types of soils mentioned in the parable; hard, dry soil; soil with rocks in it; soil with weeds in it (grass seed can be used); and good soil. Discuss the parable with the group, and speculate about how the various kinds of soils might affect the growth of a plant.

Next, plant some seeds in the four different soils. Corn seed will work fine. Make sure someone is in charge of watering the plantings as required over the next few weeks, and let the plants grow. As the weeks go by, you can chart the progress of the plants and draw comparisons to the principals taught by Jesus in the parable. It takes approximately 80 days for corn to grow, so you might want to take some pictures at weekly intervals just to keep track of how they're doing. The pictures would make a nice poster at the conclusion of the experiment.

You can transplant the good corn into a garden when it's ready, and maybe even eat the corn with the group. They'll never forget the parable. *Terry Dawson*

PRODIGAL PROBLEMS

Next time you're doing a study or talk on the parable of the prodigal son, use the pop quiz on page 61 to get everyone's attention. It's fun and educational, too! Here are the answers:

1—e. The story is in Luke 15, not Mark 15.
2—b. Verse 12.
3—b. Verse 12 says he divided his property "between them."
4—c. Verse 15.
5—c. Verse 20.
6—d. Verse 22.
7—c. Verse 25.
8—c. Verse 25.
9—c. Verse 29.
10—c. Verse 19.
11—d. The calf wished he'd never come home, too!
12—c.
13—b. Verse 28.
14—d. Verse 18 says, "Father, I have sinned against heaven and against you. Besides, have you ever known someone named "uncertain"? "Heaven" must have been his mother's name, right?
15—c. Verse 30.

David P. Mann

SO YOU WANT TO CUT AN ALBUM?

This activity will take 30 to 45 minutes. You will need to divide into groups of three to five people. Bibles, paper, pencils, and great imaginations are needed.

Each group will select a chapter from the Bible and then "produce" a CD that reflects the themes of that chapter. Each group reads the passage and selects eight to 10 song titles to be put on the album. Encourage originality and creativity. Next, each group must design a CD cover with proper credits. The album also needs to be entitled.

Here are a few sample passages of Scripture that could be used:

Matthew 18	Acts 10
Acts 2	John 10
Luke 15	Mark 16
Acts 16	Acts 3
John 15	John 3
Luke 10	Romans 12

When the groups are finished, allow them to share their results with each other. For added fun have them perform one of their songs. *John Peters*

THERE IS A TIME

The following activity works well as a way to help your young people realize how they use their time. It also allows them an opportunity to compare their own lifestyles to the lifestyle of Christ.

Have the kids choose a typical day of the week. It could be any day, Monday through Saturday. Then give them the chart on page 62. Have them evaluate how much time they spend in the various activities that are listed for their typical day, making sure that the hours total 24. They should put this information in the column labeled YOURSELF.

When they've finished doing this, have them label the column at the far right JESUS. They should now imagine how much time they think Jesus would spend in the same activities if he were living as a human being today in our culture and community.

Next, they should compare the two columns and see if they can come to any conclusions about their own use of time. Do a quick study of Romans 8:28-30 and emphasize the point that they need to do their best to imitate Christ. This can either lead into a study of the life of Christ or end with a discussion about how to be more like Jesus at school, home, work, and church. *Joe Harvey*

UPPERS AND DOWNERS

For an excellent exercise in community building, have the kids in your group fill out the chart on page 63.

Ask the kids to think of a time when someone said something to them that was really a downer—something that made them feel bad. This could be a put-down, an angry comment, anything. Then have them think of a time when someone said an upper to them—something that made them feel good. If they can think of several entries for the first two columns, encourage them to write them in.

Next, have the kids do the same thing in the third and fourth columns, only this time they should think of times when they said an upper or downer to someone else.

Chances are your young people will be able to think of many more downers than uppers, if your

Prodigal Problems

1. According to the parable of the prodigal son found in Mark 15:11-31, how many sons were there?
   a) 1
   b) 2
   c) 3
   d) multitudes
   e) none

2. Which son is considered the prodigal?
   a) oldest
   b) youngest
   c) middle
   d) the one with the earring

3. When did the oldest son get his inheritance?
   a) when Pop died
   b) at the same time as the other
   c) when the sun stood still

4. What job did the prodigal son take once his wealth ran out?
   a) youth pastor
   b) farming
   c) pig slopper
   d) carnival barker

5. (Fill in the blank.) "But while he was a long way off, his father saw him and was filled with _____ for him..."
   a) disgust
   b) totalitarianism
   c) compassion
   d) punishments

6. What items did the father give his returned son?
   a) robe, gold chain, and sandals
   b) ring, sandals, and Walkman
   c) ring, robe, and 'rithmetic
   d) sandals, ring, and robe

7. Where was the older son when the younger son returned home?
   a) BMX racing
   b) tending the cattle
   c) in the field
   d) out somewhere

8. The older son knew something was up when he heard...
   a) the doorbell
   b) music
   c) music and dancing
   d) a still, small voice

9. What did the older son say his father never gave him so he could celebrate with his friends?
   a) fattened calf
   b) party hats
   c) goat
   d) lamb

10. What didn't the younger son feel worthy to be called any longer?
    a) chicken lips
    b) Jewish
    c) son
    d) prodigal
    e) Buford

11. Who was unhappy at the homecoming?
    a) the fattened calf
    b) the homecoming queen
    c) older son
    d) a and c

12. According to verse 19, who did the younger son want to be like?
    a) big brother
    b) Dad
    c) hired servants
    d) Pastor Dave
    e) Buford

13. Where did the older brother refuse to go?
    a) Africa
    b) in the house
    c) to the party
    d) Bismarck High
    e) Sodom

14. According to verse 18, what was the mother's name?
    a) Mildred
    b) Rachel
    c) Hildegaard
    d) heaven
    e) uncertain

15. What did the older son say the younger son spent his money on?
    a) video games
    b) friends
    c) women of the evening
    d) wine, women, and song

There Is a Time

TIME ANALYSIS FOR AN AVERAGE DAY (24 HOURS)

ACTIVITIES

	NUMBER OF HOURS	
	Yourself	Jesus
School		
Homework		
Church		
Prayer		
Bible study/reading		
Sports, play		
Watching TV		
Listening to music		
Playing games		
Dating		
Extracurricular school activities		
Sleeping		
Hanging out		
Eating		
Driving around		
Other		
TOTAL		

OTHERS		ME	
Upper	**Downer**	**Upper**	**Downer**

UPPERS & DOWNERS

OTHERS		ME	
Upper	**Downer**	**Upper**	**Downer**

UPPERS & DOWNERS

OTHERS		ME	
Upper	**Downer**	**Upper**	**Downer**

UPPERS & DOWNERS

group is typical. Discuss what this means. Talk about how easy it is to discourage or to put down others without a second thought—how damaging our tongue can be, and how the damage takes so long to repair.

Follow up with a look at Hebrews 10:23-25, which deals with encouragement, and then discuss practical ways to put it into practice.

You can also help kids identify the things they say to each other as an upper or a downer. This will encourage them to be more careful about what they say. If you are on a weekend retreat, challenge them to confront each other during the retreat when they hear someone giving someone else a downer. This can cut down on the negativism that often ruins youth group meetings and activities. *Bill Williamson*

WILL THE REAL GOSPEL PLEASE STAND UP?

As an intro to the book of Galatians, particularly chapter 1:6-9, this adaptation of the old TV game show, "What's My Line?" works great. Have six people come to the front of the room, each representing the Christian gospel. They read their "affidavits" as printed on page 65 (modify them as you see fit), and then the group discusses the pros and cons of each one. For best results, have each person know the role well enough to defend his or her position when questioned by group members. Finally, let the group vote on which one (or ones) they feel best represents the gospel. *Jack Schultz*

BIBLE RAPS

Rap is a musical form that can be used for all kinds of youth group applications—Bible study, announcements, skits, and so on. Rap is basically a rhythmical poem performed, but not exactly sung, against a musical background

To do a rap with your youth group, you'll need to get a music track (record or tape) that you can rap to. Some kids in your group might have one, If they don't, go to your local record shop and ask for a single of any rap group, and see if it has an instrumental version of the song on it—the label should tell you if it does.

Then let the youth group make up a rap that can be done to the music. If you do it as a Bible study, give the kids a Bible passage or story and let them translate it into rap. After they have written the rap, have them perform it to the music. For added fun, video-tape it and let them see how well they did. *David C. Wright*

CORINTHIAN MAD LIBS

The next time you discuss the love chapter in the Bible (1 Cor. 13), make it come alive by turning it into a mad lib. First, get your group's responses to the questions listed on page 66 and then read the chapter aloud as given on the same page (based on *Today's English Version*), filling in the blanks with their answers. The exercise can help teens gain a fresh understanding of Paul's words on love. Take care, however, that the Scripture doesn't become trivialized by overly silly responses. Follow up with your own questions about what kids think that various phrases in the passage mean. *Alan C. Wilder*

IT'S ALL GREEK TO ME

Is Acts 2 in this quarter's lessons? Need an effective, realistic illustration of the coming of the Holy Spirit to the disciples? Your group can get the feel of what it must have sounded like when out-of-towners heard the mighty works of God proclaimed in their own languages.

First, translate a Bible verse into several languages. (See sample of John 3:16 translated into six languages. This verse, by the way, is translated into the most common languages in the front of most Gideon Bibles.) Then ask some students in your group who can speak a foreign language to read the verse in that language. There are enough kids taking Spanish, French, or German in most groups for you to find a few. And perhaps some of your kids are from families with strong ethnic ties—such as Italian or Swedish families, for instance—and who have retained some of their native languages or you may have students who know sign language.

In any case, your group members need not understand the words in the verse they read—all they need to do is read it aloud as best they can with a correct pronunciation. Try to have at least three or four languages represented. (Don't forget English!) Try to distribute the verses ahead of time so that readers can practice. After you've explained the tongues phenomenon in Acts 2, have everyone simultaneously read

Will the Real Gospel Please Stand Up?

1. I am the gospel of hope. Knowing that mankind is utterly sinful and lost, I claim that Jesus died on the cross and rose from the dead to give all people everywhere forgiveness of sin and eternal life. God does it all, mankind does nothing—therefore, all people everywhere will be saved.

2. My gospel teaches that Jesus died and rose for the forgiveness of all mankind. Those who believe in Jesus will have this forgiveness and eternal life. I also expect you to follow Jesus' command, "Go and sin no more" (John 8:11).

3. I am the gospelof grace. Jesus suffered, died, and rose that mankind might have forgiveness and life. If you believe, it doesn't matter what you do. You are under a blanket of forgiveness and grace. Enjoy yourself, don't worry how you're doing—Jesus did it all!

4. My gospel teaches that Jesus died and rose for the sins of mankind. This gospel creates a relationship with God in which a person repents and believes in Jesus. This believer's life is one of repentance and faith, expressing itself in love (Gal. 5:6).

5. My gospel is one of action. The same Jesus that suffered and died for the forgiveness of our sins, also said, "Let your light shine before men, that they may see your good deeds and praise your Father in heaven." I teach that unless your faith is active, it is no faith at all. Your faith must be visible.

6. I am the gospel of faith. Jesus died and rose for the sins of all who believe. All that God requires of us comes freely through the death and resurrection of his Son. We need only to believe that. Romans 5:1, "Therefore, since we have been justified through faith, we have peace with God through our Lord Jesus Christ." And from John 6:28, "Then they asked him, 'What must we do to do the works God requires?' Jesus answered, 'The work of God is this: to believe in the one he has sent.'"

Corinthian Mad Libs

1. Name an animal. _____
2. Name another animal. _____
3. Name a loud musical instrument. _____
4. Name a percussion instrument. _____
5. Name a talent you would like to have that you don't. _____
6. Name something that some people have lots of. _____
7. Name your hardest subject in school. _____
8. Name something very, very big. _____
9. Name your most cherished possession. _____
10. Name something that lasts a long time. _____
11. Name something else that lasts a long time. _____
12. Name something else that lasts a long time. _____
13. Name something a small child would do. _____
14. Name something else a small child would do. _____
15. Name something else a small child would do. _____
16. Name something shiny. _____

1 CORINTHIANS 13

I may be able to speak the language of _____ and even of _____ , but if
1 **2**
I have no love, my speech is no more than a noisy _____ or a clanging _____ .
3 **4**
I may have the gift of _____; I may have all _____ and understand
5 **6**
_____; I may have all the faith to move _____—but if I have no love, I am
7 **8**
nothing. I may even give away my _____; but if I have no love, this does me no good.
9

Love is patient and kind; it is not jealous or conceited or proud; love is not ill-mannered or

selfish or irritable; love does not keep a record of wrongs; love is not happy with evil, but is

happy with the truth. Love never gives up; and its faith, hope, and patience never fail.

Love is eternal. There are _____, but they are temporary; there are _____,
10 **11**
but they will cease; there is _____, but it will pass away. These things are only partial;
12
but love is perfect and will go on long after these things are gone.

When I was a child, my _____, _____ and _____, were all those
13 **14** **15**
of a child; now that I'm grown up I have no more use for these childish ways. What we see

now is like a dim image in a _____; then we shall see face-to-face. What I know now
16
is only partial; then it will be complete—as complete as God's knowledge of me. Meanwhile,

these three remain: faith, hope, and love: and the greatest of these is love!

aloud their verses in their foreign languages. You can use this demonstration to convey some of the wonder that those foreigners felt upon hearing God's love proclaimed in their own languages.

John 3:16 in Seven Languages

French
Car Dieu a tant aimé le monde qu'il a donné son Fils unique, afin que quiconque croit en lui ne périsse point, mais qu'il ait la vie éternelle.

German
Denn also hat Gott die Welt geliebt, dass er seinen eingeboren Sohn gab, auf dass alle, die an ihn glauben, nicht verloren werden, sondern das ewige Leben haben.

Italian
Poichè Iddio ha tanto amato il mondo, che ha dato il suo unigenito Figliuolo, affinchè chiunque crede in lui non perisca, ma abbia vita eterna.

Spanish
Porque de tal manera amó Dios al mundo, que ha dado a su Hijo unigenito, para que todo aquel que en él cree, no se perda, mas tenga vida eterna.

Norwegian
For så har Gud elsket verden at han gav sin Sønn, den enbårne, forat hver den som tror på ham, ikke skal fortapes, men ha evig liv.

Swedish
Ty så älskade Gud världen, att han utgav sin enfödde Son, på det att var och en som tror på honom skall icke förgås, utan hava evigt liv.

English
For God loved the world so much that he gave his only Son, so that everyone who believes in him should not be lost, but should have eternal life.

To enhance the effect, have kids who are fluent in the different languages teach the verse to small groups of students, so that everyone, not just a few, can read the verse aloud at the same time in various languages. *Jeff Callen*

SCRIPTURE BOOKMARKS

One good way to help your kids get through each week is to give them Scripture bookmarks, which provide a simple thought for the week—perhaps the theme of the last youth group meeting or Bible study—and some daily Scriptures to look up and read.

Bookmarks can also be used for announcements, words of encouragement, even evangelism. Kids can give them to their friends as witness markers. *David Washburn*

MARY AND MARTHA MALPRACTICE

Here's a good role play that will help your kids better understand the difficult issues in Christianity by looking at two women characters from the New Testament—Mary and Martha (Luke 10:38-42).

Introduce the role-play this way:

Ever wonder what happened to Mary and Martha after Jesus visited them?

Well, Mary, the one who poured the precious perfume on Jesus' feet, started a convent where women can pray and worship all the time. Martha, the one who served, opened an inner-city soup kitchen. Mary never does anything to help the poor because she spends all her time praying. Martha hardly ever prays because she's too busy feeding the poor.

Because Martha has become irritated with Mary's lack of concern for the poor, she's suing Mary for malpractice of Christianity.

Now select someone to be Mary and someone to be Martha. Those two actors should select two or three attorneys each (other teens) to represent them. The rest of the group is the jury. After the two sides have had time to prepare, conduct a trial. Allow each side to present its arguments. The jury can ask questions and decide who presents the most convincing argument. *Dean Taylor*

THE UDGER FAMILY

Here's a good discussion starter based on Matthew 7:1-2 ("Do not judge..."). Write the following names on poster board or a flip chart, and introduce the members of the Udger family:
- **Billy Budger.** He tries to move people away from their faith any way he can. (1 Pet. 5:8-9)
- **Sasha Smudger.** She goes out of her way to ruin the reputation of those she doesn't like. (Eph. 4:29)
- **Fern Fudger.** Fern always cheats and alters the truth to her own advantage. (1 Pet. 2:1)
- **Jill Judger.** Jill always points out the smallest sliver of a fault in someone else. Unfortunately, she is unable to see the baseball bat in her own eye. (Matt. 7:1-2)
- **Greg Grudger.** He's notorious for holding a grudge. If you wrong him, he'll never let you forget it. (Eph. 4:26-27)
- **Nick Nudger.** He creeps around, causing everyone in his path to stumble and fall. He loves to see others fail. (1 Cor. 10:32)

Ask the kids in the discussion to decide which of these family members are most dangerous. Are any of them familiar? How can we keep this family from infiltrating our youth group? *Michael W. Capps*

UP ON THE ROOF

For an effective Bible study, take your group up onto a roof—the roof of the church or of any other building—and present a lesson like the one on page 69.

Close by asking the kids to name unusual occasions and places where they have had a significant growing experience or encounter with God. *Steve Fortosis*

FINAL FOUR FEVER

When the NCAA Final Four rolls around next March, take advantage of all the hype to conduct your own Biblical Final Four Tournament. About a month before the NCAA's Final Four, give a basketball-type pep talk—who will be the top biblical character this season?—then draw eight or 16 different biblical characters out of a hat. Perhaps start with Moses, Noah, David, Paul, Peter, Samson, Joseph (the patriarch), John, Barnabas, Stephen, Job, Solomon, Elijah,

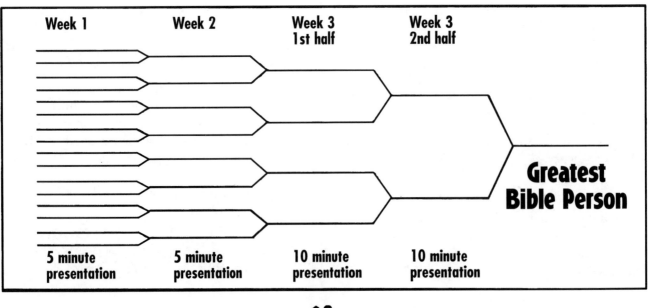

Week 1	Week 2	Week 3 1st half	Week 3 2nd half
5 minute presentation	5 minute presentation	10 minute presentation	10 minute presentation

Greatest Bible Person

UP ON THE ROOF

Did you know that in the Bible some significant things happened on roofs? Because roofs were flat back in Bible times, people ate, slept, relaxed—did all sorts of things—on top of their homes. Let's look at some Scriptures about events that took place on rooftops.

First, let's turn to 2 Samuel 11:2—here David began to lust after Bathsheba from a rooftop. Later on, when David's son Absalom led a rebellion against his father (2 Sam. 16:22), he committed adultery with David's wives on the palace roof. In Jeremiah 32:29 we read that the rooftop was a place of idolatry.

The rooftop was not always a place of sin, however. Rahab hid the Israeli spies on her roof (Josh. 2:6). In Luke 5:18-25 are some men who lowered a diseased friend through a hole in the roof for healing by Jesus. In 1 Samuel 9:25 Samuel conferred with Saul on a rooftop before he was anointed king of Israel, and in Acts 10:9-17 Peter was on a rooftop when he received a vision that taught him that Gentiles were to be included in God's plan of salvation.

The amazing thing is that God can speak to us anywhere, anytime—even on a rooftop. God is not locked up in the church. He wants to be a part of our lives everywhere, all the time.

Abraham, Timothy, Eutychus (the Final Four always has a sleeper). Instruct your students to prepare a five-minute persuasive report on why their character is the greatest in the Bible. List each character on a large tournament-type elimination chart. For extra splash make a large Biblical Final Four banner to hang in your room during March. You may want to divide characters, NCAA-like, into different divisions: women, kings, prophets, apostles, patriarchs, etc. Change categories from year to year.

Students vote at the end of the first and second weeks for the winner; eliminate half the entries at the end of week one, and half again at the end of week two. Divide the Final Four meeting in half—eliminate two characters during the first half, then during the last half let the final pair go head to head.

Conclude the tourney (or debrief the next week) by looking at Scriptures like Matthew 18:1-14, Mark 10:35-45, John 13:1-17, and other passages that deal with greatness in the kingdom of God, servanthood, etc. *Terry Erwin, Jr.*

ORDER UP!

Begin your study of the Gospel of Mark with "Episodes in the Life of Jesus," a combination quiz/worksheet on (page 71). Let kids guess (without Bibles) the order of the episodes (left column only); then read off the correct order; then instruct kids to use their Bibles to fill in the "chapter" column on the right. *Ralph Gustafson*

POSSESSION OBSESSION

Prior to a study of Christ's words in Matthew 6:19-24, ask the manager of a Cadillac, BMW, or Mercedes-Benz dealership in town if you can bring your well-behaved group in and look around. Make sure he has a late-model car in back that's been totaled. If he doesn't, find a nearby auto-wrecker yard.

On the day of the study, take your group to tour the showroom and the lot, looking for the most expensive cars, the ones with the nicest options, their favorite models, etc. As you walk around ask your kids what they like about the cars, what the cars represent, how they perceive people who purchase such cars, why they buy them, etc.

Then take them around back and show them the wrecked one. Probe their feelings upon seeing this car. Ask them how they'd feel if they owned a luxury car that was demolished. Your kids will be especially stimulated to discuss the temporal nature of material possessions and study the Matthew passage. *Dave Mahoney*

SLAVES IN CHAINS

Bring Galations 4:7 to life. Before the meeting write the words of the verse on two-by-six-inch strips of colored construction paper, one word per strip. Do this as many times as there will be teams (a different color for each team).

Order Up!
Episodes in the Life of
Jesus
From Mark's Gospel

ORDER   CHAPTER

_____ Baptized by John the Baptist in the Jordan   _____

_____ Denied three times by Peter   _____

_____ Tempted in the wilderness   _____

_____ Resurrects the dead daughter of Jairus   _____

_____ Identified by Peter as the Messiah, God's Son   _____

_____ Teaches about the world's end   _____

_____ Heals blind Bartimaeus   _____

_____ Eats the Last Supper with his disciples   _____

_____ Feeds 5,000 listeners   _____

_____ Resurrected from the dead   _____

_____ Heals a boy tormented by an evil spirit   _____

_____ Prays in the garden of Gethsemane   _____

_____ Heals a crippled man   _____

_____ Appoints the 12 disciples   _____

_____ Tried before Pilate   _____

_____ Declares what is the greatest commandment   _____

_____ Walks on water   _____

_____ Calms a storm   _____

_____ Feeds 4,000 listeners   _____

_____ Calls children to come to him   _____

_____ Teaches a lesson about paying taxes   _____

_____ Goes early in the morning by himself to pray   _____

_____ Heals a victim of leprosy   _____

At the meeting instruct each team, first, to choose a "slave" from among them; and, second, to make a chain of the construction-paper strips—in correct verse order—and to attach one end of the chain to the wrists of the slave, the other end of the chain to a chair leg. The team that finishes first frees its slave; other slaves must remain chained throughout the ensuing discussion of Galatians 3:26 through 4:7.

Sample questions for your group to ponder:
• What does it mean to be a child of God?
• In what ways do you think of God as your father?
• In what ways are you a slave to the world?
• How has God set you free from this slavery?

Break the bonds of the slaves after the discussion—but have them serve snacks to the group. *Mary Legner*

AMAZING DISCOVERIES

Using a TV-talk-show format, offer a youth night of Amazing Discoveries that features kids who act the part of biblical characters who observed or experienced some miracles of Jesus. Prepare one student to be the host and several others to tell about the miracles they witnessed or experienced. *Bert Jones*

SAYING GOODBYE

The worksheet on page 73 will help your kids discover the good in good-bye. *John Morgan*

WATERPROOF DEVOTIONAL

After your next water event—pool party, beach trip, etc.—make enough copies of the Waterproof Devotional on page 74 for each attender. Fold the devotional so that the title shows, and then stuff each one in a Ziploc sandwich bag. The note at the end of the devotional promises those who turn in the completed devotion by a certain date will receive a prize that will save their life (give 'em a pack of Lifesavers). *Mark Adams*

WHERE CAN I PUT THE KINGDOM OF GOD?

The directive of Jesus in Matthew 6:33—seek first the kingdom of God—is illustrated with this creative devotional.

Make a mental list of all the sports, jobs, hobbies, interests, etc., that kids in your group involve themselves in. Then collect lots of objects that symbolize or depict those interests—a basketball, football, Nintendo cartridges, videocassettes, time card, pizza box, CDs, comic books, textbooks, fashion catalogs, phone books.

Open the devotional by placing on the floor a Bible opened to Matthew 6:33. For starters ask the group what sports they enjoy playing. When they answer pull from a big box the corresponding object and toss it onto the Bible. Continue the interaction, asking what classes they like the best, how they prefer to spend their leisure, the extracurricular activities they live for, etc. Each time, grab the appropriate object from the box and toss it onto the pile (which by now has probably covered the Bible completely).

A few minutes into this, ask your young people, "What happened to God?" The answer to this object lesson is obvious: God got buried under all the stuff. Once they acknowledge that, pull out the Bible from the stack of stuff and read Matthew 6:33. Ask them, "What would happen if you put the Bible—or God—on top of the pile?" Point out that if believers put God first, they still have all the other activities, but now they can see God, too. *Chuck Hawkins*

B.I.G.

Warm up your group by asking a couple kids to tell their biggest moment in life. Then read some stats from *The Guinness Book of Records* that you selected earlier—the biggest man, the biggest pizza on record, the biggest mushroom.

Have someone read Ephesians 5:1. Then ask your group what big has to do with that verse. Did they catch it? Read the verse again. God's greatest desire is for his people to **B**e **I**mitators of **G**od—**B.I.G.**—people. In small groups, students can take turns recalling how they've seen someone else imitate God. On what occasions have they themselves come close to imitating God?

End with a prayer commissioning your students to be B.I.G. people. For more study, try Ephesians 5:1-17, which challenges Christians to take three B.I.G. steps in order to be B.I.G. people for God:
1. Walk in love. (vv. 1-7)
2. Walk in light. (vv. 8-14)
3. Walk in wisdom. (vv. 15-17)

SAYING GOOD-BYE

1. THINK: Is there anything good about good-bye?
   WRITE: Describe the last time you had to say good-bye.

   _____

2. THINK: Think of a friend who has moved away with whom you still have a good relationship.
   WRITE: What was hard about that good-bye? Why is your relationship still strong?

   _____

3. THINK: Think of someone to whom you said good-bye and with whom you no longer have a relationship.
   WRITE: How did you say good-bye? What led to the loss of that relationship?

   _____

4. THINK: Read John 13:33 through 14:4 and John 14:15-31.
   WRITE: How does Jesus say good-bye? What does Jesus tell the disciples about how they should feel about his leaving? _____

5. Discuss with the group what people can do to make good-byes better.

SAYING GOOD-BYE

1. THINK: Is there anything good about good-bye?
   WRITE: Describe the last time you had to say good-bye.

   _____

2. THINK: Think of a friend who has moved away with whom you still have a good relationship.
   WRITE: What was hard about that good-bye? Why is your relationship still strong?

   _____

3. THINK: Think of someone to whom you said good-bye and with whom you no longer have a relationship.
   WRITE: How did you say good-bye? What led to the loss of that relationship?

   _____

4. THINK: Read John 13:33 through 14:4 and John 14:15-31.
   WRITE: How does Jesus say good-bye? What does Jesus tell the disciples about how they should feel about his leaving? _____

5. Discuss with the group what people can do to make good-byes better.

Youth Aquatic Day, Take-Home, Do-It-Yourself, Waterproof Devotional

By now, hopefully, all the water has drained out of your ears and you are contentedly relaxing, remembering the fun we had in the water. Yet before you hit the sack, take a few minutes to see what can be learned from this event that can help you be a better Christian.

"What can a day in the water teach me about Jesus?" you ask. You may be surprised—Jesus has a lot to do with water. In fact, the Gospels explain at least 10 significant liquid incidents in Jesus' life.

If you look closely at Jesus and H_2O, you just might wring out a spiritual truth or two. Here goes.

Now here's what you do:

- Get your Bible.
- Read each reference.
- In the space provided after each statement, write down what this example has to do with your life—what lesson can you learn that will make wakin' up tomorrow better?

Need a hint? The first example (Jesus was born of water) reminds us that, although Jesus was 100 percent God, he was also 100 percent human. That means he was born just like any human, lived life just like us—and so he knows what it is to suffer pain and bust a gut laughing. It also means that when you pray, you pray to someone who understands.

You do the other seven examples yourself. **If you bring me your completed devotional this Sunday, I will give you a tasty prize that will save your life!**

Jesus...

1. **was born of water. (Luke 2:7)**

2. **turned water into wine. (John 2:9)**

3. **was baptized in water. (Matt. 3:16)**

4. **drank water. (John 4:7)**

5. **calmed stormy water. (Luke 8:24)**

6. **wept water. (John 11:35)**

7. **walked on water. (Mark 6:48)**

8. **on the cross when Jesus' side was pierced with the spear, water and blood flowed out. (John 19:34)**

Tommy Baker

CPAS FOR GOD

Okay, so your teens aren't all aspiring certified public accountants—but they can all become CPAs for God using this Bible study from the third chapter of Joshua.

Use these questions to start the discussion: What's the most amazing thing—

- you've ever seen?
- you've ever done?
- you've ever heard about?
- God has done in history?
- God has done in your life?
- God has done for someone you know?

Now on to explore some amazing things God can do through us as "CPAs."

The focus of this study is on Joshua 3:5, so familiarize your students with the context by reading the entire chapter.

When you've read Joshua 3, now explain to the kids what's involved in being a CPA for God. First, the C.

Commands

1. Ask a volunteer to read Joshua 3:5. In order to be God's CPA, we must know his commands. Not only is it important to know the commands, but we must want to obey them more than we do.

2. In Joshua 3:5, Joshua delivers a command given by God. What is the command?

3. Ask a volunteer to read John 14:15. Why is obedience so important to God? What does this passage say about the need for or importance of obedience? Why does God link love with obedience?

4. Divide your students into small groups with a supply of poster paper and some felt pens. Ask them to remember or look up some other commands in the Bible. After five or 10 minutes, ask the small groups to read their responses to everyone.

5. Because God loves us, we can be confident that there is a reason for every command. Ask another volunteer to read Joshua 3:5 again. Notice the progression: the command to "consecrate yourselves to the Lord" comes first. Then the promise *follows* the command.

Promises

6. Everyone loves to claim God's promises in the Bible. What's one of your favorites?

7. What is God's promise in this passage in Joshua?

8. Do you think the Israelis slept the night before the crossing? What would have been going through your mind? Do you think they tried to guess what would happen? What amazing thing did God do here in Joshua 3?

9. Ask the groups to return to their lists of commands and determine what promise is linked with each command, or what God's reason is behind each command. Again, each small group then tells the others what they came up with.

10. In Joshua 3 God delivered on the promise the very next day. What preceded the promise? In other words, what were the people of Israel asked to do?

11. God has given the command and made a promise—but when does the promise come true? First thing the next morning? As they approach the river? Let's look into this passage a little further.

Action

12. God's Word is full of commands with promises to be claimed, but they are of no value unless we obey God. God could have parted the water during the night to have it ready for them the next day. He could have parted the water as they approached the river. But he didn't, possibly because he wanted the Jews' obedience to demonstrate their love—because love proves that there is trust. The waters didn't part until their feet touched the water, which proved the Israelis trusted their God. (Note that the waters were at flood stage, and if the people touched the ark of the covenant, they would die.)

13. Because they don't obey, many fail to see God do amazing things in their lives—not because God can't do it, but because people don't claim his promises or don't obey.

14. God did an amazing thing that day—but he isn't through yet. God will do amazing things through you if you obey his commands and claim the promises in his Word.

And that's how to be God's amazing CPA! This could be a perfect opportunity for students to consecrate themselves to the Lord. In fact, you may want to conduct right then, or schedule for later, a special service of consecration. *Tommy Baker*

BIBLE DIVING

I have used Bible Diving over and over again to acquaint the students in my youth group with general Bible concepts and some of the more unusual passages.

The only materials needed are Bibles for each individual and a supply of Bible commentaries from your church library.

Divide into small groups of three to six. Explain that the students will have 10 minutes to find a Scripture passage that qualifies for one of the following categories:

1. There is a significant question regarding the meaning of the passage.
2. The passage is unusual in some way.
3. The passage is challenging or upsetting in some way.
4. There is a meaningful message in the passage that relates to the participant's current experiences or feelings.
5. The passage is just plain weird.

After 10 minutes stop the groups. Have students take turns sharing the Scripture passages that they found with the rest of the small group. The group can look up the Scripture passage together. If there are questions about biblical passages that no one in the group can answer, call on the experts: Bible commentators. You may have to give a few initial instructions about how to use those books available to you. Have someone read aloud what the Bible scholar has to say and everyone will learn some background and meaning in a researched context. It's like bringing in seminary professors to comment on strange passages of Scripture for your kids.

Allow plenty of time for the group to share. Many times my youth group reaches the end of the evening and not even half of the young people have been able to share the Scriptures they found because the group has become so involved in a discussion.

The conversations become quite interesting when kids discover parts of the Bible that they have never read before, especially the bizarre laws found in Leviticus and the love poetry in the Song of Solomon. *Michael Bell*

AQUA BIBLE STUDY

Supply copies of the Aqua Bible Study on page 77 (one for each student) and cover them with clear contact paper. Then take your group, along with these waterproof Bible study sheets, to the nearest swimming pool for a refreshing way to study the Bible. "Diving into God's Word" will have new meaning.

- **Floating on the surface.** Divide the group into small schools of fish. Give them opportunity to come up with a fishy name.
- **Games.** Hold competitions for the most creative dive, biggest splash, most consecutive underwater

somersaults, longest underwater breath holding, and longest water treading. Let the youths develop a point system and have turns judging competition.

- **Getting your feet wet/going deeper.** Work through the Bible study sheet on page 77.
- **Take the plunge.** "Practice" each mode of baptism.

    1. Sprinkle: Have a splashing fight.
    2. Pour: Have a splashing fight with buckets.
    3. Submerge: Dunk one another.

Other appropriate topics for Aqua Bible Studies include Noah and the flood, the parting of the Red Sea, Jesus turning water into wine, and Jesus the living water. *Larry Stoess*

DON'T S-L-I-P

After an evening of banana games or water games, use the devotional on page 78 to emphasize "Don't Slip," and "Stand Firm." Divide your group into three teams and give each team one of the following passages of Scripture for each letter. They are to read the passage and come up with a key word or phrase that begins with the appropriate letter and that capsulizes the concept of the passage.

Briefly review the main idea of each passage as a whole group. *James L. Wing*

INSTRUCTIONS FOR LIFE

This idea was the basis for our morning devotions at camp. First we purchased copies of *Life's Little Instruction Book*, volumes I and II, by H. Jackson Brown, Jr., (1991 and 1993, Rutledge Hill Press).

Next, we explained to the youths that the instructions for life found in these books were compiled from those a father had shared with his son to help him cope with life while away at school.

Sample instructions from the book:
- Be brave. Even if you're not, pretend to be. No one can tell the difference.
- Beware of the person who has nothing to lose.
- Spend less time worrying who's right and more time deciding what's right.

Then we informed them that another valuable set of instructions for life could be found in Proverbs. We indicated that these were gathered from elders who wished to share their wisdom and insights with young people to help them cope with

AQUA BIBLE STUDY

Getting Your Feet Wet

Throughout church history people have been baptized in different ways. How people are baptized in a local church depends on the individual church's theology of baptism and its tradition. Unscramble the words to find out three modes of baptism.

PKIESRLN

UORP

MGEESBRU

Which method of baptism fits with each of the following passages?

I will sprinkle clean water on you, and you will be clean; I will cleanse you from all your impurities and from all your idols. I will give you a new heart and put a new spirit in you; I will remove from you your heart of stone and give you a heart of flesh. And I will put my Spirit in you and move you to follow my decrees and be careful to keep my laws. *Ezekiel 36:25-27*

No, this is what was spoken by the prophet Joel: "In the last days, God says, I will pour out my Spirit on all people. Your sons and daughters will prophesy, your young men will see visions, your old men will dream dreams. Even on my servants, both men and women, I will pour out my Spirit in those days, and they will prophesy." *Acts 2:16-18*

Or don't you know that all of us who were baptized into Christ Jesus were baptized into his death? We were therefore buried with him through baptism into death in order that, just as Christ was raised from the dead through the glory of the Father, we too may live a new life. *Romans 6:3-4*

Going Deeper

➤ Were you ever baptized? If so, answer the following questions:
➤ How were you baptized?
➤ Why were you baptized?
➤ What does your baptism mean to you?

Don't Slip

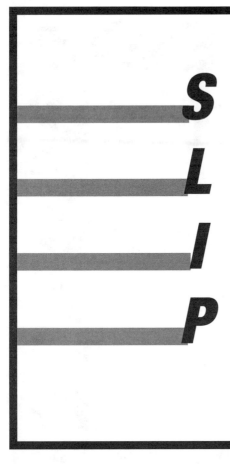

S Serving money *Luke 16:13-15*
Selfishness *Philippians 2:3*
Secret sin 2 *Corinthians 4:1-2*

L Laziness *Titus 1:12-14*
Lying *Proverbs 6:17; Colossians 3:9*
Law breakers *Romans 13:1-10*

I Idleness *Proverbs 31:27; Ecclesiastes 10:18*
Injustice *Psalm 82:3; Micah 6:8*
Intoxication *Ephesians 5:18*

P Perverse language *Psalm 19:14* and perverse heart *Psalm 101*
Presumption *Psalm 19:13; Proverbs 13:10*
Pride *Proverbs 16:18; 1 John 2:16*

Stand Firm

S Scripture memory *Psalm 119:11*
Self-control *Galatians 5:23*
Submit to God *James 4:7*

T Test your faith 2 *Corinthians 13:5*
Thank God in every circumstance *1 Thessalonians 5:16-18*
Turn away from sin *1 Peter 3:11*

A Abstain from appearance of evil *1 Thessalonians 5:22*
Accept one another *Romans 15:1-3 ,7*
Ask God for wisdom *James 1:5*

N Neglect not your spiritual gift *1 Timothy 4:14*
Need for other Christian friends *1 Corinthians 12:12-27*
Notice God's work in your life *Psalm 139:14*

D Devote yourselves to prayer *Colossians 4:2*
Desire the greater gifts *1 Corinthians 12:31*
Decide to stay sexually pure *1 Thessalonians 4:3*

life in Old Testament times.

Sample instructions from Proverbs:
• Do not withhold good from those to whom it is due, when it is in your power to do it.
• Do not envy the violent and do not choose any of their ways.
• Let another praise you, and not your own mouth.

Each day students were given the opportunity to choose several instructions from Brown's books and from Proverbs. They were given time to reflect on the instructions they chose and then share in small groups why they found theirs to be valuable for them. It was interesting for the youths to discover that the biblical teachings were as rich in meaning for them today as the teachings found in the more recently published popular books.

It is also fun to let the teens act out some of their favorite instructions, letting the rest of the group guess what the instructions are. *Carolyn Peters*

CROSS WALK

Cross Walk can be conducted quickly as a discussion starter or extended as a more elaborate project in itself. In this creative yet everyday way of helping your teenagers become more aware of the meaning of the cross of Christ, first read this quote from the British Christian writer Malcolm Muggeridge:

I would catch a glimpse of a cross—not necessarily a crucifix; maybe two pieces of wood accidentally nailed together, on a telegraph pole, for instance—and suddenly my heart would stand still...

Now send your kids on a walk around the neighborhood; ask them to notice the everyday objects and arrangements that form crosses (telephone poles, intersecting power lines, clothes poles, lines on the sidewalk, etc.). Have them jot down a brief description of what they see. Or they can make sketches or take Polaroid shots of the crosses they find. Have kids discuss what they found and display any sketches or photos.

Wrap up the experience with a discussion of the cross and its significance as a symbol of the Christian faith. *Keith Curran*

YARN CIRCLE

Here is a good suggestion for a meaningful communion service, lesson on the body of Christ, or a time of sharing with the youth group. The group should be seated in a circle, either on the floor or in chairs. Each person is given a piece of yarn, about 18 inches long, to represent their individuality. After a time of sharing with each other, each person, one at a time, ties their string to the person's string next to them to form a circle. This symbolizes the unity of the group and the fact that we are one in Christ. The group may then enter into a time of reflection on Christ, the cross, the Resurrection, or participate in the Lord's Supper.

To close, the leader goes to each person and cuts a section off of the string, leaving one knot on each person's section to represent the change that has happened during the experience. The piece of string that the young person receives represents the fact that we leave the meeting as individuals, but reminds us that we belong to the body of Christ and are connected to others in the group. *Tracy Wiser*

79

FULL
LESSONS

Here are ideas for creating *entire* sessions—from openers to closings, including provocative discussion questions, creative Bible studies, and sessions on relevant topics facing kids today (love, peer pressure, security, witnessing, serving, seeking God, etc.)

LOVE PROGRAMS

The following two program ideas deal with relationships in a creative way that is strong on personal application. They might be especially useful if there is evidence of cliques or snobbery building in your group.

Loving the Unlovely

Part 1—Role play:

This role-play uses three characters: Joe Director (leader of the group); Gunky Gertrude (dirty, unmatched clothing, out of style); Mod Mary (fashionable, neat, pretty).

Joe is getting ready for the youth meeting to start when Gunky Gertrude walks in. Joe says hello, but then keeps busy setting up chairs, etc., ignoring Gertrude. She follows him around relentlessly, telling him about her day—she got a "D" in Home Ec, went to a worm wrestle after school, lost a chess tournament, got to buy lunch at school instead of taking a bag lunch. Joe is cold toward her.

Mod Mary arrives. Joe meets her with a big smile and handshake. He asks her questions and listens sympathetically. He invites her to have dinner with his family that week. Gertrude tries to join in the conversation, but is not acknowledged by Joe and Mary. Mary sits down. Gertrude looks for a seat, but they are all taken. Joe suggests that she sit on the floor on the far end of the circle. Joe and Mary enthusiastically start singing, "We Are One in the Spirit." Gertrude sits with a dejected, puzzled look on her face.

Part 2—Discussion:

Lead the group in discussing their response to the role-play by asking these questions: How did they feel toward Joe, Gertrude, and Mary? Did anyone identify with one of the characters? Should any of them have acted differently? How? What would Jesus have done? Have you seen this type of behavior in our group? What can you personally do to prevent it?

Part 3—Wrap-up:

Turn to James 2:1-13 and 1 Samuel 16:7. Conclude the lesson with a brief explanation of the principles of love at work in these passages.

Being Kind

Part 1—Preliminaries:

During the opening minutes of your youth group (games, announcements, singing), plan for a few leaders and a group of kids to make cruel remarks, critical comments, belittling cuts, and to be generally sarcastic toward the activities. Hand out paper and pencils to the group after this and have them answer the following questions:

• How do you feel about the group today? Why?

• Does anything seem unusual about the group today?

• Are you glad you're here or do you wish you had stayed home?

Part 2—Group discussion:

Go over the questions and expand on the subject of cutting and criticizing. Ask the kids to describe a time when they felt really cut down.

Part 3—Role play:

Using the story of the good Samaritan as a model, act out the responses of three passersby to a victim who has been robbed and beaten on the street. The first person to come along throws a Bible to the man and tells him to read it. The next one acts snobbish and turns away. Another kicks him and complains about drunks on the street. Finally, someone comes to the victim's aid.

Part 4—Discussion:

Review the various options of the characters and discuss how your kids might respond in similar situations.

Part 5—Wrap-up:

Read Ephesians 4:31-32, 1 Peter 3:8-12, John 13:35. Suggest that the kids look for opportunities to be kind to others and have them keep track of the kindnesses done to them during the coming week. *Vaughn Van Skiver*

PEER PRESSURE STUDY

No youth group can afford to ignore the subject of peer pressure and conformity. The power that one's age group has to consciously or unconsciously force others to conform and act in harmony with the group can be a major obstacle in the spiritual development of your kids. The study on page 85 is helpful as a means of opening up discussion on the topic. It also presents some valuable tools that can be used by your kids to battle peer pressure. *Greg Platt*

SECURITY FIRST

Here's a plan for a youth meeting which deals effectively with the subject of security.

Begin with a stuffed animal contest. Have the young people bring their favorite stuffed animals to the youth meeting and share them with the rest of the group. If they don't have a favorite now, have them bring one they had when they were younger. Most parents save them, so everyone should be able to bring one. Animals can be entered in a variety of categories: cutest, ugliest, most loved, most huggable, best bear, and best "other" animal. The winner can be judged by applause from the group.

Next, divide into small groups, and play a few "trust" games, like a trust walk (one partner is "blind," another is "dumb," and they guide each other through a maze); a trust drop (blindfolded, you drop backward into your partner's arms); or Wind in the Willows (in a circle of six, one person stiffens his body and is passed around the circle).

These activities can then be followed by a discussion. Here are some sample questions:

1. How did you feel during the games?

2. How do you feel (physically and emotionally) when you are secure?

3. How do you behave when you feel secure? Rejected?

4. When do you feel most secure? Most rejected?

5. What are some ways you ensure security?

6. Does God make you feel secure or rejected? How do you know?

7. Did Christ feel accepted all the time? When did he feel rejected and why? What did he do when he felt rejected?

8. Christ teaches that to find our lives, we must

Peer Pressure Study

Part One—A Quiz

Take this survey to see how you react to peer pressure:

(1) When faced with a decision to act or not to act like others my age, I usually:
   a) Flip a coin
   b) Panic and hide under my bed
   c) Think it over
   d) Pray and ask God to show me what to do
   e) Other _____

(2) I (often/sometimes/never) feel pressured to do something that others are doing in order to be accepted.

(3) There is a right and a wrong choice for each decision that I must make. (Yes/No)

(4) All peer pressure is bad. (Yes/No)

(5) There is peer pressure to act a certain way in our group. (Yes/No)

(6) The pressure I face most often is _____

(7) A Christian writer named Søren Kierkegaard once wrote, "There is a view of life which conceives that where the crowd is, there is also the truth. There is another view of life which conceives that wherever there is a crowd there is untruth." Which view do you agree with?

(8) In order of their importance to you, list five values or priorities you have that you could use to guide you in making a decision:

   1.

   2.

   3.

   4.

   5.

PART TWO—TWO BIBLICAL EXAMPLES

In the Old Testament we read how Daniel and his three friends were taken prisoner when the Babylonian army defeated Israel in 604 B.C. (Daniel 1). Daniel was probably about 16 years of age at the time. He was taken from his country, his home, his school, and his parents and carried several hundred miles away to the Babylonian capital. He and his three friends were to be trained to serve the king.

They were suddenly faced with an intense test of their values. Would they continue to worship God or bow to the Babylonian idols? Would they break the Jewish dietary laws that they knew God had given them to keep them healthy and undefiled for his service? How would they react to the immoral practices of their captors?

They could easily have gone along with the crowd and compromised their values. But years before they had decided to put God's values above the values of other people. Daniel and his three friends had already set their priorities; there was no further decision to make.

In the New Testament (John 7:1-7) Jesus was encouraged by his brothers to visit the believers in Judea. No doubt, the argument presented by his brothers was a persuasive one. Jesus, however, was in touch with the larger plan and more perfect will of God the Father. Nothing, not even the pleas by his brothers, could veer him away from that plan.

PART THREE—MAKING DECISIONS

Facing peer pressure comes down to answering one question—Where are your priorities? What values do you place the most importance on? In Matthew 6:33, Jesus tells us to "seek first his [God's] kingdom and his righteousness." As Christians, we should put God and his will for our lives first, above everything else.

So there are three questions you can ask yourself before making decisions:
1. How does it affect me as an individual?
2. What will be the effect it has on others?
3. How will it affect the cause of Christ?

There are three tests to apply to each choice you face:

1. The test of secrecy. Would you feel different if someone else you knew was aware of what you were doing?

2. The test of individuality. Would you still do it even if all of your peers did not?

3. The test of prayer. Can you ask God to go with you and bless you in this?

And finally, there are three sources of spiritual guidance available to you:

1. From within—your conscience and the Holy Spirit.

2. From without—your parents (they do know something), Christian friends, and church leaders.

3. From above—your relationship with Jesus Christ and your understanding of what the Bible has to say.

lose them. Substitute the word "security" for "life." Is this a true saying? How does it apply to you?

9. Can we as Christians feel secure all the time?

10. How does the church help us feel secure? How does our youth group help us feel secure?

The meeting can be closed with a community-building exercise of some kind, or a time of prayer, allowing each person the opportunity to give thanks for the security they have in Christ. They can also give thanks for one or two other people in the room or elsewhere who provide them with security. *Beth DuBois*

PETER AND THE WOMAN AT THE WELL

For an interesting way to begin a discussion on witnessing, read John 4:7-42 with your group—then read the narrative on page 88.

Use these questions to generate discussion about both versions of the passage.

• In verse 7, why didn't Jesus begin the conversation by telling the woman who he was?

• Why did Jesus talk about "living" water, a term the woman didn't understand?

• In verse 15, the woman seemed to ignore or not realize that Jesus had just mentioned eternal life. How do you account for this?

• In verse 16, why do you think Jesus asked her to go get her husband?

• How would you have responded after discovering that the woman was living with someone after having been married five times?

• What do we learn from the exchange in verses 31 to 38?

• What is the significance of Jesus staying with the Samaritans for two days before continuing his journey?

• Name at least three principles we can learn about witnessing from this story.

Close by encouraging each teenager to pray for a friend who needs to hear the Good News. Then tell kids to look for chances to practice what they've learned from this study. You may want to pass out a "water drop" (made of heavy stock and colored blue on one side, one to two inches wide) to all students and suggest that they write on the back the name of a friend who needs help—one who needs some "living water." They can carry these "drops" with them during the week to remind them to share what they have in Christ. *James Wing*

YOUTH GROUP MVP

Hand out a slip of paper to each student and announce that they are going to vote for the Most Valuable Person in the youth group. Voters may list on their slips their first, second, and third choices. Each first-place vote is worth three points, a second-place vote is worth two points, and third-place votes receive one point each. (For example, Judy Smith received two first-place votes, seven second-place votes, and six third-place votes. Her total score is 26 points.)

Don't explain the balloting in any more detail. Let the students judge on the basis of their own standards.

Collect the ballots when they are completed and total the individual scores. Announce the top three finalists for MVP, and ask each of them to prepare a 15-to-30-second speech on "Why I Should Be Chosen Most Valuable Person to the Youth Group."

Following the speeches, read aloud Luke 9:18-36. Ask: Who would you have voted for as MVP among the 12 disciples?

Discuss the reasoning behind their choices. Read Luke 9:37-46. Ask: Why do you think the disciples were arguing about who was the greatest? (Hint: Think about Peter's confession, the "privileged" disciples taken by Jesus to witness the Transfiguration, and the testimony of the father of the child—"I begged your disciples to drive it out, but they could not.")

Conclude by reading Luke 9:47-48 and Matthew 20:26-28. Ask: If we were to vote again for MVP in the youth group, would you vote differently this time? Why or why not?

Just before dismissal, either lead the group in a foot-washing service or distribute a small piece of towel to each student: ask them to carry it with them until the next meeting to remind them that the greatest is the one who serves. Close by praying for opportunities for the members to be MVPs in the coming week. *James Wing*

DISCOVERING LIFE

This idea could be used in an informal Sunday school class, at a Bible study, a Sunday night fellowship, or a youth group meeting. First, instruct your group to look up Matthew 7:7-8 (or Luke 11:9-11). Let them dwell on this passage by reading it through two or three times and then meditating on how this wisdom applies to their life.

Peter AND THE Woman AT THE Well

*Y*es, Jesus gave us an example here of how to witness. Yet how would the conversation have run if one of us had been there with her instead of Jesus? To save us the embarrassment, let's pretend Peter stuck around at the well while Jesus and the remaining disciples went into the city for food. Listen as I read the passage again—though this time from the Revised Fumbled Version.

There came a woman of Samaria to draw water. Peter said to her, "Do you believe that Jesus is the Messiah? Do you have eternal life? He is God's only Son, you know."

The Samaritan woman said to him, "You are indeed weird. Get lost before I crown your head with this water pot." Peter then asked her for a drink of water. "Only if you quit talking about religion," she said. Peter agreed.

(While this conversation was taking place, incidentally, Jesus and the other disciples had gone away into the city to buy food.)

Then the woman said, "How is it that you, being a Jew, are talking with me, since I am a Samaritan woman?" For Jews, you see, had no dealings with Samaritans.

"Well, you are the only one around, and I have a goal of talking to five people each day about Jesus," Peter replied. "I tell everyone that he can give them living water."

"Who is this Jesus?" the woman asked. "And does he get the living water from this well? I hope he has something to draw the water with, for this well is deep. At any rate, he is not greater than our father Jacob, is he? Jacob gave us the well, and drank of it himself, and his sons and his cattle."

Peter said, "Everyone who drinks of this water will thirst again. But whoever drinks of the water that Jesus has will never thirst again. This water that I'm speaking of will become in him a well of water springing up to eternal life."

"Sir," the Samaritan said, "show me how I can get this water that Jesus has, so I will not be thirsty, nor come all the way here to draw."

"No, lady," Peter explained, gesturing to the well. "I'm not talking about this kind of water. Go get your husband. I'm sure that he'll understand."

"I have no husband..." She paused. "I've been married five times, and now I'm living with someone."

"You're what?" Peter blurted. "You ought to be ashamed of yourself...I can't believe you'd sin like this—and then openly admit it. You're on you way to hell, lady. You need Jesus more than you think." The woman never heard whatever else Peter had to say. She turned and walked away while he was still speaking.

Next break into groups of four or five. Inform these groups that they are to find in the Gospels a factual incident where a person "sought and found." Use the whole Bible if you want. Then have the groups discuss how they would act out this happening—be creative! Stress that this can be anything from a comedy to a serious drama. After 10 to 20 minutes, have the groups come together and share what they discovered from the Scriptures by presenting their short play or skit and Scripture. When the skits are finished (after much thought, laughter, clapping, and excitement), bring them together in a serious mood by introducing and discussing three questions within their group or as a general group.
• What personally could you do this week to "seek and find" for God?
• Is there any certain answer you are seeking from God or doors that you would like opened?
• Commit yourself now and during the next week to prayer and study of the Word for an answer. Come back to the next meeting ready to share what has happened.

Andy Hansen

GOOD SAMARITAN

The following material can be used to plan a meeting around the parable of the Good Samaritan (Luke 10:25-37). You should familiarize yourself with the parable and get as much background material on Samaritans as possible. Since this is one of the most familiar of the parables, one of the chief objectives of this meeting will be to provide new insights and understanding to details that enrich the story, but which are often lost in the telling.

The meeting may include the following exercises:
• As the group enters, seat all the left-handed members (or any other obvious distinguishing characteristics that might make up a minority group) separate from the rest. This should be preferably in the worst chairs, on the floor, behind some obstacle, facing the wrong way, or any other undesirable place. No explanation is needed at this time.
• Begin with a discussion on "Samaritanism." Use a concordance to find four or five references to Samaritans. Have the group read them, and ask what general attitude toward Samaritans prevailed in New Testament times. Why? Have the group list five or six parallels (contemporary) to this situation

(e.g. Catholics in Northern Ireland, Turkish people in Cyprus, Palestinians in Israel, etc.).
• Give each person a slip of paper and pencil. Ask the group to write their answers (without signing their names) to this question: In the last six months, have you ever acted like the "priest" or the "Levite" in the parable? Then have them pass their papers around. Each person should then silently read the answer he ends up with. Have the kids share with each other their reactions to this exercise—how they identify with the writer of the one they received.
• Ask the group how they feel about the "left-handers" (the "Samaritans") in the room. Did they do anything for them? How do the "Samaritans" feel?
• Have the class break into groups of four and discuss the two questions, "Who is my neighbor?" and "What does it mean to be a neighbor?" If necessary reread the passage and point out that Christ's response to the first question might help answer the second.

Keith Geckeler

THE DISEASE OF DIOTREPHES

Does your youth group have "Diotrephes Disease?" Are there dictators or bosses in the bunch who insist on having their own way? That type of personality can be disastrous in a youth group. Here's a Bible study that allows kids to evaluate their lives and attitudes to avoid this ancient form of "illness," described by the Apostle John:

> I wrote to the church, but Diotrephes, who loves to be first, will have nothing to do with us. So if I come, I will call attention to what he is doing, gossiping maliciously about us. Not satisfied with that, he refuses to welcome the brothers. He also stops those who want to do so and puts them out of the church (3 John 9-10).

After reading together these words about Diotrephes, have the group consider the following six characteristics that can cause problems in the Christian community:

1. He loves to be first (v. 9). How does this desire usually show itself? Why do you think people want to be first? Is it possible for Christians to have this attitude? What did Jesus say to the disciples who had this problem? (Mark 9:33-35) Instead of wanting to be first, what attitude should we have? (Phil. 2:3-4) How can we develop this attitude?

2. He would have nothing to do with us (v. 9). The "us" refers to John and his companions. Who was John? Why do you think Diotrephes would want to reject one of Jesus' apostles? Do we ever reject leaders in the church today? If so, how? What should our attitude be toward leaders in God's church? (Heb. 13:7,17) How can we be more supportive of our leaders?

3. He is gossiping maliciously (v. 10). How would you define gossip? What happens in a group when gossip is a habit? What does God have to say about gossip? (James 3:1-12, Eph. 4:25,29) How can we stop gossip in our group and begin practicing useful, helpful, encouraging speech?

4. He refuses to welcome the brothers (v. 10). Does this ever happen today? If so, how and why? Is there ever a time when we should separate ourselves from fellowship with certain believers? (Rom. 16:17-18, Titus 3:9-11) Why is fellowship with other believers so important? What can we do to improve our fellowship? What can we do to make new believers welcome?

5. He stops those who want to do so (v. 10). There were those who wanted to welcome John and the others, which obviously is the right thing to do. Do Christians ever keep fellow Christians from doing the right thing? If so, how? What keeps us from doing what we know is right? What does God say about knowing the right thing and not doing it? (James 4:17) How can we develop a willingness to do what is right every time? How can we encourage one another to do what is right?

6. He puts them out of the church (v. 10). Read 1 Corinthians 5:1-5 and Matthew 18:15-17 to discover when and why church discipline should be practiced by the local church. If it's practiced correctly, how does it help a church? Can church discipline ever harm a church? If so, how? What can we do to ensure that correction of erring members is done in the right way for the right reason to accomplish the right results? How can our youth group practice this right kind of discipline?

With these insights in mind, every youth group member should ask himself, "Am I ever a Diotrephes? Is there another Diotrephes in our group I could help in some way?" Then consider together whether your youth group as a whole suffers from the Diotrephes disease. If so, how can you be cured? How do visitors or new members see your youth group? What can be done to make your youth group more attractive and encouraging? *Doug Newhouse*

FAMILY MATTERS

Here is a Bible study that can help you build personal relationships within your youth group by focusing upon the "family" responsibilities that are called for in the church. Begin by brainstorming this question: What are some ways a church is like a family? Allow several responses. Affirm each.

Then announce that you're going to examine the concept that a church should have intimacy like a family and this intimacy should carry over into your youth group. Have them turn to Matthew 18.

Divide students into groups. Assign each group one of the following passages and topics:

> Matthew 18:1-4 "Family Attitudes"
> Matthew 18:5-14 "Family Concern"
> Matthew 18:15-20 "Family Discipline"
> Matthew 18:21-35 "Family Forgiveness"

Instruct the groups to read the passage assigned to them and write down how the church, and specifically their youth group, is to fulfill these responsibilities. They should also make note of how this illustrates the intimacy of a family. Encourage them to pay special attention to key words, concepts, or statements.

After several minutes of study, allow each group to share their findings. These questions may be used to stimulate further discussion.

Family Attitudes
1. What is the key attitude described here? Why is it so essential? If it is present, what will it do?
2. Define the "children" in the kingdom.

Family Concern
1. According to verse five, what is the first concern?
2. Who are the "little ones" in the kingdom?
3. Why is leading others to sin such a serious thing? Do you think most Christians today recognize this? Why or why not?
4. What does verse 10 tell you about angels?
5. How faithfully should a church pursue "lost ones?" Do we do this? Why or why not?

Family Discipline
1. What is the purpose of this passage?
2. What is the role of the witnesses?
3. How would you explain verses 18-20?

4. Do you think this should be practiced today? Why or why not?

5. If this were practiced regularly, what do you think would happen?

Family Forgiveness

1. How does Peter's question in verse 21 relate to Jesus' teaching about discipline?

2. What prevented one servant from giving forgiveness? Does this happen today in the church? Why?

3. How easily do Christians forgive each other? What hinders forgiveness in the church?

Close your study by suggesting that all these responsibilities are given to individual Christians. If you must fulfill them, an intimacy will be created and developed within your youth group that will be like the intimacy of a family. Then ask, "What are some ways we can begin to do these things?" Allow the kids to brainstorm some answers, and close the meeting with prayer. *Doug Newhouse*

DRESSED FOR DEFENSE

Divide your youth group into three equal groups. Group one dresses a teammate as a defensive player of football (linebacker); group two, as a defensive player of baseball (catcher); group three, as a defensive player of hockey (goalie). Groups dress players with construction paper, scissors, clear tape, and any other creative materials you want to provide. Groups dress their defensive players with helmets, masks, pads, gloves, etc., appropriate to each player's sport. Encourage your athletic fashion designers to be creative!

Now discuss these questions:

- **What is the purpose of each item of protection?**
- **What areas of the body are protected?**
- **What is defense?**
- Why are the players covering only the front of their bodies?

After discussing the homemade costumes, read to your group Ephesians 6:10-20 (about the armor of God) and discuss the following questions:

- What is the purpose of each item of protection (girdle, breastplate, shoes, shield, helmet, sword)?
- What areas of the body are protected?
- Why isn't the back of the body protected?

Conclude your discussion by calling attention to the weaknesses in the Christian armor (the rear, the back, Achilles tendon, back of neck—the same weaknesses of the protective gear of the defensive players). These areas of our bodies are susceptible to injury if exposed to an external force and subject to severe pain when injured.

Reread verse 11—we wear God's armor to "stand against the devil's schemes." To do this we must face the enemy, not retreat; use our defenses, not run; use our weapons, not surrender. Our armor protects as long as we face our enemy, but our unprotected areas are easy targets if we turn and run.

We are in a daily battle with Satan. If we let down our defenses or expose our backsides, we are more likely to fall instead of standing our ground when the evil comes. *Rick Sanders*

MULTIPLE SESSION IDEAS

UNDERSTANDING DISABILITY

To encourage sensitivity toward those with disabilities, use the following outline over the course of five sessions. Combine or drop sessions or create your own as needed.

Session I: How do I feel about disabled persons?

Objectives:

1. To identify how you feel about the disabled.

2. To identify how you react to disabled individuals and how you tend to treat them.

3. To discover how you and the disabled are alike.

Step 1: Distribute 3x5 index cards. Have students write out the first few thoughts that come to mind when they think of a person with disabilities. Collect the cards and read them aloud. Identify and discuss the more common statements and those of interest. Write them on a chalkboard or a large piece of newsprint. Keep these notes for future reference.

Step 2: Role-play one or more of the following situations:

1. Two or three students are talking in the hall at school. A new student walks in the door with a parent and is looking for the office. They stop to ask directions. The boy speaks with an unusual voice and you notice hearing aids in both ears. How do you react to this situation? What are your thoughts about this new boy?

2. You are at the mall and it is very crowded. You get behind a girl who walks with crutches and

has braces on both of her legs. She is walking very slowly and you are in a hurry. How do you feel? What do you do?

3. You are with a group of friends on the first day back at school. A boy with cerebral palsy (walking with an uneven gait and one arm seems to jerk continuously) approaches you for directions to the gym. He is difficult to understand because of a slight speech defect. How do you react to him? How do your friends react to him?

4. You are having lunch with some friends and notice a person in a wheelchair at the next table. He also has a device attached to his hand to help him eat by himself. He has finished eating and seems to be having some difficulty getting around the table to leave. What do you do?

5. You are walking down the street with a few friends and notice a girl with a cane walking in front of you. She makes a turn and comes to the wall of a building. She seems to be a little disoriented. What do you do? How do you feel?

After each role-play discuss the feelings of all the individuals in the situation. How did it feel to be disabled? How did you want other people to react to you? What are some of the typical ways we react to those who are different from us?

Step 3: List the ways in which those who have disabilities are like us. When we meet others who have a noticeable handicap, our first reaction, often, is to observe how different that person is from us. However, when you think about it, people with disabilities are more like us than not. Some similarities are: (a) We all feel the need to be loved and accepted. (b) We all need shelter. (c) We all need food. (d) We all want to be liked. (e) We all want to be entertained and have a good time. (f) We all need clothing. (g) We all want to look as nice as possible.

Step 4: Identify and discuss ways you can begin to look beyond a person's disability to see a person's gifts, talents, expectations, disappointments, joys, and sorrows.

Session II: What is it like to be disabled?
Objectives:
1. To see life through the eyes of a person who is disabled.
2. To talk with a disabled person in a nonthreatening situation.
Step 1: Call your local state division of vocational rehabilitation or a private rehabilitation agency in

your area and invite a representative along with one or two clients to explain to your group what it is like to be disabled and how they manage in your own community. Explain your objectives to these visitors. Through this activity your group can gain a better understanding of what it is like to have a specific disability.

Session III: What is it like to be disabled? (cont.)
Objectives:
1. To experience firsthand some of the difficulties people encounter.
2. To become aware of the way our communities cater to people without disabilities and how it excludes the disabled population.
Step 1: Set up several simulations to build an awareness of the barriers disabled individuals face. You could take your group to a mall, divide into small groups so as not to be disruptive, and try the following experiences:

1. Take turns using a wheelchair. Move in and out of stores, go to a movie, a restroom, or a second floor. Get a drink of water.

2. Have several people wear earplugs while the other kids observe them as they try to communicate with each other, salespeople, and other shoppers.

3. Blindfold several of your kids. Have guides lead them to elevators, restrooms, etc. You can also try this in familiar surroundings to show that it can be just as difficult to find one's way around.

4. Distribute crutches. Have a few kids use them to get from one end of the mall to the other.

5. Tell kids using the wheelchairs that they can't use their arms to get around. They have to find another way...

You may be able to borrow wheelchairs or crutches from a local rehabilitation agency if you explain your purpose. They can also be rented. Discuss the experience. What was most difficult? How did others react to you? Were there any surprises? How did you feel?

Session IV: What is rehabilitation?
Objectives:
1. To learn about the facilities available to rehabilitate those who are disabled.
2. To learn to interact with disabled people in a positive way.
Step 1: Visit a local rehabilitation agency and discover what is being done to help disabled individ-

uals attain their highest level of functioning, adjust to their disability, and eventually find employment or some other meaningful activity in life. This would also be a good time to meet some other individuals with disabilities and talk with them. Call a local agency and arrange a tour of the facility as well as an opportunity to interact with the clients there.

Session V: How do I further handicap people with disabilities?

Objectives:

1. To learn the difference between a disability and a handicap.
2. To learn how we handicap others.
3. To make a decision to act in the interest of disabled individuals, being sensitive to their feelings, wants, needs, and rights.

Step 1: Explain the difference between a disability and a handicap. A disability is the actual physical condition (loss of a leg, paralysis, blindness, etc.). That disability becomes a handicap when it keeps people from doing something they need or want to do. All disabilities do not have to become handicaps. Sometimes, due to our attitudes toward disabled people, we handicap them. That is, we interfere with their ability to live and work to their full potential.

Step 2: In what ways do we tend to handicap disabled people (remember the simulations)? Some possible answers are:

1. By ignoring them we keep them from enjoying regular interactions with others.

2. By assuming that they can't do things as well as we can, we interfere with their accomplishments and perhaps even their jobs or careers.

3. By failing to make buildings accessible to the disabled, we keep them from doing certain tasks for themselves, from enjoying some forms of entertainment, from shopping for themselves, and so on.

4. By being too helpful, we keep them from meeting us on equal ground and enjoying a relationship of equality.

5. By expecting less of them, we keep them from attaining the most for themselves.

Step 3: Repeat the first step from Session I. Compare answers. Have perceptions changed? If so, how?

Step 4: Have groups of three or four people list on paper ways to become more sensitive and helpful to the disabled. Share the ideas with the whole group.

Mary Jo Davidson

WHO KILLED JESUS?

"Who Killed Jesus?" is a four-week Bible study and mock trial.

Week 1: Team Research. Divide your group into three equal teams, each with an adult advisor. One team is assigned to the perspective of Judas, one is assigned to the religious leaders, and one is assigned to the Roman authorities. The object of each group is to examine the biblical and historical evidence surrounding the crucifixion of Christ and prepare to defend its suspect or suspects in a mock trial setting. Provide Week 1 worksheets (pages 94-97) for each team (notice that they present identical information at the top but the bottom portion varies) in addition to resources such as Bible dictionaries, Bible handbooks, encyclopedias, commentaries, and concordances. The worksheets present issues and questions, and introduce the roles that the groups will present at the mock trial.

Week 2: Team Trial Preparation. Get your groups together again for more research and preparation for the mock trial. The second handout (page 98) outlines the strengths and weaknesses of the groups' defendants (Judas, the religious leaders, or the Roman authorities) and describes the trial procedure. Each group will need to assign individuals to role-play various characters who will be called to the witness stand during the mock trial. They must also select someone to be the group's defense attorney during the mock trial. Each group is to attempt to present their defendant as "not guilty" and focus blame on the other groups.

Week 3: Mock trial. Hold the trial in an actual courtroom if you can arrange it. As the youth group leader, play the part of the judge yourself. Select another adult leader to play the role of the prosecuting attorney. There are three handouts for the week. "The Judge's Opening Comments" (page 99) are distributed to everyone. "Trial Questions for the Prosecution" (pages 100-101) are given to the prosecuting attorney and the judge. "The Verdict" (page 102) is distributed to everyone at the end of the trial. Be prepared for a lot of reaction from each of the groups as the verdict is read.

Week 4: Debriefing and Follow-up Session. The handout for the week (pages 103-104) is designed to reemphasize the facts surrounding the crucifixion, to analyze the feelings of the participants, and to discuss the verdict. Hand out another copy of the verdict at this time. During this follow-up session the students are not in their defendant groups or roles. *Tom Lytle*

Who Killed Jesus?

WEEK 1 / GROUP 1

You will be the witnesses, the defense, the prosecutors, the plaintiffs, and the defendants as we explore the greatest injustice of all time: the execution of Jesus Christ. But who was responsible? We'll explore the biblical evidence and the historical background as the following suspects are investigated.

Judas Iscariot One of the chosen disciples who betrayed Jesus by turning him over to Jewish authorities.
The Jewish Leaders Herod Antipas, the Scribes, the Pharisees, the Sadducees, and Caiaphas the High Priest, all desired the death of Jesus Christ, "the religious fanatic."
Roman Authorities Caesar, Pilate, and the Roman guards all played a major role in this crime.

1. From information found in Scripture and the resources provided, discuss the following issues and questions. See in particular Matthew 26-28, Mark 14:43-15:47, Luke 22:47-23:56, and John 18-19.

   ➤ Who was Judas?

   ➤ What kind of relationship did he have with Jesus? With the other disciples?

   ➤ What made Judas betray Jesus?

   ➤ What part did he play in the killing of Jesus? Was *he* responsible?

2. Choose someone in your group to play the role of Judas. Make sure this person knows the events of Judas' life, especially the betrayal, and could defend himself in a trial setting.

3. Choose one or two others to play the parts of witnesses or to give character testimonies for Judas. These testimonies can be positive or negative, but must reflect scriptural truth.

4. Choose someone from your group to act as the defense attorney. This person's role is to ask questions and present evidence that will make Judas look innocent and cause the other suspects to appear guilty.

5. Decide how your group will act during the trial. What defenses will you use? What accusations against other suspects will you bring?

Who Killed Jesus?

WEEK 1 / GROUP 2

You will be the witnesses, the defense, the prosecutors, the plaintiffs, and the defendants as we explore the greatest injustice of all time: the execution of Jesus Christ. But who was responsible? We'll explore the biblical evidence and the historical background as the following suspects are investigated.

Judas Iscariot One of the chosen disciples who betrayed Jesus by turning him over to Jewish authorities.
The Jewish Leaders Herod Antipas, the Scribes, the Pharisees, the Sadducees, and Caiaphas the High
  Priest, all desired the death of Jesus Christ, "the religious fanatic."
Roman Authorities Caesar, Pontius Pilate, and the Roman guards all played a major role in this crime.

1. From information found in Scripture and in the resources provided, discuss the following issues and questions. See in particular Matthew 26-28, Mark 14:43-15:47, Luke 22:47-23:56, and John 18-19.

   ➤ Who were the Pharisees?

   ➤ Who were the Sadducees?

   ➤ Who were the Scribes?

   ➤ Who was Herod Antipas?

   ➤ Who was Caiaphas?

   ➤ What roles did each of them play in the crucifixion of Christ?

   ➤ Why did Jesus not get along with the religious leaders of his day? What did they have against him?

   ➤ What charges did the Jews bring against Jesus? What did Jesus do to cause them to see him as a false messiah and as a threat to their power and religion?

   ➤ What was the political relationship between the Jews and the Roman empire at the time of Jesus? How is it significant in relation to the crucifixion?

  95

2. Choose individuals in your group to play the roles of the following people:

    ➤ A Pharisee

    ➤ A Sadducee

    ➤ Herod Antipas

    ➤ Caiaphas

    Make sure each person knows details about his identity and the important events of the conflict with Jesus well enough to defend his actions and positions in a trial setting. Remember, they wanted Jesus killed, but didn't want to assume responsibility for it.

3. Choose someone from your group who will act as a defense attorney. Her job is to ask questions and present evidence which will make your suspects look innocent and cause the other suspects to appear guilty.

4. Decide how your group will conduct themselves during the trial. What defenses will you use? What accusations against the other suspects will you bring?

Who Killed Jesus?

WEEK 1 / GROUP 3

You will be the witnesses, the defense, the prosecutors, the plaintiffs, and the defendants as we explore the greatest injustice of all time: the execution of Jesus Christ. But who was responsible? We'll explore the biblical evidence and the historical background as the following suspects are investigated.

Judas Iscariot One of the chosen disciples who betrayed Jesus by turning him over to Jewish authorities.
The Jewish Leaders Herod Antipas, the Scribes, the Pharisees, the Sadducees, and Caiaphas the High
   Priest, all desired the death of Jesus Christ, "the religious fanatic."
Roman Authorities Caesar, Pontius Pilate, and the Roman guards all played a major role in this crime.

1. From information found in Scripture and the resources provided, discuss the following issues and questions. See in particular Matthew 26-28, Mark 14:43-15:47, Luke 22:47-23:56, and John 18-19.

   ➤ What was the relationship between the Jewish nation and the Roman empire?

   ➤ Who was Pontius Pilate? What role did he play in the crucifixion of Christ?

   ➤ In what sense was Jesus' claim to be the Messiah a political issue?

   ➤ What was involved in a Roman crucifixion?

2. Choose someone from your group to play the role of Pontius Pilate. Make sure the person understands the events and issues well enough to defend himself in a trial setting.

3. Choose someone to play the role of the Roman guard responsible for actually carrying out the order to crucify Jesus. Make sure he can describe what crucifixion involved.

4. Choose someone from your group who will act as the defense attorney. This person's job is to ask questions and present evidence which will make your suspects appear innocent and the other suspects to appear guilty.

5. Decide how your group will act during the trial. What accusations against the other suspects will you bring? What defenses will you use?

JUDAS ISCARIOT DEFENSE PREPARATION

Who Killed Jesus?

WEEK 2 / GROUP 1

1. Important evidence to present

➤ Judas was paid by the *Jewish authorities* to betray Jesus.
➤ The Bible speaks of Satan filling the heart of Judas. Could this be a case of demon possession?
➤ Crucifixion is a form of *Roman* execution. Judas is Jewish.

2. Weaknesses in your defense

➤ Judas apparently was at odds with Jesus and his concept of the kingdom of God.
   When he realized Jesus was not going to lead a political revolt, he wanted no part of him.
➤ Judas sought out the Jewish officials and made the arrangements.
   He took the initiative, not the Jews (Luke 22:1-6).

3. Trial procedure

➤ The following witnesses and defendants will be called for questioning in this order:

Judas Iscariot
Judas' character reference #1
Judas' character reference #2
A Pharisee
A Sadducee
A Scribe
Herod Antipas
Caiaphas, the high priest
Pontius Pilate
Roman guard/soldier

➤ A court-appointed prosecuting attorney will question the witnesses and defendants.
➤ Following the testimonies given to the prosecuting attorney, the witnesses and defendants
   can be questioned by your group's defense attorney.
➤ Before being dismissed from the stand the other two defense attorneys may question the
   witnesses and defendants.

JEWISH LEADER DEFENSE PREPARATION

Who Killed Jesus?
WEEK 2 / GROUP 2

1. Important evidence to present

➤ Judas Iscariot, one of Jesus' own followers, turned Jesus over to the Jewish leaders. He made the first move.

➤ In turning Jesus over to the Roman authorities, the Jewish leaders were merely being good citizens and keeping peace in Israel for Rome. If Jesus were allowed to continue his ministry and teaching, a rebellion against Rome could have resulted.

➤ Crucifixion is a Roman form of execution and the charges against Jesus that led to his death were political (treason) not religious (blasphemy).

2. Weaknesses in your defense

➤ The Jews wanted Jesus killed, but had no political power to carry it out (Luke 22:1-3).

➤ The political charges the Jews brought against Jesus were a cover for the real issues which were religious. Jesus was a threat because he blasphemed (he claimed to be the Son of God and the Messiah), he broke the Sabbath (healing), and he was a friend of tax gatherers and sinners. Jesus was also a threat to the Jewish leaders because he called them hypocrites and contradicted their concept of what the Messiah would be.

3. Trial procedure

➤ The following witnesses and defendants will be called for questioning in this order:

Judas Iscariot
Judas' character reference #1
Judas' character reference #2
A Pharisee
A Sadducee
A Scribe
Herod Antipas
Caiaphas, the high priest
Pontius Pilate
Roman guard/soldier

➤ A court-appointed prosecuting attorney will question the witnesses and defendants.

➤ Following the testimonies given to the prosecuting attorney, the witnesses and defendants can be questioned by your group's defense attorney.

➤ Before being dismissed from the stand, the other two defense attorneys may question the witnesses and defendants.

ROMAN AUTHORITY DEFENSE PREPARATION

Who Killed Jesus?

WEEK 2 / GROUP 3

1. Important evidence to present

➤ The Jewish leaders brought Jesus to Pilate with phony political charges as a cover for their religious charges (blasphemy).

➤ Pilate tried several times to release Jesus, having found no crime worthy of death, but the Jewish crowd, led by their religious leaders, insisted on his crucifixion (Luke 22:66-23:25).

➤ Pilate tried to stay out of the conflict by sending Jesus to Herod (a Jewish official) for trial.

2. Weaknesses in your defense

➤ Pilate was a coward. He had the power to release Jesus and knew that he was innocent, but gave in to the crowd.

➤ Rome was the political power at that time and had the only authority to execute. Jesus was executed on a Roman cross for a political charge—treason. He had claimed to be "King of the Jews" instead of Caesar.

3. Trial procedure

➤ The following witnesses and defendants will be called for questioning in this order:

Judas Iscariot
Judas' character reference #1
Judas' character reference #2
A Pharisee
A Sadducee
A Scribe
Herod Antipas
Caiaphas, the high priest
Pontius Pilate
Roman guard/soldier

➤ A court-appointed prosecuting attorney will question the witnesses and defendants.

➤ Following the testimonies given to the prosecuting attorney, the witnesses and defendants can be questioned by your group's defense attorney.

➤ Before being dismissed from the stand the other two defense attorneys may question the witnesses and defendants.

Who Killed Jesus?

WEEK 3 / MOCK TRIAL

This court will now come to order. We are here to investigate the historical and biblical evidence surrounding the greatest injustice of all time: the crucifixion of Jesus Christ. On trial as defendants are Judas Iscariot, the Jewish leaders, and the Roman authorities. The court has appointed _____

NAME

as the prosecuting attorney who will call the following witnesses and defendants to the stand in this order:

➤ Judas Iscariot

➤ Judas' character reference #1

➤ Judas' character reference #2

➤ A Pharisee

➤ A Sadducee

➤ A Scribe

➤ Herod Antipas

➤ Caiaphas, the high priest

➤ Pontius Pilate

➤ Roman guard/soldier

The prosecuting attorney will question the witnesses and defendants. Then the defense attorney will cross-examine them. All attorneys are free to object at any time if the questions are inappropriate or are leading the witness. I will sustain or overrule the objections based on the reasoning of the objecting attorney.

After all of the witnesses and defendants have been questioned, I will render my verdict.

Mr. Prosecutor, call your first witness.

TRIAL QUESTIONS FOR THE PROSECUTION

Who Killed Jesus?
WEEK 3 / MOCK TRIAL

Questions for Judas Iscariot
1. For the court records, please state your identity and tell us about yourself.
2. So, you were one of Jesus' followers, one of his disciples, is that correct?
3. What attracted you to Jesus? Why did you follow him?
4. So, you lived with him, you watched him perform miracles, you heard his teaching about the kingdom of God, you believed he was the Messiah. What caused you to change your mind?
5. Isn't it true that when Jesus failed to live up to your expectations, when he wasn't going to bring an end to the Roman government and restore the nation of Israel to political power, you took matters into your own hands and betrayed him to the Jewish leaders who also sought to kill Him!?

Questions for Judas' Character Reference #1
1. What relationship did you have with the defendant, Judas Iscariot?
2. Was Judas a trusted, loyal disciple as far as you could tell?
3. What kind of relationship, in your estimation, did Jesus have with Judas? Did he love Judas?

Questions for Judas' Character Reference #2
1. What was your relationship with Judas Iscariot?
2. Did Jesus and Judas ever have a difference of opinion? (If the answer is "no" then ask the third question.)
3. Isn't it true that on one occasion, when Jesus was anointed by Mary, that Judas suggested instead that the ointment be sold and the money given to the poor? Wasn't his real motive greed, not concern for the poor? And didn't Jesus rebuke him for that?

Questions for the Pharisee
1. For the court records, please state your identity and tell us about yourself.
2. So, you are a religious leader in Israel, is that correct? As a Jew, weren't you looking for the Messiah to come?
3. Jesus claimed to be that Messiah. What was it about Jesus that, in your understanding, disqualified Him as the true Messiah? What did you have against Him?

Questions for the Sadducee
1. For the court records, please state your identity and tell us about yourself.
2. So, you too are a Jewish religious leader. What was it about Jesus' teaching and ministry that threatened you enough to want him killed?
3. Isn't murder against your law?

Questions for the Scribe

1. For the court records, please state your identity and tell us about yourself.
2. So, another Jewish religious leader. How did you feel when Jesus, a miracle worker, prophet, and as some felt, the long-awaited Messiah of the Jews said, and I quote: "Woe to you teachers of the law and Pharisees. You hypocrites! You are like whitewashed tombs which look beautiful on the outside but on the inside are full of dead men's bones. On the outside you appear to people as righteous, but on the inside you are full of hypocrisy and wickedness?"

Questions for Herod Antipas

1. For the court records, please state your identity and tell us about yourself.
2. Then you are a Jewish ruler over the regions of Galilee and Perea. So you must have been at least curious when you heard about the ministry and popularity of Jesus in your area. How did you feel when Pilate sent Jesus to you for questioning?
3. How did Jesus react to your questions? What did he say?
4. What did you then do with Jesus?

Questions for Caiaphas

1. For the court records, please state your identity and tell us about yourself.
2. So, as High Priest and leader of the Jewish courts, you had the responsibility and authority to try Jesus as a criminal against your religious laws, isn't that correct? What happened during this trial?
3. What finally was the charge brought against Jesus? What was your verdict? What is the penalty for that crime?

Questions for Pontius Pilate

1. For the court records, please state your identity and tell us about yourself.
2. How did you, a Roman official, get involved in the affairs of this religious issue? Why did the Sanhedrin bring Jesus to you?
3. What charge against Jesus did the Jewish leaders bring to you?
4. Interesting. This religious group was bringing a political charge, treason, against a fellow Jew. What did you do?
5. When Herod questioned Jesus and then sent him back to you, what happened then?
6. You had the power and authority to release Jesus. Why didn't you?

Questions for the Roman guard/soldier

1. For the court records, please state your identity and tell us about yourself.
2. So, you were actually the one given the order to carry out the death sentence issued by Pilate, is that correct? Would you explain please exactly what is involved in a Roman crucifixion? What did you do to Jesus?

Who Killed Jesus?

WEEK 3 / MOCK TRIAL

This is a very unusual and difficult case on which to render a decision for several reasons. First of all, instead of one defendant on trial, there are three defendants—and two of those three are distinct groups with their own laws, traditions, and motives.

Second, from the evidence presented there was obviously a conspiracy at work—a conspiracy that involved two groups, the Jews and the Romans, who hated one another, but found in each other the means to carry out their unholy purposes.

Finally, the biblical and historical evidence presented, though detailed and accurate, is ambiguous—no single individual or group can be held solely responsible.

For these reasons we are compelled to render the following verdict:

This Court finds Judas Iscariot guilty for the killing of the Messiah, Jesus Christ. Judas you acted ignorantly when you betrayed Jesus for not being the kind of Messiah you expected. Ignorance of the Bible and its prophecies of the suffering servant Messiah is, however, no excuse, especially from one who was chosen by and loved by Jesus as much as you. Furthermore, Judas, you acted selfishly in turning over Jesus to the Jewish authorities for a mere 30 pieces of silver. Our verdict of guilty therefore carries with it the sentence of *death*.

This Court also finds the Jewish leaders: the Pharisees, Sadducees, Scribes, Caiaphas, and Herod Antipas, all guilty for the killing of the Messiah, Jesus Christ. Jewish leaders, you are at fault for rejecting the very Messiah you had so long awaited, simply because he did not conform to your religious expectations and dared to put people ahead of your laws and traditions. He did and claimed what only God could do and claim. But religion blinded you to truth, and you manipulated your mortal enemies into carrying out your despicable plot. You will be forever remembered as hypocrites for your actions and for using your power against the meekest, kindest man who ever lived. Our verdict of guilty, therefore carries with it the sentence of *death*.

This Court also finds the Roman authorities: Caesar, Pilate, the guards, and soldiers guilty for the killing of the Messiah, Jesus Christ. You Romans pride yourselves in your justice and civilization, but the execution of Jesus Christ on a Roman cross was the most unjust and inhumane act carried out on a human being, especially one as innocent as Jesus. Furthermore, your concept of government is not only abusive to its subjects, but also a blasphemous institution which claims Caesar is a god. Pilate, you are a coward. You knew Jesus was not guilty, yet you buckled to the pressure of a hostile crowd, and feared for your own safety and position of power. The act of washing your hands cannot take the stain of blood away in this case where you stand *condemned*.

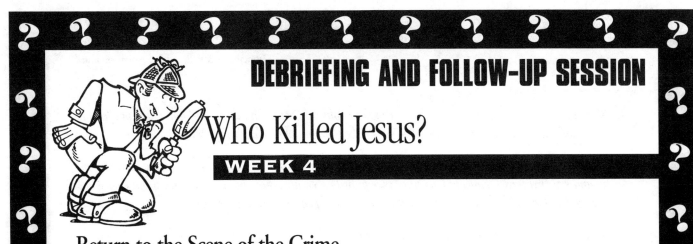

Who Killed Jesus?
WEEK 4

Return to the Scene of the Crime

1. Who was on trial? *Judas, the Jews, and the Roman authorities.*

2. What was the political situation during the time of Christ's death? *The nation of Israel was part of the Roman Empire and subject to its rules and laws. To keep peace, Rome allowed the Jews some autonomy, especially in religious areas. They still had to pay taxes and were limited in their legal system. The most significant limitation in relation to the trial issues was the fact that the Jews were not allowed to practice capital punishment in accordance with their own laws.*

3. Who was Judas Iscariot? Why did Judas want Jesus killed? *Apparently Judas was disappointed that Jesus did not match up with his messianic expectations as a political revolutionary. When it became apparent that Jesus had another means of bringing about the kingdom of God, Judas responded with betrayal and led the Jewish authorities to him.*

4. What lessons/warnings can we learn from Judas? *Our expectations may not be in God's plan. Judas did not have any faith in Jesus or patience with his concept of the coming kingdom. Demon possession is real. If Judas had repented, Jesus would have forgiven him. (Sorrow for sin is not enough.)*

5. Who were the Jewish leaders at the time of Christ's death? *Pharisees, Sadducees, Scribes, the Sanhedrin, Caiaphas, and Herod Antipas.*

6. Why did they want Jesus killed? *According to their traditions and interpretations of Scripture, Jesus was an impostor, a false Messiah. They accused him of breaking the Sabbath, of being a friend of tax gatherers and sinners, of being a false prophet, and especially of blaspheming. They clearly understood Jesus' claims to be the Son of God, to be equal to God the Father himself, but they rejected him and actively sought to remove him. They also were offended by Jesus' evaluation of their religious system and moral code. His charges of hypocrisy, ignorance, and selfish motives were especially repulsive to them. So, they attempted to take his life on several occasions but did not succeed. Judas' betrayal provided the opportunity they were looking for to remove him.*

7. What charge did they bring against Jesus at their trial before Caiaphas, the high priest? *"Blasphemy" is a religious charge meaning "to speak against the holy name of God." Jesus was accused of this because he claimed to be equal to God (John 10:33; Mark 14:61-64).*

8. What charge did the Jewish leaders bring against Jesus at their trial before Pilate? *"Treason" is a political charge meaning "to be disloyal and to be a threat to the government" (Luke 23:1-3).*

9. Why did they change the charges? *Because of their political limitations, they could not legally put Jesus to death and because treason was a capital crime for the Romans while blasphemy was not.*

10. What lessons can we learn from the Jewish authorities? *It is possible to appear religious but really be sinful and evil (hypocrisy). Faith in God must take priority over our expectations of what we think God should be and do. God's will will be accomplished despite the evil plots of men. He is in control.*

11. Who were the Roman authorities? *Caesar, Pilate, and the Roman soldiers.*

12. What part did they play in the killing of Christ? How were they responsible? *In the trials before Pilate the Jews brought the charge of treason against Jesus as a threat to Caesar, the Roman emperor. Jesus stood trial twice before Pilate, both times being found not guilty. Because of pressure from the Jewish crowds and fearing for his own security, however, Pilate allowed another criminal, Barabbas, to be released and ordered Jesus to be beaten and executed. The Roman form of execution, crucifixion, was carried out by Roman soldiers.*

13. What lessons can we learn from these Roman authorities? *Peer pressure is dangerous and promotes cowardice. Elevating oneself or another to the place of God is also dangerous. Blindly following the orders of another person is dangerous.*

Personal Reflections/Observations and Lessons Learned

1. How did you feel playing the role or representing the defendants?

2. What did you learn personally that you did not know?

3. Did you enjoy the trial itself? Was this activity a good learning experience? Why or why not?

The Verdict Revisited
Review "The Verdict" sheet from Week Three.

1. What do you think of the verdicts?

2. Do you agree with them? Why or why not?

3. If you were the judge, what verdicts would you render? Why?

THE BIG FISHERMAN—ON LOCATION

Try a series of studies over a period of weeks or at a retreat on the life of Simon Peter. Each study is held at a location that relates to the incident being examined. Study his call to be a disciple by the side of a lake or at the beach; his reaction to Jesus' Transfiguration at the top of a mountain; put him on trial for denying Jesus at a courthouse; and conclude with breakfast on the beach for a study of his restoration (John 21). *David Scott*

ARE YOU SERIOUS, DR. SEUSS?

No, this is not an idea for young children. This one is for the big kids—junior high, high school, college age, or even older. It incorporates the use of some of the popular Dr. Seuss tales. (The books are published by Random House, New York.)

Most people are familiar with Dr. Seuss' nonsense books, like *The Cat in the Hat*, but he also has a number of excellent books that deal with topics that are ideal for discussion and Bible study groups.

The discussion questions that follow are based upon several of these Dr. Seuss stories. *Sneetches* is a book that deals with racism, sexism, cliques, and so on. *Yertle the Turtle* deals with pride, vanity, taking advantage of others, etc. All of these issues are approached by Dr. Seuss in a humorous yet profound way. You will have to have your own Dr. Seuss books in order for you to make much sense out of the discussion questions published here. Some stories are also available on video. Check your local library.

One great way to use this material is to put on a Dr. Seuss Retreat that would feature the use of these books and the following discussions. Along with the more serious discussions can be a variety of Dr. Seuss games (Just change the names of your favorite games. Capture the Flag could become The Sneetch Snatch). You might have some of the youths act out the stories while they are being read to the group. Another possibility is to obtain enough copies of each book for everyone or for each study group.

But regardless of how you use these learning experiences, you'll be surprised to find just how effective and interesting they are. Most young people enjoyed Dr. Seuss when they were children, but are just now getting old enough to really appreciate what he has written. *Barry DeShetler*

The Sneetches

1. In your school, home, community and nation, who are the Star-Bellied Sneetches?

2. Who are the Plain-Bellied Sneetches in your home, community, school, and nation?

3. Are you a Plain-Bellied Sneetch or a Star-Bellied Sneetch? Why?

4. What really made the Star-Bellied Sneetches feel superior and Plain-Bellied feel inferior? How can the Plain-Bellied Sneetches overcome this?

5. Name some stars that exist in our society. Are they good or bad?

6. Who or what might be a Sylvester McMonkey McBean in our society?

7. What is this story really about? What is one of the points of the story?

8. What advice does this story give for handling the problems between different groups such as women and men, rich and poor, Christians and non-Christians?

9. What does the Bible say about pride? See Luke 18:9-14, 1 John 2:15-17, and 1 Peter 5:5-6.

10. What does Galatians 3:26-29 mean and how does it apply to Sneetches?

11. What happens regarding Sneetch attitude when a person is a Christian and motivated by the Holy Spirit? See 2 Corinthians 5:16-21.

12. For homework, read John 15:11-17 and then find a Plain-Bellied Sneetch and befriend him or her by inviting him or her to join in on a game after this session is over.

Horton Hears a Who

1. What is the main point of this story?

2. Pretend you are either a Who or someone trying to help a Who at school or in your neighborhood. Who are the Wickershams and Kangaroos? What do they represent?

3. Why couldn't the Wickershams and the Kangaroos just leave Horton alone?

4. Who are some Whos that you know? Name one time when you were the only one able to hear them. How did you feel then?

5. Why did Horton feel an obligation to the Whos? What drove him on?

6. Suppose that you are a Who in Whoville, but your speck is really a poison ivy seed. Christ is Horton. Will Horton still go to all the efforts he did to save the seed—even though he will surely get terminal poison ivy? Why or why not? See Romans 5:6-9.

7. Since you are a Who and have been saved from disaster because of Horton, what is you obligation and behavior toward other Whos and specks you should see (in light of John 15:11-17)?

8. What is the point Jo-Jo adds to the story? Name some Biblical figures like him—small but able to do great things.

9. For homework, find a Who and stick with him or her "through thin and through thick."

Yertle the Turtle

1. Describe the type of turtle Yertle was and was becoming before he fell. Name his emotions, characteristics, and attitudes up to the falling time.

2. What kid of turtle was Mack? Describe his emotions, attitudes and characteristics.

3. If Mack is turtle 1 and Yertle is turtle 10, write down what your number is between 1 and 10.

4. What was Yertle's real problem? Are people as a whole like this? Why or why not?

5. What was Mack's real problem? Do you know people who have this same problem?

6. According to Genesis 3:1-5, what promise did the snake in the pond make to Eve the Turtle? Is this still our basic problem?

7. In the story of the Prodigal Turtle (Luke 15:11-24), what things was the son seeking before he left home? Do you consider these bad things or good things?

8. When the Prodigal Turtle landed in the mud, what did he realize?

9. Imagine you are Yertle and are at the top of the pile and see the moon over you. But instead of trying to be higher still, you realize the God of the turtles gave us everything we have and are and that he made us not kings over other turtles but brothers with them. Realizing this and that God is above all, you become converted. What do you do and say to get down off the throne? What do you say to the other turtles when you are down? After you have written your answer, read Matthew 5:21-24.

10. For homework, sometime during this retreat go find a place to sit down outside and think of yourself as a little (or a lot) like Yertle and then have a conversation with the King of the Turtles.

The Lorax

1. Write two of the main points this story has to offer.

2. Who do you think Dr. Seuss thinks the reader is in this story and why? Does he think we are Once-lers, the Lorax, or the little boy?

3. Which character do you feel like you are while reading the story? Why?

4. What do truffula trees represent? What are some of America's truffula trees?

5. A hydroelectric plant is being built that will provide you and 100,000 others in your area with electricity. It is learned that a small endangered species of fish will be eliminated if the dam is built. There is a conflict between the neighbors who need electricity and some young conservationist who wants to protect the fish. Whose side are you on and why?

6. What does the Lorax symbolize? What was his job and who does it (or should do it) today?

7. What are some reasonable guidelines for individuals and businesses about using our natural resources?

8. The word on the Lorax's last standing place said, "Unless." Unless what?

9. Read Genesis 1:26-31 and Genesis 2:15. What are our duties to the earth according to God?

10. What was the Once-ler's main character flaw? What do you consider to be the chief cause of sin? See 1 Timothy 6:10.

"Gertrude McFuzz" (in Yertle the Turtle)

1. Name three bad characteristics or evil desires of Gertrude's.

2. What is the real difference in Gertrude from the very beginning of the story and its end since she still only has one plain tail feather?

3. Imagine you are Gertrude but instead of wanting tail feathers you want something that some other bird has and you do not. What is it you want and why do you want it?

4. What did Doctor Drake say to convince Gertrude not to seek to have a different tail? How can this apply to human Gertrudes?

5. If you were Gertrude and could have eaten between 0 and 36 pill-berries to get what you wanted, at what number would you stop eating and why?

6. What did Gertrude want to do immediately after she had all the feathers she wanted? Name two times when you did what Gertrude wanted to do.

7. What was Gertrude's cure and what warning might it give to us when we behave like Gertrude?

8. Write one of the 10 Commandments that could best be applied to this story (Exodus 20:7-17).

9. Find a Bible with an Old and New Testament and read 1 Samuel 16:6-7 and then 1 Peter 3:1-5. What would Gertrude say if she had read this before she had eaten a pill-berry? What would she say now?

10. For homework, the next time you see someone trying to show off their tail feathers ask, "Have they seen Gertrude lately?"

"The Zax" (in Sneetches)

1. What is this story really about? What is the point?

2. Who was at fault in this argument? Who won the argument?

3. If you were a Zax and you met another, how would you solve the difference if only one of you were willing to compromise? Would you negotiate, use force, persuasion, or some other creative idea?

4. By arguing, stubbornness, and focusing exclusively on one another, what are the Zaxes failing to see going on around them? Can you relate this to your life? To the church?

5. Have you ever been in an argument when you would not give in? When? Why wouldn't you give in? How did it end?

6. After you have read Luke 6:27-36, pretend you meet a Zax coming from the other way. In the light of Luke 6, what do you do and why?

7. How does the King of all the Zaxes want us to behave? Read John 13:1-17 before you answer.

8. Are there any times when giving in to the other Zax is not acceptable? If so, when?

9. For homework, to help humorously solve conflict, the next time you find yourself in a confrontational situation or argument, as soon as you can remember to do so ask the other person, "Are you a north-going Zax or a south-going Zax?"

THEME
LESSONS

Build an entire lesson on a specific theme. Try "Feet Meeting" (page 118)—foot games followed by a lesson on the symbolic importance of washing each other's feet. You aren't into feet? Okay, what about boxes? Or the hands of Jesus? Or light versus darkness? They're all here!

HANDS OF JESUS

Using the theme "The Hands of Jesus," have kids dig through the New Testament to find as many passages as possible where Christ used his hands to help others. After finding them, have the passages read and discuss each.

Then divide the group into smaller groups and work on a collage, with the title "The Hands of Jesus." Kids are given magazines, paste, scissors, paint and brushes, and marking pens. They are to cut out photos of hands or draw them, with words or without, to illustrate the theme. These should not be too large, so as to save time. Limit to about 30 minutes.

Next, discuss how modern-day Christians act like the hands of Jesus in the world. Songs dealing with hands can be sung either to open or close this meeting.

BOXES

Here's a meeting idea that can be introduced by reading Matthew 13:31-35. Have boxes placed around the meeting room. They can be all the same size or of various sizes. Having introduced the idea of the parable, ask the group to think and meditate and discuss the following questions which can be given to them before the discussion time.

1. What did you think as you came into our meeting place and saw these boxes?
2. What experiences have you had with boxes? (Other areas to consider—size of box, closed, open, shape, etc.)
3. What do boxes illustrate about the church?
4. What do boxes illustrate about our relationship to God; our relationship to each other?
5. Have you ever felt boxed in?
6. Is the Christian life in a neat package?

This is an opportunity for a group to share things, listen, or discuss. The use of boxes can lead to many areas of discussion. Use the idea of being "squeezed" (Romans 12:2) to develop the whole idea that the boxes are objects to be used and are most useful when open and available to be filled. You can close with the idea that Christ was born and put in a type of box, but he outgrew that one and nobody was able to box him...not even his disciples. Even when he was crucified they put him in a box and then placed a boulder there to keep him. He broke out of that box and continues today to break out of the boxes people put him in. *David Worth*

FEET MEETING

This creative program idea combines some fun with serious learning about servanthood and discipleship. The theme of the meeting is feet. Start the meeting with some feet games:

• **Foot Signing.** Kids take off their shoes and socks, and receive a felt tip pen (the kind that will wash off). On a signal, the group has one minute to see how many signatures they can get on the bottom of their feet.

• **Foot Wrestling.** Kids pair off and sit down with right feet together. They lock toes. On a signal, they try to pin the other person's foot, like regular arm-wrestling.

• **Feet by the Foot.** Teams line up with their feet in a single file line, heel to toe, to see which team has the most footage. Longest line wins.

• **Lemon Pass.** Teams remove shoes and try to pass a lemon down the line without using their hands; only feet. The lemon cannot drop or teams have to start over.

• **Foot Drawing.** Each team chooses some object in the room. Using only feet for patterns, they trace parts of the feet on paper to create that object. Other teams must then try to guess what the object is.

Following the games move to a Bible study, using whatever Bible study method your group prefers. A good passage would be John 13:1-17. Talk about the significance of feet in the passage. What was so unusual about Jesus being willing to wash the disciples' feet? What does that say about servanthood?

Following the Bible study gather the group around a large paper cross that has been taped to the floor. Place a pan of colored poster paint around it. Use a different color in each pan. Then talk about what it means to be a part of the cross—to be willing to walk as a servant in the same way Christ did. Invite the kids to choose a color, and (one at a time) dip in their feet and walk across the paper, leaving their footprints on the cross. This can be done as an indication of their decision to follow in the way of the cross.

Next you can conduct a foot washing ceremony, as kids wash the paint off each other's feet. Provide pans, towels, soap, etc.

This exercise can be followed up with good discussion, of course. As you view the cross together, you can talk about the significance of the different kinds of footprints upon it, how they are all unique, the blending of colors in the middle section, the plain cross that is now bright with colors, etc. You can close by allowing the kids to cut the cross into small poster-size pieces and to take them home to hang on their walls as a reminder of their commitment to walk with Christ. *Ruth Staal*

WALK A MILE IN MY SHOES

Here's a clever idea for a retreat or series of meetings. The shoe theme can be tied in with a focus on walking with Christ or putting yourself in the shoes of others, and so on.

You might even want to create shoe-shaped publicity posters or name tags for your event. The title of this activity, "Walk a Mile in My Shoes," is the name of an old song by Joe South, which you might want to sing as a group if you can find a recording of it in your local music store.

• **Shoelace Sharing.** Give each player a shoelace. One at a time, kids should slowly wrap their shoelaces around one of their fingers and reveal one fact about themselves with each full circle. Make sure the shoelaces vary in length.

• **Shoe Search.** Have kids sit in a tight circle with their legs extended toward the middle. Have each player choose a shoe within the circle that he feels says something about his life and why.

• **Important Steps.** Give each person a sheet of paper and a pencil. Have each student write down 15 to 20 important steps (events, people, decisions) that have taken place in their lives and that have affected their lives. Invite volunteers to explain the items on their lists.

• **When the Shoe Fits.** Distribute the list on page 120 to each person. Allow kids time to complete the sentences, and then have them pair off and share their answers.

• **Wear My Shoe.** Mix up a boxful of slips of paper on which kids have written about a personal problem. Each kid withdraws one slip of paper from the box, reads the problem aloud, and offers a solution. You may want to fatten the box with extra problems. Spend five minutes or less on each problem.

• **Walking with God.** Distribute the following, one to each student.

• **Coat of Feet.** Have kids create their own coat of arms with the outline of a shoe. Have them divide it into sections and write a statement in each section according to these guidelines (place one statement in each section of the coat of feet).

Something you learned:
• about yourself.
• about someone else.
• about God.

In one of the shoe sections, they should write a statement that summarizes their personal experiences over the last week and in another section, they should describe a dream or goal they have for themselves.

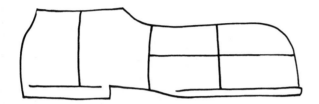

You can also use other foot terminology to enhance the session. Here are a few examples:
• Shoebox—a small group
(for sharing and discussion)
• Shoelaces—a summary time
(to tighten things up)
• A Really Big Shoe—a talent show
• Happy Feet—a dance you make up

Susan Norman

LIGHT OVER DARKNESS

The following is an effective way to present the metaphors of light and darkness found in Scripture. You will need one 18-by-11-inch cross, one medium candle that cannot be blown out (you can get this at a magic shop), and one regular candle for each person.

Set the cross on a table and put the candle that won't blow out in front of the cross. Have kids sit facing the cross and give each of them a regular candle. Light the candle in front of the cross and turn off all lights. Then follow this procedure:

Explain that light represents good (God) and darkness represents the evil forces of this world (Satan).
• Read Genesis 1:3-4. Light the first person's candle; have the first person light the next candle and so on until all the candles are lit.
• Read John 8:12. Explain that if you put your trust in Jesus, you will walk in the light, but if you put your trust in the world, you will walk in darkness.
• Read 1 John 1:6. Explain how if you merely say you are a Christian and go through the motions of walking in the light, you're only fooling yourself because God knows your heart.
• Have your kids blow out their candles and experience darkness. Ask the question, "Can you silently identify a sin that is making your life dark? Think for a minute about the darkness Satan is putting in your pathway. Jesus was tempted by Satan to join him in the darkness also."
• Try to blow out the main candle three times. Explain how attempts to extinguish the candle represent Satan's attempt to cause Jesus to sin. Jesus did not succumb to the temptations; his light kept shining and is still shining today.
• Explain that in 1 John 1:5 God is light and in him there is no darkness.
• Ask teens if they will let the eternal light of the world reignite their faith. (Have them come forward one at a time, relight their candles, and return to their seats.)
• Challenge teens to commit themselves to the light of the world and to the work of sharing the light with those in darkness.
• Read Isaiah 2:5 and end with a prayer.

Chip King

Walk a Mile In My Shoes

I often feel worn out because...

One thing I am really strict about is...

One thing (from my sole) that I would like to share with others is...

One thing in my life that may be wearing a hole in me (putting a lot of strain on me) is...

One thing I really like to wag my tongue about (talk a lot about) is...

A time that I feel that I was stepped on was when...

A memorable step (time) in my life was...

One thing I've been a real heel about lately is...

A person's shoes that I would really like to fill is...

Walk a Mile In My Shoes

Have each student complete the following sentences:

God first felt close to me when...

The time I felt closest to God was when...

The time I felt farthest away from God was when...

I would like my relationship with God to be...

120

BIBLE
GAMES

These games won't speed your kids into seminary, but they certainly go a long way toward making the Bible interesting to your students. Group members with extensive Bible knowledge may have an advantage in these games, but you can compensate for them with creative rules and team assignments.

BIBLE MATHEMATICS

Sometimes it is a good idea to use Scripture search games with young people to familiarize them with their Bibles, and to give them practice at looking up verses and finding information in Scripture. It's definitely not the best way to learn Scripture, but it does get kids into their Bibles. The following four games are math problems that are solved by looking up the verses and finding the necessary numbers then doing some simple arithmetic. Print them up and give them to the kids in your group. They will, of course, need Bibles and pencils. Pocket calculators are optional. They can be solved individually or they can be worked on in teams. The object is to be first to arrive at the correct answer.

Here are the answers. The numbers needed for each step are provided, plus the final answer. *Pat Andrews*

Game One	Game Two	Game Three	Game Four
1. 50,000	1. 430	1. 603,550	1. 318
2. 100	2. 30	2. 50	2. 962
3. 16	3. 600	3. 962	3. 120
4. 14	4. 2000	4. 209	4. 400
5. 450	5. 300	5. 10,000	5. 50
6. 4	6. 46	6. 10	6. 3
7. 200	7. 14	7. 40	7. 40
8. 8	8. 5		8. 90
Final answer: 15	Final answer: 350	Final answer: 50	Final answer: 110

Bible Mathematics

Game One

1. Locate the number of gold pieces the burned books were calculated to be worth in Acts 19:19.

2. Divide that number by the age of Abraham when Isaac was born (Genesis 21:5).

3. Add to that number the number of years Ahaz ruled in Jerusalem (2 Chronicles 28:1).

4. Add to that number the number of generations from Abraham to David (Matthew 1:17).

5. Subtract from that number the number of years the Israelites were in possession of their land (Acts 13:20).

6. Multiply that number by the number of days that Lazarus had been in the tomb (John 11:17).

7. Subtract from that number the number of years that Serug lived after the birth of Nahor (Genesis 11:23).

8. Divide that number by the number of oxen in Numbers 7:8.

   Final answer: _____

Bible Mathematics

Game Two

1. Locate the number of years that Eber lived after the birth of Peleg (Genesis 11:17).

2. Subtract from that number the age of David when he became king (2 Samuel 5:4).

3. Add to that number the number of men armed for war in Judges 18:11.

4. Add to that number the number of pigs that ran down the cliff and drowned in the lake (Mark 5:13).

5. Divide that number by the number of years Enoch walked with God after he had Methuselah (Genesis 5:22).

6. Add to that number the number of years it had taken to build the sanctuary according to John 2:20.

7. Add to that number the number of days that Paul and the crew on the boat had gone hungry (Acts 27:33).

8. Multiply that number by the number of sparrows two pennies would buy according to Luke 12:6.

   Final answer: _____

Bible Mathematics — Game Three

1. Locate the number of the total of the 12 tribes of Israel in Numbers 1:46.

2. Divide that number by the number of just men Yahweh asked Abraham to find in the city of Sodom (Genesis 18:26).

3. Subtract from that number the number of years Jared lived (Genesis 5:20).

4. Subtract from that number the number of years that Peleg lived after the birth of Reu (Genesis 11:19).

5. Subtract from that number the number of men who stayed with Gideon (Judges 7:3).

6. Divide that number by the number of Joseph's brothers who went down to buy grain from Egypt (Genesis 42:3)

7. Subtract from that number the number of years the land enjoyed peace after the battle led by Deborah and Barak (Judges 5:31).

   Final answer: _____

Bible Mathematics — Game Four

1. Locate the number of the members of Abram's household (Genesis 14:14).

2. Add to that number the number of years that Jared lived (Genesis 5:20).

3. Add to that number the number of talents of gold that Hiram sent to Solomon (1 Kings 9:14).

4. Subtract from that number the number of years the descendants of Abraham would be oppressed (Acts 7:6).

5. Divide that number by the number of loops along the edge of the tabernacle curtain in Exodus 26:10.

6. Multiply that number by the number of times Paul was shipwrecked (2 Corinthians 11:25).

7. Subtract from that number the number of years the Israelites enjoyed peace in Midian (Judges 8:28).

8. Add to that number the age of Enosh when he became the father of Kenan (Genesis 5:9).

   Final answer: _____

STEAL THE BACON BIBLE GAME

Divide the group into two equal teams and have them count off. Then seat the teams in two parallel rows of chairs, facing each other with about six feet between the rows. Players should be seated in order of their numbers, with the players who have the number one seated at opposite ends of the rows. Place an upside-down garbage can at the midpoint of the rows and halfway between them, then set a chalk eraser on the can.

When the leader calls out a number, the player from each team with that number must race to get the eraser first. Whoever gets it has the chance to earn his or her team a point by correctly answering a Bible-knowledge question. You can make up your own questions, or use some from one of the popular Bible trivia games. The team with the most points after all the numbers have been called out twice wins. *Laurie Christian*

20 QUESTIONS WHO AM I?

Divide the group into two teams. One person from each team must draw from a box containing slips of paper, each with the name of a Bible character written on it. Then the two players have 45 seconds to huddle with their teammates and find out as much as possible about the person whose name has been drawn. They should not let the opposing team know who it is.

At the end of that time, teams take turns asking each other a yes/no question about the identity of the opposing team's character, and are given one chance after each question to guess who it is. Questions can only be answered by the player who drew the name, and the only answers which can be given are "Yes," "No," or "I don't know." If the player doesn't know the answer, or if the answer given is wrong (you'll have to be the judge), the opposing team gets to ask another question. The team that guesses the correct character first wins a point for that round; highest score after 10 rounds wins. Each round should involve a different pair of players.

Some useful questions might be:
•Is this character in the Old Testament?

Is this character human (as opposed to God, angels, devils, or animals)?
•Is this character a woman?

•Is this character a political leader?
•You might want to have someone from each team record the answers—it's easy to forget in the excitement of the moment! *Laurie Christian*

BIBLE QUIZ Q'S

Basic Bible knowledge helps students feel confident about locating important events, people, and truths in God's Word. The following list of questions can be used during a Tic-Tac-Toe tournament or other quiz games. *Alan Rathbun*

•Which book tells about Moses leading God's people out of Egypt?
Exodus

•Which Gospel was written by a doctor?
Luke

•Which book lists all the food and ceremony laws for Israel?
Leviticus

•Which book of the New Testament is shorter: 2 John, 3 John, or Philemon?
2 John

•Which book tells the story of Samson?
Judges

•Which book describes the life and thoughts of a man who faced very difficult suffering?
Job

•Which two books list the 10 Commandments?
Exodus and Deuteronomy

•Which book describes what the end times will be like?
Revelation

•Which book tells about a runaway slave and the forgiveness requested of his owner?
Philemon

•Which book was a letter written to the pastor of the church at Crete?
Titus

•Which book contains the words, "The Lord is my shepherd"?
Psalms

•Which book is "the book of beginnings"?
Genesis

•Which book relates the account of a man being stoned while he preached?
Acts

•Which book is well known for its teaching about wisdom?
Proverbs

•Which book is about the love between a husband and wife?
Song of Solomon

•Which book tells about Abraham?
Genesis

•Which book contains the verse, "For all have sinned and fall short of the glory of God"?
Romans

•Which book gives the account of three men in a fiery furnace?
Daniel

•Which two books report genealogies (family trees) of Jesus Christ?
Matthew and Luke

•Which book states that life under the sun is meaningless?
Ecclesiastes

•Which books chronicle the lives of the kings of Israel after Saul and David?
1 and 2 Kings, 1 and 2 Chronicles

•Which book narrates the account of a missionary being swallowed by a big fish?
Jonah

•Which book tells about rebuilding the wall around Jerusalem?
Nehemiah

•Which book recounts the life of Joseph, son of Jacob?
Genesis

•Which book contains the story of Moses standing before the burning bush?
Exodus

•Which book describes the history of Israel before it was ruled by kings?
Judges

•Which book contains the verse, "For God so loved the world that he gave his one and only son, that whoever believes in him shall not perish but have eternal life."
John

•Which book tells how 12 spies from Israel scouted out the promised land?
Numbers

•Which book recounts how a Jewish queen saved Israel from a holocaust?
Esther

•Which prophet responded to God by saying, "Here am I. Send me"?
Isaiah

•Which book describes the flood that covered the whole earth?
Genesis

•Which book gives the account of the man thrown into a lion's den for his faith in God?
Daniel

•Which book tells us what Jesus' great assignment to believers is?
Matthew

•In which Gospel does Jesus say, "I am the way and the truth and the life. No one comes to the Father except through me"?
John

INTERCHURCH ESPIONAGE

The following is a simulation game designed to teach the internal unity among the true members of the body of Christ. The game is set up as a fun activity, the players being unaware that the game has been rigged to teach a profound truth. Although the game's instructions are somewhat elaborate, this is only to disguise the simplicity of the game. Here's how it works.

Before the game:

• Prepare enough slips of paper to enable everyone in the crowd to have one. Select about four sets of numbers, such as:

53	207
219	21
21	119
107	53
121	129
107	101
49	47
123	123

Write one set on each slip of paper. The important thing is that all the number sets add up to the same sum (in this case, 400). The players are unaware of this, of course. Fold the papers and shuffle them so they are all mixed up.

• Get enough pennies for everyone to have one. Part of the game involves flipping coins.

• Have golf pencils on hand for everyone who needs one.

Explain the game to the crowd as follows:

1. You are all spies. In a moment you will receive a slip of paper with numbers on it. By adding the numbers, you will know the code number of the country you are spying for. The person next to you could be an enemy spy or he might be a friend from your country. You don't know. Don't reveal your code number until you have to, and make sure you add the numbers correctly.

2. The object of the game is to: (a) eliminate enemy spies from the game, (b) locate and team up with your fellow spies, and (c) avoid being eliminated from the game. In other words, whichever country survives without being eliminated is the winner.

3. You will also receive a coin and a pencil with your code number. When the game begins, add up your numbers and write the total on the paper. Next, go up to any person in the room. One of you calls "Odd," one "Even." Flip your coins. If they both turn up the same, whoever called "Even" is the "aggressor" and the other person is the "responder." If, when flipped, the two coins

turn up different (one heads and one tails), whoever called "Odd" becomes the aggressor.

4. After you determine who the aggressor is, the aggressor asks "friend or foe?" The responder must then show her code number. If it is the same as the aggressor's, the responder remains in the game because she is a friendly spy and on the same team. She now joins the aggressor by holding onto his waist and following behind. If the responder's code number is different from the aggressor's, the responder is out of the game.

5. At this point, if you are still in the game, you find other survivors and the process is repeated. If you have a fellow spy behind you, then you work as a group. You are the spokesman for the group, however, if you were the original aggressor. You approach another individual or group, flip coins (per instruction 3), and you will either eliminate, be eliminated, or form a larger group.

6. Keep this procedure going until only one group is left. This will be the winning country.

Play the game:

• Make sure there is enough room for the snake-like groups to form and move about. Of course, as the game progresses, no one will be eliminated, and all will be absorbed into one long group.

• Try to keep the game going. The players will eventually wise up to the fact that there aren't any enemy spies before the game is completely over. It doesn't take long for the game to be played.

Discuss:

1. What did you assume about the game that wasn't true? (That there were different countries, when actually there was only one.)

2. If you had known ahead of time that there weren't any enemy spies, how would it have affected your play? (Probably wouldn't have been threatened, therefore, no need to compete or be suspicious of others.)

Application:

• We are all members of the same team, but often we forget and are threatened by the unknown responses of others.

• As Christians we are all members of one body (1 Cor. 12), yet we have fractured it on all levels (denominations, cliques).

• On a broader scale, we are all members of the human family. We should seek to understand others better and learn to live in harmony. *Tom Grey*

Owl Island

The following simulation game can be played just for fun, or it can be used as a discussion starter on the subject of communication, teamwork, cooperation, etc. It could also be tied in quite nicely with a devotion on the church as the body of Christ and the importance of each member.

To introduce the game, explain that a mad scientist has cloned a deadly bacteria, and everyone in the world has been infected with it.

Divide the young people into groups representing the different countries of the world. Each country is to have theoretical biochemists, bionic men and women, and pharmacists. The theoretical biochemists are located in a top secret lab on the mysterious Owl Island. A vaccine effective against the bacteria has been synthesized at the Owl Island lab.

The task is for the theoretical biochemists to relate information about the vaccine via the bionic men and women back to the pharmacist in their respective countries. The pharmacist then reconstructs the vaccine using the information given to them by the bionics. The information they are sending is a description of the vaccine's structure (made of colored toothpicks and marshmallows).

The vaccine could look like this:

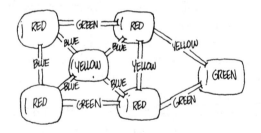

The task must be completed within a given time limit. A country "dies" if the reconstructed vaccine is not exactly as the original or the country is not finished before the time is up. The time limit can be made so that everyone or no one can have an opportunity to finish, depending on the leader's discretion.

Other rules:

1. Bionic men and women are used to transmit the information because Owl Island is surrounded by defenses such as booby traps, electrified fences, dangerous animals, etc. Therefore, only bionics can move between the island and their home country.
2. Only theoretical biochemists are allowed to view the structure, no one else. There should be some sort of screen set up so that no one else can see.
3. The pharmacists are supplied with toothpicks and marshmallows.
4. The bionics are not allowed to touch the toothpicks or the marshmallows. Only the pharmacists are allowed to touch them.

Suggestions:

1. It's best to have about four to five people per group: one theoretical biochemist, two to three bionics, and one pharmacist.
2. The biochemists should relay the information a little bit at a time to relieve the confusion.
3. The distance that the bionics have to travel between the island and home country can be varied depending on how much you want to exercise the kids, and how much territory you have available. It's great for camps.
4. The difficulty of the game is determined by the complexity of the vaccine. The more complex the vaccine, the more time should be allotted. *Milton Hom*

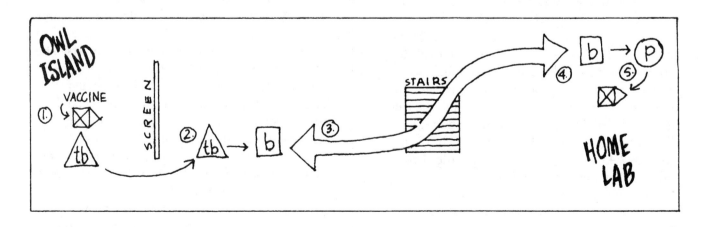

WAR AND PEACE

This is a simulation game that deals with conflict, cooperation, trust, and a number of other topics as well. On top of that, it is exciting and lots of fun to play.

The game can be played with any size group. For larger groups, divide into "continents" of eight people per continent. Each continent is then divided into four separate countries, with two people in each country. Each continent will then have its own game going. If your entire group is smaller, like 12 people, then just divide into four countries of three people per country, or whatever you need to do to get four small groups.

The object of the game is for each country to improve its economic situation (in other words, to win money) by declaring war or peace on each of the 10 successive rounds in the game. To begin, pass out the game score sheet on page 131 to each country.

The rules on the game score sheet should be self-explanatory. Each country simply declares war or peace during each round, and the first chart determines how much money it wins or loses. For example, on round 1, if one country declares war and the other three declare peace, then the country that declared war would win three million dollars, and the other three countries would each lose a million dollars.

Make sure everyone knows how to play the game before starting. You as the leader should act as timekeeper and announce each round and the payoffs. On rounds 4, 6, 8, and 10, there is a bonus payoff which will increase the amount that each country wins or loses on that particular round. For example, on round 8, you would multiply each country's winnings or losses by five.

On each round, the countries have either one minute or two minutes (see chart) to make up their minds as to what they will declare. They then must write in their declaration in the space provided. After everyone has decided, each country announces its declaration, and the winnings or losses are determined and written in, and the balance recorded. Everyone starts out with nothing. When countries are conferring with each other (rounds 2,4,6,8,10), they may try to mislead each other if they want to. That's up to them.

When playing, don't stress the idea of "beating" anyone—that is, trying to defeat the other countries. Stress instead that the object of the game is to improve your own country's position and to win as much money as possible. They must decide during the course of the game whether or not they want to improve themselves by clobbering the other countries, making them lose money. Usually by the fourth or fifth round, nobody trusts anybody, and each country is trying to outsmart the other. It's a lot of fun.

Follow up with a discussion of the game and try to apply some scriptural principles regarding trust and cooperation, and our basic tendency to look out for ourselves more than others. Talk about reasons why we usually do what's wrong, even when we know what's best for everybody. The discussion can go in all kinds of directions. *Alex Rollins*

THE DEVIL MADE ME DO IT

This simulation game can be used to explore a number of different topics, including the role of Satan in temptation and the role of Scripture in resisting temptation. Here's how it is played: Divide into two equal groups. If there is an odd number of people, then one of your adult sponsors may have to participate. One group will be designated the "Devils" and the other group will be designated the "Pilgrims." Give each Pilgrim a game sheet (see page 133) containing the list of 20 instructions. Half of these are good deeds and the other half are no-no's. Unfortunately, the Pilgrims don't know which is which. The Devils are given the same list, but they are informed as to which ones are no-no's and which ones are not. The no-no's on the list are numbers. 1, 2, 6, 8, 9, 12, 15, 16, 18, and 19.

Now pair the kids off, with each Pilgrim getting a personal Devil to follow him around, give him advice, and tempt him in one way or another. The object of the game for the Pilgrim is to score more points than his Devil by doing as many good deeds as possible and by avoiding the no-no's. The Devil can score points by getting his Pilgrim to do no-no's. Here's how the points are awarded: for the Pilgrim—100 points are given for every good deed performed; 200 points are subtracted for every no-no committed. For the Devil—200 points are awarded for every no-no committed by the Pilgrim. Have nice prizes available for the highest scorers to provide some incentive.

Pilgrims can make decisions about what to do based on their own judgement, advice from their

WAR AND PEACE

Directions: The game consists of 10 successive rounds. On each round, your country must declare either war or peace. You will win or lose money on each round, depending on how the other three countries declare. This chart shows the payoffs that apply for each round:

POSSIBLE RESULTS	PAYOFF
Four Countries Declare War	Lose $1 million each
Three Countries Declare War One Country Declares Peace	Win $1 million each Lose $3 million
Two Countries Declare War Two Countries Declare Peace	Win $2 million each Lose $2 million each
One Country Declares War Three Countries Declare Peace	Win $3 million Lose $1 million each
Four Countries Declare Peace	Win $1 million each

You are to confer with your partners on each round and make a joint decision as to whether you want to declare war or peace. Before rounds 2, 4, 6, 8, and 10, you are to have a summit meeting and confer with all the other countries on your continent. After conferring with the other countries, and after you have come to an agreement (if you do), you may change your mind if you so desire. That is your international privilege. You may not change your mind, however, after you have written your declaration in the column below.

ROUND	STRATEGY		YOU DECLARE: (war or peace)	WON $	LOST $	BALANCE $	
	TIME	CONFER WITH					
1	2 Min.	Country Only					
2	1 Min.	Country and Continent					
3	1 Min.	Country Only					
4	2 Min.	Country and Continent					BONUS x two
5	1 Min.	Country Only					
6	2 Min.	Country and Continent					BONUS x three
7	1 Min.	Country Only					
8	2 Min.	Country and Continent					BONUS x five
9	1 Min.	Country Only					
10	2 Min.	Country and Continent					BONUS x ten

Devils, or a copy of a Good Book, which contains all the verses that are referred to on the game sheet. If a Pilgrim has a Good Book, then he will know exactly what to do and what not to do. (The instructions for making the Good Books are on page 134.)

But, here's the catch. The time limit for the game is only 15 minutes. In order to obtain a Good Book, it is necessary to memorize 1 Thessalonians 5:22, which says, "Avoid every kind of evil." That verse must then be quoted perfectly to the Good Book Giver who is handing out all the Good Books, plus a 60-second speech must be given to the Good Book Giver on why that verse is important to modern-day Pilgrims. To make things even more difficult, Pilgrims must line up single file in the Good Book line and be taken one at a time. The Good Book Giver presents a Good Book to each Pilgrim after he completes the 60-second speech, and then the next Pilgrim gets an opportunity to receive one in the same manner. Some Pilgrims may consider this to be too difficult and time-consuming.

Before the game begins, the Devils can meet separately and be informed that they can use any means they want (except physical force) to get their Pilgrims to do no-no's. They can lie, act as if they don't really want to win, keep a fake score for themselves, convince the Pilgrims that they don't have enough time to get a Good Book—that common sense will do, etc. At the same time, the Pilgrims can be given instructions on how to obtain Good Books.

Once everyone understands the rules, blow the whistle and start the game. Let things develop in a natural sort of way. The game itself is a lot of fun with all sorts of crazy things happening. After the time limit is up, stop the game and reveal to the Pilgrims the good deeds and the no-no's so that players can tally up their scores. Award prizes; then discuss the following questions:
1. How many of you decided to get a Good Book and why? Why did some of you choose not to get a Good Book?
2. Was getting a Good Book as hard as you thought it would be?
3. For those of you who did not a get a Good Book, how did you determine which activities to do?
4. Was it easy or difficult to tell when your Devil was lying?

5. Did your Devil force you to do anything?
6. Can the Bible frustrate Satan in this same way as the Good Book frustrated the Devils? How?
7. Did any of you go to other Pilgrims for counseling? What was the response you received?
8. What methods did you Devils use to try to convince your Pilgrim to sin?
9. Can we modern-day Pilgrims (Christians) learn something from this game about the importance of Scripture?

You can no doubt think of other questions besides these. In each case help the group to make the connection between what happened in the game and what happens in real life. In other words, in response to question 4, you might follow that up with another question, like, "How can we know when Satan is deceiving us?" You might wrap it up with some thoughts on how Satan's activity is ultimately limited by God (see 1 Cor. 10:13; book of Job; etc.) *Greg Thomas*

LEGAL BALL

This game was created to illustrate how we cannot expect to please God only by living according to a set of strict rules or do's and don'ts. The game is a form of softball that is best played with a Wiffle Ball or Nerf ball and a light bat. It can be played indoors or outdoors. Lay out the ball diamond (bases, etc.) and divide into two teams of any number.

Before the game begins, read the following rules of the game and state that you will strictly enforce them. Players caught breaking a rule will be called "Out!" and their team will be penalized one run.

The rules:
1. Thou shalt play the game with one hand and one eye. Example: A right-handed person must cover his right eye with his right hand and use his left hand and eye. A left-handed person vice versa.
2. Thou shalt not run! You may only walk at all times.
3. Thou shalt not throw the ball. You may only hand it to another person.
4. Thou shalt receive one pitch. If you do not hit the ball, you are out.
5. Thou shalt ask permission to walk the bases. If you hit the ball, you must turn to the umpire and ask permission to walk to first base. If the umpire says "No!" you are out.
6. Thou must apologize to thy teammates each time you make an out.
7. A foul ball is an out.

The Devil
MADE ME DO IT

You have 15 minutes to complete as many tasks as possible. Each time you complete a task, get your Devil to initial your sheet. For each good deed you receive 100 points. For each no-no you lose 200 points and your Devil receives 200 points.

   In order to get a Good Book, you must wait in line, memorize the Scripture (1 Thess. 5:22) and quote it without looking. Then, give a 60-second talk on the importance of that verse for us today.

____ 1. Blow in someone's ear.
      Melchizedek 4:16

____ 2. Untie someone's shoelace.
      2 Malachi 3:12

____ 3. Do 10 jumping jacks.
      Hezekiah 1:5

____ 4. Stand on a chair and shout,
      "Alfred E. Newman,
      eat your heart out."
      Maher-Shalal-Hash-Baz 11:9

____ 5. Lay on your stomach and act as if
      you're swimming for 10 seconds.
      Jeconiah 10:17

____ 6. Invite someone of the opposite sex
      out for frog legs.
      St. Mike 2:1

____ 7. Get down on all fours and shout,
      "I ain't nothing but a hound dog."
      Josiah 6:12

____ 8. Find someone's real Bible and
      give it to them.
      1 Samson 7:7

____ 9. Sit quietly for 15 seconds.
      2 Samson 9:14

____10. Skip across the room from one set
      of windows to the other.
      Synthesis 20:56

____11. Go to the microphone and sing,
      "There's a sweet, sweet odor in
      this place."
      Exclamation 14:7

____12. Go up to someone, pound your
      chest, do a Tarzan yell, and say
      "Thanks, I needed that!"
      Bereans 16:40

____13. Find one of the Devils and say,
      "You handsome Devil, you!"
      Chaldeans 1:1

____14. Sit in the front row and shout
      "Amen, preach it brother."
      Macedonians 5:8

____15. Get someone to shake hands with you.
      1 Philip 8:14

____16. Find someone with a Good Book
      and shout "Fanatic!" five times.
      2 Philip 13:11

____17. Take one shoe off and balance it on
      your head for five seconds.
      Hilkiah 5:3

____18. Go to the microphone and whistle,
      "Give me oil in my lamp."
      St. Stephen 1:15

____19. Kiss one of the chairs three times.
      Facts 28:42

____20. Go to someone, hold your nose,
      and pass out from the smell.
      Naomi 19:1

Make Good Book by cutting apart all of the following verses and stapling them together with the title page (The Good Book) on the front.

Synthesis 20:56 The soul that skippeth, it shall reach the other side.	**St. Mike 2:1** One thing is an abomination to the Lord, even frog legs.
Facts 28:42 Even a chair if it is kissed will become a slobbery mess and displease the Lord.	**Maher-Shalal-Hash-Baz 11:9** He that standeth on a chair and shouteth shall hear it and be blessed.
Hezekiah 1:5 Bodily exercise is of great value: it exercises the body.	**Jeconiah 10:7** Learn much from those who swim, for they are those who do not drown.
Macedonians 5:8 He that shouteth "Amen!" is like a platform: he supporteth the preacher.	**2 Philip 13:11** He that shouteth "Fanatic!" shall suddenly be declared lunatic and that without remedy.
2 Samson 9:14 Let not quietness be heard in your midst.	**1 Philip 8:14** A shaking hand is unto the Lord as a cow pie: It stinketh.
Exclamation 14:7 Sing unto the Lord as a sweet smelling odor in his nostrils.	**Bereans 16:40** Be ye not unequally yoked to Tarzan, for what fellowship does an ape have with a man.
Chaldeans 1:1 Even the Devils get compliments and are blessed. Where does that leave you?	**Naomi 19:1** He that smells overpowering odor shall be crowned with life after the smelling salts are applied.
2 Malachi 3:12 To untie a shoelace is to loose the wrath of God.	**Josiah 6:12** Learn a lesson from the hound dog: "He that barks now, shall be heard later."
1 Samson 7:7 Hear the commandment of God, "You touch strange Bible, you die."	**Hilkiah 5:3** A shoe on the head is like soothing ointment for sunburn: both are runny.
Melchizedek 4:16 The wind that blows through the ear is despised by the Lord.	**St. Stephen 1:15** He that whistles into microphone shall die suddenly from flying eggs and tomatoes.

134

8. Thou shalt not disagree with the umpire or question any of the calls.
9. Thy team must score four runs each inning.
10. Thy team must score 15 runs to win.
11. Thy team must win.

Following the game (play it as long as the group can take it), discuss what it means to live in the Spirit according to Galatians 5. You might also use Romans 7 and 8, or other Scripture for further Bible study.

The game can be both fun and frustrating. The experience will open up good discussion on the futility of the law to provide abundant living. Good luck and may the most religious team win! *Don Thomas*

THEOLOGICAL FICTIONARY

If your young people sometimes get stumped trying to figure out the meanings of those big theological terms, here's a game that will whittle those words down to size. It's played like the game Dictionary found in another volume of the *Ideas* Library.

Simply distribute a list of such words (justification, atonement, sanctification, vicarious, transfiguration, and so on). Have each student define each word, one word at a time. Kids can write phony definitions when they don't know the real definitions, but the phony ones should sound as realistic as possible to score points. Have kids read aloud their definitions for the first word; then they can vote for what they think is the real definition—one vote per student. Tally the votes, reveal the real definition, and award points as follows:

• Kids who write correct definitions earn five points for each one.
• Kids whose phony definitions receive votes earn five points per vote.

If your group is so large that it is hard to keep track of definitions, create smaller groups. As the game progresses give each player an opportunity to vote first (to improve the first player's chances of persuading others to vote for his or her definition).

The person with the most points is the winner of the game. You might be surprised by your kids' ability to come up with believable new theological definitions. You can use this game with ordinary words, too. *Rick Harris*

THE TRADER GAME

Here is an allegorical simulation that teaches several spiritual abstractions in a very concrete way. The game is easily adaptable, so you can change the rules of the game in order for it to reflect your church's theology.

The object of the game is to trade tokens with two Traders and each other in order to amass the most value. You need at least five players, but the more the better. Tokens—whose values are not revealed at the beginning of the game—are red, purple, blue, green, yellow, and orange (or whatever colors you prefer). There should be twice as many tokens of each color as there are players.

Two tokens of each color—except purple and red—are given to each player. The two Traders stand behind their tables. At Trader A's table are all purple tokens; at Trader B's, all red tokens.

When all are ready, you say this: "In a moment you can begin to trade tokens with the two Traders and with each other in order to obtain the greatest value. You're on your own to determine how to do this—even though you don't yet know what the different tokens are worth. If you trade at the tables, you must obey all agreements you make there. You have five minutes during which to deal [for less than 10 players, shorten the time]. Begin!"

Prior to the game, secretly tell the two Traders how they must conduct business:

Trader A should propose the same, unchanging offer to all clients in a kind yet firm manner: "I will give you two purple tokens for all the red and blue tokens you have. You must sign your name to one of the purple tokens and keep it for the rest of the time. You may use the other purple token as you wish—but if you trade it to someone who plans to keep it, he must sign it."

Trader B should make any deal she can in a hurried, sometimes rude manner. Her only restriction is that she cannot accept signed purple tokens. Her unspoken goal is twofold: she wants to put as many red tokens as possible into clients' hands, and she wants to take unsigned purple tokens out of circulation. She should offer two-for-one, three-for-one, or other inviting deals to accomplish her goals and keep business brisk around her table. Neither Trader may reveal the tokens' values.

When trading is finished, gather the group, distribute a scorecard (see page 137) to each player, and ask players to total their scores.

In the ensuing discussion, explain (or lead your students in discovering) possible meanings of the different tokens. Here are some suggestions:
- Signed purple token: eternal life accepted
- Unsigned purple token: eternal life offered
- Green token: career or work
- Orange token: family
- Yellow token: leisure and recreation
- Blue token: sin
- Red token: more sin

As the discussion unfolds, include ideas like these:
1. You had to give up all your blue and red tokens in order to get a purple token to sign; similarly, salvation (or eternal life) is available to all, but we must give up our sins—that is, have them forgiven—in order to receive it (Acts 20:20-21).
2. Once you signed a purple token, you could not surrender it; salvation is ours forever once we obtain it (Eph. 1:13-14).
3. No other token could negate the value of a signed purple; even though Christians fall into sin, they do not lose their salvation (John 10:27-29, 1 John 2:1-2).
4. Business was brisk and lively at the Red Trader's table; though the church—those from whom we learn of eternal life, salvation, and forgiveness—may not appear as exciting as the world, its joys are eternal (1 John 2:16-17).
5. The Red Trader tried to take unsigned purple tokens out of your hand and out of circulation so that others would have no access to them; the world will try to cause words from Christians to be ignored, words that may persuade some to receive Christ and his eternal life (Mark 4:3-4,14-15).
6. The volume of business and excitement at the Red Trader's table may have discouraged some players from looking elsewhere; the world—Satan's tool—tempts people to neglect God's offer of eternal life by offering what looks like a good deal and a lot of action (Mark 4:7, 18-19).
7. The Red Trader gave you red tokens for, among others, blue ones—and the reds cost you even more; sin leads to more sin (James 1:14-15, 1 John 3:8).
8. Green, yellow, and orange tokens were an asset if they were accompanied with a signed purple token; without a signed purple token, they were a liability.

Accordingly, the lives of saved people produce good fruit (1 John 3:7, Matt. 12:35), and the lives of the lost produce bad fruit (Gal. 5:19-21, Matt. 12:35).
9. Some players didn't want to share an unsigned purple token, even though it was of no value for them to keep; and others were too busy trading to think about sharing an unsigned purple. Christ wants all Christians to overcome their thoughtlessness and instead share their faith (Acts 1:8).
10. The kingdom of God is of the highest value. Will you give all you have to possess it? (Matt. 13:44-46)
David Tohlen and Doug Thorne

LABOR GAME

This game is based on the parable of the laborers in the vineyard (Matthew 20:1-16). This sometimes perplexing parable can become real by allowing your youths to experience the frustration of the workers who complained about equal distribution of pay at the end of the day, even though all did not work as long or as hard. The owner (God) was just and kept his promise—paying exactly what he said he would. This would have satisfied the workers until greed crept in. The following simulation game will help kids to understand this parable more fully.

As the kids enter the room, have several tables prepared with a puzzle, "brain teaser," or skill to do on each one. Some should be very easy, others impossible. Have points for each puzzle—depending on the difficulty—and each person is to keep track of his own score. After 20 or 30 minutes call a stop. Go to each young person, ask how many points he has, and then reach into a bag and give him a prize. The prize can be very small, just be sure every prize is exactly the same for everyone in the group.

As you slowly do this, it will soon be obvious to everyone in the group what is happening. No matter how high or low the score they tell you, they are all receiving equal payment. Allow free talk as you distribute the reward. Follow by discussion, prodding with questions such as "How do you honestly feel?" "What is your attitude toward the "prize-giver?" "How do you feel toward the other young people?" Ask the one that scored the highest and the one that scored the lowest how they feel. Follow by reading the Scripture account of the parable and discuss greed, envy, lust, and competition, and how these things can foul up our relationship with God. *Jim Bourne*

The Trader Game

COLOR	NUMBER	VALUE	SCORE
signed purple	only 1 allowed	1,000,000	
purple		0	
green w/S.P.		1	
green		-1	
orange w/S.P.		1	
orange		-1	
yellow		1	
red		-500	
blue		-100	
TOTAL			

The Trader Game

COLOR	NUMBER	VALUE	SCORE
signed purple	only 1 allowed	1,000,000	
purple		0	
green w/S.P.		1	
green		-1	
orange w/S.P.		1	
orange		-1	
yellow		1	
red		-500	
blue		-100	
TOTAL			

THE BEATITUDES GAME

Divide your group into several small groups and supply each one with a set of the nine Beatitudes cards on page 139.

Each group shuffles their deck of cards and distributes one card to each person. Set any extras aside. Based solely on the card they receive, each person constructs a collage (using magazines, glue, marking pens, etc.). Allow 10-15 minutes. The card is placed in an envelope and taped to the back of the collage. Also tape an identification number onto the front of each collage.

In a large-group setting, each player is given $1,000 in play money. Explain that the collage will be auctioned off to the highest bidder. No one is to bid for their own collage or a collage constructed from their group. Everyone must buy a collage.

The auction begins by proclaiming bids open on a selected collage. Bidding continues on the collage until the "price" reaches top bid and is sold to the highest bidder. Continue until all collages have been bought.

Ask each buyer to explain what their "bought" collage means to them. Ask all players to identify collages that possibly describe particular Beatitudes (other than their own), and why. What is the meaning of this particular Beatitude? Why proclaim it? Of what use is it? Compare the collages and their intended corresponding Beatitude (in sealed envelopes). Ask the collage designers to explain their work in terms of how they interpret the Beatitude. Do they agree with the auction price? What value do they place on their work? On their Beatitude? Do they agree with what others have said about their collage and Beatitude? How can we become a Beatitude? *John Washburn*

LOST AND FOUND

This event will help your group discover what it means to find the lost even as they struggle themselves to walk by faith. It's a fitting activity to precede or follow a study of the three lost-and-found stories in Luke 15.

The objective is for each team to make it as far along a course as they can in five minutes—blindfolded—while in the process finding as many items as they can.

Preparation

What you'll need: large room with lots of tables and chairs, fishing line, 10 items from your office (pencil, cassette, key, aluminum can, dart, coffee cup, coat hanger, book, etc.), Bible, masking tape, blindfolds (two to four), watch, prizes (optional). Set up as follows:

1. Trash the room. Turn all the tables and chairs on their sides. It should be hard to walk through.
2. The path through this chaos will be a fishing line. Tie one end of the fishing line to a chair leg just inside the door. Then run the line all over the room, wrapping it around numerous tables and chairs to keep the line taut. The line should not cross over itself.
3. Mark 10 locations along the path (though not on the fishing line itself) with pieces of the masking tape. At these sites you'll put the "lost" items for each group to find; then you'll replace them after each group goes through the course.
4. Put your 10 items on the tape-marked sites.
5. Blindfold the teams before they travel the course.

Introducing the lesson:

If you haven't already studied Luke 15, tell the kids that Christians walk by faith. Though we do not always know where the Lord is leading us, if we study the Bible and stay tuned into the Spirit, we will be led to where God wants us.

One thing is certain—we will encounter the lost. Then share with your students the highlights of your study of the three lost-and-found stories in Luke 15.

Playing the game:

To start the game, divide your group into teams of two, three, or four. Tell them that in a nearby room you have lost 10 items; list them for the teams. Each team has five minutes during which to find as many of the 10 items as they can. When one team member finds an item, the whole team is to whoop it up (Luke 15:6-7, 9, 23-24, 32). The catch is that the teammates wear blindfolds and the lights are out. On the other hand there is a fishing line strung throughout the room that, if they can locate it by feel, will lead them to at least the vicinity of all 10 lost objects. Furthermore, they'll encounter obstacles along the way—they may have to step over chairs, tables, and the fishing line itself.

Blindfold the first group, release them into the darkened room, and let them have a go at their task. After five minutes, turn on the lights and allow the team to remove their blindfolds. Count the number of items they found, and how many (if

Beatitudes

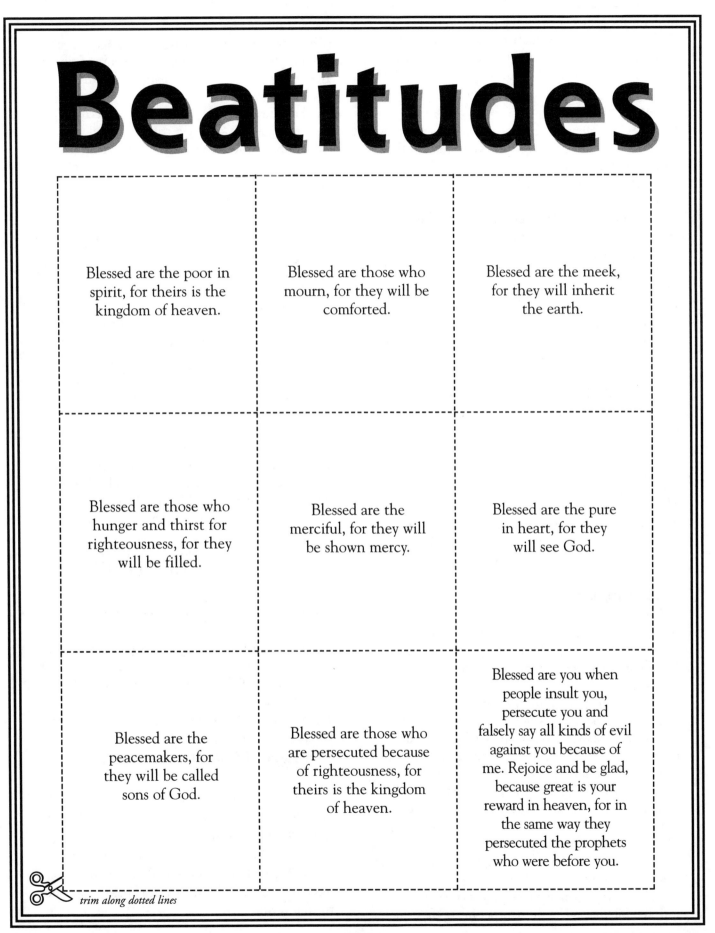

Blessed are the poor in spirit, for theirs is the kingdom of heaven.

Blessed are those who mourn, for they will be comforted.

Blessed are the meek, for they will inherit the earth.

Blessed are those who hunger and thirst for righteousness, for they will be filled.

Blessed are the merciful, for they will be shown mercy.

Blessed are the pure in heart, for they will see God.

Blessed are the peacemakers, for they will be called sons of God.

Blessed are those who are persecuted because of righteousness, for theirs is the kingdom of heaven.

Blessed are you when people insult you, persecute you and falsely say all kinds of evil against you because of me. Rejoice and be glad, because great is your reward in heaven, for in the same way they persecuted the prophets who were before you.

trim along dotted lines

139

any) finished the course. If the fishing line needs to be drawn taut again, have that team help you. Then allow this team to watch the next team go through.

After all the teams have finished, award a prize to the team that found the most items.

Postgame ponderings:

Assume that following the line represented walking by faith, and that the objects the kids found in the dark room were lost people we encounter. Your observations may resemble the following:

• "Brad made it almost all the way through, but he never found a single lost item. Walking by faith is a struggle in itself, and sometimes you struggle so hard that you go right past the lost."

• "When Lisa and Tanya lost the line, John helped them find it again. Sometimes we stray from our walk with God, and then we become ones who need to be found."

• "When Michelle started humming the theme song to 'The Twilight Zone,' it distracted Clay enough that he stopped following the line. It reminded me how the world diverts us from our walk with God."

Then turn it over to your group to share their own observations. You may want to close by reading the Great Commission (Matt. 28:18-20). *Doug Partin*

GOD TABOO

This game is based on the commercial game, Taboo. It can be a very effective tool for teaching teens because it gets them involved with making the game. It's also a blast to play.

Preparing the game:

Before the students arrive compile a list of verses that describe God (e.g., 1 John 4:9-10, Psalm 8:1, Isaiah 66:13; Acts 17:24). You may also provide a list of corresponding attributes that they can choose from.

Divide the group into two teams. Give each team blank God Taboo cards, the list of verses, and the list of attributes. The group members look up the verse, determine the corresponding attribute of God, and write it on the blank card. Then the group lists five words that will be forbidden when describing the attribute. Taboo words are defined as the five most common words that players would be likely to use in explaining the attribute. Keep the cards of each group separate and give to the other team for guessing.

The game preparation gets students involved with the Bible *and* gives them ownership of the game.

Playing the game:

Wait until the next meeting, if possible, to begin playing the game. This will allow plenty of time for the young people to forget many of the attributes and taboo words.

Each team picks a volunteer, who needs to get her teammates to say the attribute of God without saying any of the taboo words. This student is the only one on the team to see the card. The other team's members can look over the clue-giver's shoulder to ensure that taboo words are not used, to keep time, and to make the player nervous. The volunteer can use any words not on the taboo list to get her teammates to guess the attribute. If she says any of the taboo words, she is buzzed. An annoying buzzer is included in the commercial game, but kids can be just as effective without one! The student continues to give clues for as many attributes as possible in the time allowed, usually three minutes.

According to traditional Taboo rules, players cannot use hand motions or acting. Students may have difficulty with this restriction, so you may want to allow them to act.

The teams keep track of Taboo cards completed, and alternate turns. The winning team is the one with the most correctly guessed attributes of God.

You can be creative and adapt God Taboo to many topics: attributes of Jesus, Old Testament characters, miracles, etc. Happy Tabooing. *Duane Steiner*

TEN-PLAGUE RELAY

Whether you're studying the life of Moses or just playing for fun, your group will know the 10 Egyptian plagues when they finish this relay. Before playing create a set of game sheets for as many teams as you expect will play. Each set consists of 10 sheets (index cards will do); on each sheet write one of the 10 plagues along with its corresponding task.

• **The Plague of Blood.** Drink a glass of red punch before returning to your team.

• **The Plague of Frogs.** Hop like a frog all the way back to your team.

• **The Plague of Gnats.** Return to your team waving your hands in front of your face as if swatting gnats.

• **The Plague of Flies.** Make buzzing sounds, flap your arms like wings, and fly back to your team.

• **The Plague on Livestock.** Get down on all fours, moo like a cow, and roll over dead before returning to your team.

GOD TABOO
The Game of Unspeakable Fun!

1. Look up the passage of Scripture.
2. Get the general meaning of the passage.
3. Match the passage to the list of attributes you have been given.
4. Write that word in the box below.
5. Write five taboo words in the bottom section of the card. Taboo words are defined as the five most common words that you would be likely to use in explaining the attribute.

Bible Verse _____

Attribute

Taboo Words

GOD TABOO
The Game of Unspeakable Fun!

1. Look up the passage of Scripture.
2. Get the general meaning of the passage.
3. Match the passage to the list of attributes you have been given.
4. Write that word in the box below.
5. Write five taboo words in the bottom section of the card. Taboo words are defined as the five most common words that you would be likely to use in explaining the attribute.

Bible Verse _____

Attribute

Taboo Words

GOD TABOO
The Game of Unspeakable Fun!

1. Look up the passage of Scripture.
2. Get the general meaning of the passage.
3. Match the passage to the list of attributes you have been given.
4. Write that word in the box below.
5. Write five taboo words in the bottom section of the card. Taboo words are defined as the five most common words that you would be likely to use in explaining the attribute.

Bible Verse _____

Attribute

Taboo Words

- **The Plague of Boils.** Place four Band-Aids on your body and then return to your team.
- **The Plague of Hail.** Empty a cup of ice on your head before returning to your team.
- **The Plague of Locusts.** Flap your arms like wings and fly in circles back to your team.
- **The Plague of Darkness.** Keep your eyes closed as you return to your team.
- **The Plague on the Firstborn.** Drop to the floor as though you are dead.

When you're ready to play, divide your group into teams of 10 or less. Place each team's set of game sheets on a chair 30 feet or so in front of each team. A few feet beyond the chairs, place on a single table one glass of red punch and one cup of ice per team, and four Band-Aids per team. Instruct players to line their teams up behind the starting point.

At a signal, the first member of each team runs to the stack of game sheets (stacked, by the way, in order of plague) on the chair in front of his or her team, grabs the top sheet and reads it, yells out the name of the plague, and then follows the instructions on that game sheet. When the first player tags the next person on the team, that person runs for the chair of game sheets and follows its instruction, and so on. (If there are less than 10 team members, let some run twice.)

The first team to have a team member drop to the floor as though dead is the winner. Capture this relay on video for a hilarious promotion of youth group activities. *Tommy Baker and Jeff Baker*

142

BOARD
GAMES

These tabletop discussion games can launch meaningful conversation among young people on a variety of topics. They're complete with reproducible "game boards."

ALLEGIANCE

This is a "table-top" discussion game that requires a gameboard (page 146) and discussion cards (page 147). The object of Allegiance is to get the players to examine the teachings of Jesus concerning the state and related topics in light of American government and individual attitudes. The only winner is the one who responds honestly and attempts to apply the teachings of Jesus and their consequences.

Each player rolls dice to determine the amount of spaces he moves his marker (any small object) around the board. He then responds according to the space he lands on:

• On a black space, the player takes a card and responds.

• On a red space he may respond to another player's response, or make comment concerning Jesus and government.

• On the other squares, the player moves as directed. (Losing or gaining a turn does not imply judgment concerning the issue, but is merely meant to add variety.)

Players may go around the board as many times as time and interest allows. *K.C. Hanson*

KINGDOMS

As "Allegiance" is about Christians' relationship to their government, "Kingdoms" campares God's kingdom to earthly kingdoms. The gameboard and playing cards are on pages 148-149. Play "Kingdoms" exactly as you play "Allegiance" (at left), with these differences:

• Scripture references on cards usually denote the source of the question rather than the answer.

• On a red square the player may comment on another player's answer or make a statement about the kingdom of God.

• On a written square the player responds as it requests.

K.C. Hansen

Allegiance

BEGIN HERE

Tell the group what you think the relationship should be between a Christian and Government.

Red

Black

Black

If you have prayed for the nation's leaders in the past week, take another turn.

If you could hold political office, go to Washington. Lose one turn.

Red

Black

If you have considered withholding part of your taxes that go for war, you must pay the price. Go to Jail. Lose one turn.

Black

If you voted in the last election, go forward one space.

CARDS HERE

Black: Take a card.
Red: Respond to another player's answer or make a statement about Jesus and Government.

Black

Black

Red

Black

Red

If you could go into combat, go to War. Lose turn.

Black

CARDS

1. Does "Render unto Caesar" include military service?

2. Could you have been a tax collector for Rome? Why or why not? (Luke 19:2-10)

3. Would you be willing to go to jail because your convictions were not compatible with the government? (Matt. 5:10)

4. Is politics a legitimate means of achieving the goals of the Kingdom of Heaven? (Matt. 11:12)

5. Was Jesus a "politician" in any sense of the word?

6. Name something you could not render unto "Caesar" (i.e., the government).

7. Would you consider Jesus an anarchist? Why or why not? (Luke 23:2)

8. Is withholding part of your taxes because of your convictions legitimate?

9. How is a servant greater than a king? (Matt. 20:25-28)

10. Name three figures of authority over you. Which are by your choice?

11. Do you believe in amnesty? How does that relate to forgiveness? (Matt. 18:21-35)

12. Could you as a Christian hold a political office? Why or why not?

13. Should you as a Christian take a stand against corruption and hypocrisy in high places? (Luke 13:32; Matt. 23:27-28)

14. Would you consider Jesus a civil disobedient? Why or why not? (John 9:13-16)

15. Is civil disobedience legitimate for a Christian?

16. To what extent is the public responsible for oppression,

Kingdoms

START HERE

Red

Black

Red

Red

Black

Black

Red

Black

Red

Red

Name a specific difference between the kingdoms of this world and the kingdom of God.

Black

Devise an original simile of the kingdom of God (The kingdom of God is like...) and explain why.

If you have prayed for the coming of the kingdom this week, take another turn.

If you thought that Jesus' kingdom was of this world, lose one turn and read John 18:36.

CARDS HERE

Black: Take a card.

Red: Respond to another player's comment or make a statement about Jesus and the kingdom.

148

Kingdoms
C A R D S

1. Since the masses did not hear Jesus' interpretation of the parable of the sower, how would you interpret it? (Matt. 13:3ff)

2. Is the kingdom of God without order or rules? Do the 10 Commandments still govern us?

3. In what way have you made preparations for entering the kingdom like the five wise virgins? (Matt. 25:1-13)

4. How was (or will) Jesus' prophecy that some of his disciples would not die before he came into his kingdom be fulfilled? (Matt. 16:28)

5. In what ways, and in what areas, does the kingdom demand our all?

6. Name some of the attributes of people who will inherit the kingdom. (Matt. 5:3-10)

7. How does "Seek ye first the Kingdom..." relate to capitalism? (Matt. 6:33)

8. What is the "will" of the Father? Is that synonymous, or in some other relationship with the "kingdom"? (Matt. 6:10)

9. How and why is John the Baptist referred to as having a different position in the kingdom? (Matt. 11:11)

10. Was the kingdom inaugurated with the coming of Jesus and his signs? (Matt. 12:28)

11. Do you feel more like a sheep or goat and why? (Matt. 25:33)

12. Why did Jesus differentiate between his disciples and the masses for interpreting the parables and mysteries of the kingdom? (Matt. 13:10, Mark 4:11, Luke 8:10)

13. What do you think the substance of Jesus' message was when he "preached the kingdom"? (Matt. 4:23, Luke 19:11)

14. How could Jesus speak of the kingdom in varied time sequence (i.e., in you, at hand, near, to come)? (Luke 17:21, 21:31, Mark 1:15, Matt. 6:10)

15. How will the kingdom of God bring the fulfillment of the Passover? (Luke 22:14-16)

16. Have you ever been guilty of "castling" (i.e., making the kingdom of God so other-worldly that it has no present significance?)

DOUBTING GAME

Here's a fun learning game that provides a lot of thought and discussion on the subject of doubt. Print up the gameboard (page 151) and Growth Cards (page 152), cut the Growth Cards out, and you're ready to go.

To play the game, divide the group into teams. Each team throws a die and moves along the game board the appropriate number of spaces, like any other board game. As a team, they must do what the space suggests, rotating team members so that everyone gets involved. If the team is unable to do what the space says, they must move back two spaces (just to sit and wait until the next turn). If they can do what is on the space, then they get to draw a Growth Card and do what it says.

You could also divide the cards into good cards and bad cards. If the team is unable to answer, they must draw a bad card. If they are able to answer, they get to pick a good card. Be sure to allow plenty of time for questions, answers, and discussion. The game can take up to two hours. *Jim Walton*

MISSION IMPROBABLE

This learning game can be used with teens or with teens and their parents. It is a lot of fun to play and it opens up good discussion on the topics of motivation and communication. The game board is provided here and the basic directions and rules for the game are printed on it. To play, create your own game board or copy the one on page 153, and copy the "task," "energizer," and "squelch" cards (page 154-156). Use different colors of paper for the three different kinds of cards.

The object of the game is to complete various tasks by accumulating enough "motils," which you get on the energizer cards. The squelch cards take motils away. If you get too many negative motils, you may fail to complete the task. Incidentally, all the sayings on the squelch cards (insults, for the most part) were suggested by a group of high school students. Perhaps your group can think of others. Make up a few cards of your own.

One great way to use this game is to print it up so that each young person in your group has one to take home. Encourage kids to play it at home with their parents. The game is great for family interaction. It can be used effectively at a family retreat. *Mike Jarrett*

MONOPOLY MORALITY

An ordinary Monopoly game (available in department stores, toy stores, etc.) can be used very effectively as a way of understanding the significance of unjust distribution of goods in the world.

The rules of the game have to be altered in the following way. There should be four teams. Two of the teams (Teams 1 and 2) should only have two or three players at the most. The other two teams (Teams 3 and 4) should be much larger, with the rest of the group divided between those two teams. All decisions regarding strategy, etc., must be made by the entire team as a unit.

The money should be distributed as indicated below, but its value should be multiplied by 1000. In other words, a $1 bill is now worth $1000 and a $5 bill is actually worth $5000. But all of the prices for property, etc., are multiplied by 1000, thus "Virginia Avenue" now costs $160,000. This makes the game a bit closer to reality.

• Team 1 and Team 2 receive the following:

> Six $500 bills
> Ten $100 bills
> Five $50 bills
> Ten $10 bills
> Ten $5 bills
> Ten $1 bills

This amounts to a total of $5,530,000 (with the 1000x inflation).

• Team 3 and Team 4 each receive the following:

> Zero $500 bills
> One $100 bill
> Two $50 bills
> Two $20 bills
> Two $10 bills
> Two $5 bills
> Two $1 bills

(continued on page 157)

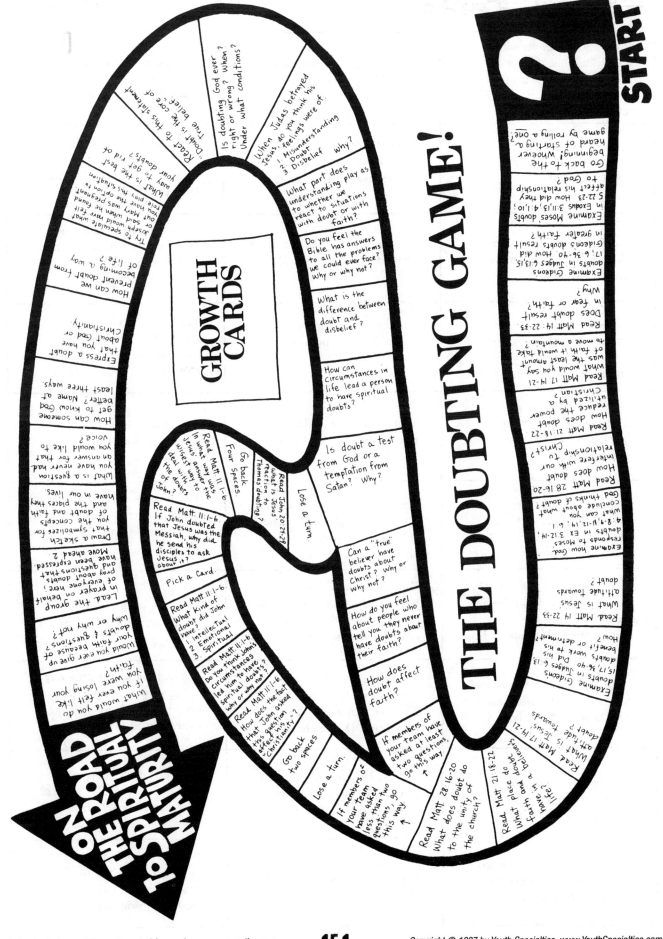

THE DOUBTING GAME!

ON THE ROAD TO SPIRITUAL MATURITY

GROWTH CARDS

START

Go back to the beginning! Whoever heard of starting a game by rolling a one?

Examine Moses' doubts in Exodus 3:11,13, 4:1,10; 5:22-23. How did they affect his relationship to God?

Examine Gideon's doubts in Judges 6:13,15, 17, 6:36-40. How did Gideon's doubts result in greater faith?

Read Matt 14:22-33. Does doubt result in fear or faith? Why?

Read Matt 17:14-21. What would you say was the least amount of faith it would take to move a mountain?

Read Matt 17:14-22. How does doubt reduce the power utilized by a Christian?

Read Matt 21:18-22. How does doubt interfere with our relationship to Christ?

Read Matt 28:16-20. God thinks about what can you conclude about doubt?

Examine how God responds to Moses' doubts in Ex 3:12-14, 4:8-9,11-12,14; 6:1. What is Jesus' attitude towards doubt?

Read Matt 14:22-33. Did his doubts work to his benefit or detriment? How?

Examine Gideon's doubts in Judges 6:13, 15, 17, 36-40. What is Jesus' attitude towards doubt?

Read Matt 17:14-21. What place does believing faith and doubt have in life?

Read Matt 21:18-22. What does doubt do to the unity of the church?

Read Matt 28:16-20. What does doubt do to the unity of the church?

Lose a turn.

If members of your team have asked less than two questions, go this way.

If members of your team have asked at least two questions, go this way.

Go back two spaces

Read Matt. 11:1-6. How does the fact that John asked this question affect his "Christianity"?

Read Matt. 11:1-6. Do you think John's circumstances led him to have spiritual doubts? Why or why not?

Read Matt. 11:1-6. What kind of doubt did John have?
1. Intellectual
2. Emotional
3. Spiritual

Pick a Card.

Read Matt. 11:1-6. If John doubted that Jesus was the Messiah, why did he send his disciples to ask Jesus about it?

Read Matt 11:1-6. In what way was John's answer the wisest way to deal with the doubts of John?

Go back Four Spaces.

Read John 20:24-29. What is Jesus' reaction to Thomas' doubting?

Lose a turn.

How does doubt affect faith?

How do you feel about people who tell you they never have doubts about their faith?

Can a "true" believer have doubts about Christ? Why or why not?

Is doubt a test from God or a temptation from Satan? Why?

How can circumstances in life lead a person to have spiritual doubts?

What is the difference between doubt and disbelief?

Do you feel the Bible has answers to all the problems we could ever face? Why or why not?

What part does understanding play as to whether we react to situations with doubt or with faith?

When Judas betrayed Jesus, do you think were of:
1. Misunderstanding
2. Doubt
3. Disbelief   Why?

Is doubting God ever right or wrong? When? Under what conditions?

"...Doubt is the core of true belief." React to this statement.

What is the best way to get rid of your doubts?

Try to speculate what Joseph would have felt or said when he found out Mary was pregnant. Did you have the option to role-play this situation.

How can we prevent doubt from becoming a way of life?

Express a doubt that you have about God or Christianity.

How can someone get to know God better? Name at least three ways.

What is a question you have never had an answer for that you would like a voice?

Draw a sketch that symbolizes for you the concepts of doubt and faith and the places they have in our lives.

Move ahead 2. Lead the group in prayer on behalf of everyone here's doubts and questions that have been expressed.

Would you ever give up your faith because of doubts & questions? why or why not?

What would you do if you ever felt like you were losing your faith?

151

Growth Cards

If you knew someone with unanswered questions and doubts about Christianity, you would advise him to try another religion. (Move back 3)	It is your opinion that people should keep their questions to themselves. (Move back 2)	You spend time with other Christians to help get you through serious doubts. (Move ahead 2)
Complete faith extinguishes doubt. (Move ahead 1)	You realize that doubt doesn't increase faith, but that faith relinquishes doubt. (Move ahead 3)	Your doubt rules your life. You become too cynical to improve your relationship with Christ. (Move back 3)
You are satisfied with what you "don't know." (Don't move anywhere)	You doubt that God knows what he is doing. (Move back 2)	You have a lot of deep questions about Christianity and you raise them as often as you can. (Move ahead 3)
You believe that God answers prayer. No matter how slowly or how seemingly wrong his answers are. (Move ahead 2)	You think that someone who doubts is just a complainer. (Move back 2)	You expect God's plan to always be so clear-cut that there will never be any place for doubting. (Move back 1)
You sometimes doubt your doubts just like you doubt your faith. (Move ahead 2)	Your advice to a doubter is to read his Bible more. (Move ahead 1)	Your doubt gives you a raunchy attitude. (Move back 1)
You feel that doubts give us the desire to learn more. (Move ahead 2)	You discover that emotional doubts are resolved through a change in perspective. (Move ahead 1)	You are able to rise above your doubts and grow spiritually in the midst of them. (Move ahead 3)
You ignore your doubts because you feel they are a sign of unspirituality. (Move back 3)	You realize that God's ways are not our ways, and that we sometimes just have to live with our doubts. (Move ahead 1)	You doubt you will ever understand everything. (Move ahead 2)
You don't usually ask questions because of what others may think of you. (Move back 3)	You realize that doubting is normal and that people who doubt are not weird, dumb, or unspiritual. (Move ahead 3)	You realize that the only way to get answers to hard questions is to ask hard questions. (Move ahead 1)
God tolerates your doubt, but wishes you would mature in your faith. (Move ahead 1)	Your doubts remain, but you are drawn to be more dependant on God as a result. (Move ahead 2)	You feel that the more questions a person has, the more spiritually healthy he is. (Move back 1)
You think that anyone with doubt should question whether he is even a Christian. (Move back 3)	You think doubting is wrong. (Move back 1)	You look forward to the day when you will be able to ask God personally about your doubts and questions. (Move ahead 2)

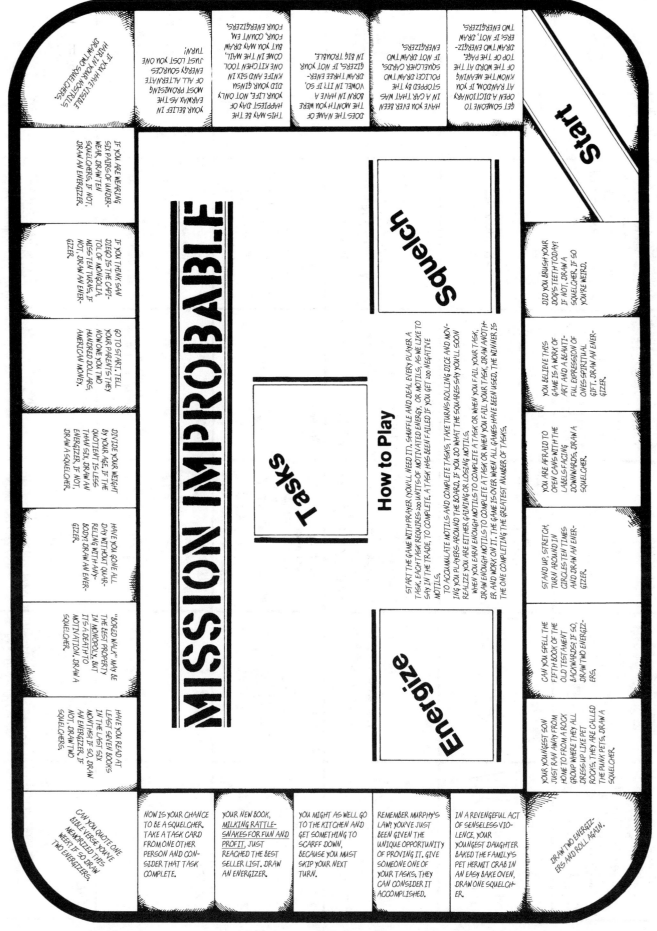

WHAT?

Card grid (values in MOTILS):

- **WHAT?** Of what use is money in the hand of a fool, since he has no desire to get wisdom? Proverbs 17:16. — 35 MOTILS
- Think through tasks first. — 35 MOTILS
- A simple man believes anything, but a prudent man gives thought to his steps. Proverbs 14:15. — 35 MOTILS
- Hope deferred makes the heart sick, but a longing fulfilled is a tree of life. Need related tasks = macho motils. Proverbs 13:12. — 45 MOTILS
- **ENERGIZER CARDS**
- A patient man has great understanding, but a quick tempered man displays folly. Proverbs 14:29. — 25 MOTILS
- Every action has eternal consequences. — 75 MOTILS

- Do not withhold good from those who deserve it, when it is in your power to act. Proverbs 3:27. — 25 MOTILS
- God keeps the books. The eyes of the Lord are everywhere, keeping watch on the wicked and the good. Proverbs 15:3. — 35 MOTILS
- Acquitting the guilty and condemning the innocent—the Lord detests them both. Proverbs 17:15. — 25 MOTILS
- RECEIVE A ONE HUNDRED DOLLAR REWARD. — 25 MOTILS
- LONG TERM GOALS CAN MOTIVATE. — 50 MOTILS
- HAVE A GOAL. Let your eyes look straight ahead, fix your gaze directly before you. Proverbs 4:25. — 50 MOTILS

- Purpose to employ means and not ends only. — 50 MOTILS
- An honest answer is like a kiss on the lips. Proverbs 24:26. — 40 MOTILS
- Good motivates the righteous person! — 25 MOTILS
- WHO ARE YOU DOING IT FOR? Commit to the Lord whatever you do, and your plans will succeed. Proverbs 16:3. — 75 MOTILS
- GET YOUR TIMING RIGHT. A man finds joy in giving an apt reply—and how good is a timely word! Proverbs 15:23. — 35 MOTILS
- ATTITUDES MAKE A DIFFERENCE. A happy heart makes the face cheerful, but heartache crushes the spirit. All the days of the oppressed are wretched, but the cheerful heart has a continual feast. Proverbs 15:13,15. — 25 MOTILS

- REWARDS WORK. The laborer's appetite works for him; his hunger drives him on. Proverbs 16:26. — 50 MOTILS
- FOLLOW THROUGH. Like clouds and wind without rain is a man who boasts of gifts he does not give. Proverbs 25:14. — 50 MOTILS
- The reason you do something is all important. All a man's ways seem innocent to him, but motives are weighed by the Lord. Proverbs 16:2. — 35 MOTILS
- WHEN YOU GIVE PEOPLE A JOB, LET THEM DO IT. Like one who seizes a dog by the ears is a passer-by who meddles in a quarrel not his own. Proverbs 26:17. — 40 MOTILS
- IT IS NOT A SIN TO OVERLOOK AN ERROR. It is a sin to keep bringing up the past. He who covers over an offense promotes love, but whoever repeats the matter separates close friends. Proverbs 17:9. — 25 MOTILS
- UNCONDITIONAL LOVE MOTIVATES. — 100 MOTILS

- WORDS HAVE POWER. Through patience a ruler can be persuaded, and a gentle tongue can break a bone. Proverbs 25:15. — 35 MOTILS
- *Variety does it!* — 25 MOTILS
- TASKS ARE A GREAT WAY OF SHOWING SOMEONE HOW MUCH THEY'RE NEEDED. TRY TO CONVEY THIS FEELING TO THEM. — 25 MOTILS
- MAKE TASKS A CHALLENGE WITHOUT BEING UNREASONABLE. — 25 MOTILS
- ALWAYS BE OPEN TO CREATIVITY. — 35 MOTILS
- EDIFY! An anxious heart weighs a man down, but a kind word cheers him up. Proverbs 12:25. — 50 MOTILS

- GIVE REASONS FOR TASKS EVEN IF THOSE REASONS ARE NOT APPARENT. — 40 MOTILS
- MAKE TASKS A GAME. — 25 MOTILS
- HAVE TRUST and FAITH. — 50 MOTILS
- UNCONDITIONAL LOVE MOTIVATES. — 100 MOTILS
- ASK DON'T TELL. — 50 MOTILS
- MIX GENTLY DON'T STIR. A gentle answer turns away wrath, but a harsh answer stirs up anger. Proverbs 15:1. — 25 MOTILS

154

SQUELCH CARDS

"BUT MOM, WHY DO YOU WANT ME TO WASH THE DISHES? WE HAVE A DISHWASHER." "I KNOW, WE HAVE A DISHWASHER DARLING, BUT IT WILL BUILD CHARACTER AND DISCIPLINE IN YOU TO WASH THEM LIKE I USED TO WHEN I WAS A CHILD." —50 MOTILS

"IS THIS THE BEST YOU CAN DO?" —30 MOTILS

DAD SAYS, "MAKE SURE YOU GET THE YARD DONE," THEN HE GOES INSIDE, SITS IN HIS FAVORITE CHAIR AND READS THE PAPER. —25 MOTILS

"REMEMBER, JOHNNY, FEEDING THE DOG IS YOUR JOB, WASHING THE DISHES IS NANCY'S JOB." —25 MOTILS

"I REALLY THINK YOU'RE BLIND, YOU JUST MOWED OVER MY FAVORITE PLANT." —25 MOTILS

"DATE THAT CUTE LITTLE GIRL YOUR MOM AND I LIKE SO MUCH INSTEAD OF THAT CREEP YOU HANG OUT WITH." —40 MOTILS

SAYING "CHEER UP, CHEER UP," DOESN'T GET TO THE BOTTOM OF A PROBLEM, IN FACT, IT CREATES A PROBLEM. LIKE ONE WHO TAKES AWAY A GARMENT ON A COLD DAY, OR LIKE VINEGAR POURED ON SODA, IS ONE WHO SINGS SONGS TO A HEAVY HEART. PROVERBS 25:20 —25 MOTILS

"THAT'S A GOOD JOB, SON, BUT...." —75 MOTILS

"I DON'T CARE IF YOU DID FINISH THE JOB, WITH AN ATTITUDE LIKE YOURS, I JUST DON'T THINK I CAN REWARD YOU." —25 MOTILS

"I CAN'T BELIEVE A GIRL YOUR AGE...." —45 MOTILS

NOBODY'S SUNG ANY PRAISES TO YOU SINCE YOUR LAST BIRTHDAY. —25 MOTILS

"DON'T FORGET, CHRISTMAS IS COMING." —50 MOTILS

PUNISHMENT STRIKES!! —25 MOTILS

NAG, NAG, GARD —25 MOTILS

"MRS. FRANKLIN SAYS YOU NEVER ACT LIKE THIS AROUND HERE." —25 MOTILS

"YOU KNOW AS WELL AS I DO, YOU DIDN'T FORGET WHAT DAY THE GARBAGE MAN COMES." —35 MOTILS

AIN'T IT FUN WHEN YOU'RE THE GUINEA PIG FOR AMATEUR PSYCHOLOGISTS. —40 MOTILS

AFTER THE JOB IS DONE: "YOU KNOW THERE WAS AN EASIER WAY TO DO THAT." —75 MOTILS

"YOU DID THAT ALL WRONG!" (SAID WHILE DESTROYING THE PROJECT) —100 MOTILS

RECESSION MAKES MONEY SCARCE —25 MOTILS

"SORRY, YOU'VE JUST BEEN YELLED AT." —75 MOTILS

"WELL, I GUESS I'LL JUST HAVE TO DO IT MYSELF." —50 MOTILS

"I REMEMBER LAST TIME..." —40 MOTILS

HAVE YOU FINISHED THAT JOB I ASKED YOU TO DO? THAT TURKEY, HE KNOWS I HAVEN'T EVEN STARTED IT YET. —25 MOTILS

"YOU NEVER DO ANYTHING AROUND HERE." "GO CLEAN YOUR ROOM." LATER "YOU NEVER DO IT RIGHT, I END UP HAVING TO DO IT OVER ANYWAY." —30 MOTILS

"WHY CAN'T YOU BE LIKE..." —50 MOTILS

"I'M SORRY I DIDN'T TELL YOU WHAT A GOOD JOB YOU DID, YOU KNOW HOW BUSY I'VE BEEN." —25 MOTILS

"A TWO YEAR OLD COULD DO THIS JOB." —30 MOTILS

"DON'T JUST SIT THERE WHEN THERE'S SO MUCH TO DO! THIS IS GENERALLY SAID WITHOUT TELLING ANYONE WHAT NEEDS TO BE DONE. —30 MOTILS

YOU HAVE THE BUSYWORK BLUES. —25 MOTILS

"WELL, I'M GLAD TO SEE YOU HAVEN'T BEEN SITTING AROUND LIKE USUAL." —30 MOTILS

I COULD ASK THAT LITTLE BRAT, BUT HE WON'T DO IT UNLESS HE'S TOLD. BESIDES HE NEEDS TO LEARN RESPECT FOR AUTHORITY. THEY WON'T TREAT HIM WITH KID GLOVES WHEN HE GETS OUT INTO THE REAL WORLD. —100 MOTILS

"I DON'T WANT TO HEAR YOUR IDEAS, DO IT THE WAY I ORIGINALLY SAID." —25 MOTILS

"WHAT HAVE YOU EVER DONE FOR US?" —75 MOTILS

MOTIVATION OUT OF GUILT: "WE ONLY ASK YOU TO DO A FEW THINGS AROUND HERE" —50 MOTILS

TASK CARDS

- COOK A MEAL.
- CLEAN YOUR ROOM. TAKE OUT EXTRA LIFE INSURANCE IF NECESSARY.
- TAKE YOUR GERBIL'S BLOOD PRESSURE.
- TAKE OUT THE GARBAGE.
- SMILE FOR FIFTEEN NON-STOP MINUTES

- TELL MOM "I LOVE YOU."
- HUG YOUR SISTER.
- OPEN A DOOR FOR SOMEONE.
- TURN DOWN YOUR STEREO.
- MOW THE LAWN.
- GO TO A REAL NERD'S BIRTHDAY PARTY.

- BECOME SKILLFUL. DO YOU SEE A MAN SKILLED IN HIS WORK? HE WILL SERVE BEFORE KINGS; HE WILL NOT SERVE BEFORE OBSCURE MEN. PROVERBS 22:29
- GET WISDOM AND UNDERSTANDING.
- MAKE UP YOUR BED.
- LISTEN TO AN OPERA.
- WRITE A LETTER TO YOUR GRANDPARENTS.
- LOSE TEN POUNDS.

- SEEK COUNSEL. MAKE PLANS BY SEEKING ADVICE; IF YOU WAGE WAR OBTAIN GUIDANCE. PROVERBS 20:18
- MAKE STRAIGHT A's ON YOUR REPORT CARD.
- HAVE A DOG WASH INSTEAD OF A CAR WASH.
- BE NICE WHEN THAT MOUNTAIN OF FLESH, AUNT BERTHA, HUGS YOU.
- TRY A FOOD YOU HAVE NEVER EATEN BEFORE.
- THROW THOSE TENNIS SHOES OF YOURS AWAY THAT HAVE THE AROMA PECULIAR ONLY TO THE CITY DUMP.

- FINISH YOUR OUTDOOR WORK AND GET YOUR FIELDS READY; AFTER THAT BUILD YOUR HOUSE. PROVERBS 24:27
- PACKAGE THE LEFTOVERS FROM TONIGHT'S SUPPER AND MAIL THEM TO INDIA.
- WASH BEHIND YOUR EARS.
- BUY SOMEONE A FLOWER.
- CALL AN OLD FRIEND ON THE TELEPHONE.
- WEAR A TIE.

- MAKE A POINT OF STUDYING MOTIVES: THE PURPOSES OF A MAN'S HEART ARE DEEP WATERS, BUT A MAN OF UNDERSTANDING DRAWS THEM OUT. PROVERBS 20:5
- PICK YOUR NOSE CONTINUOUSLY FOR THREE DAYS.
- GET YOUR HAIR CUT.
- WASH AND WAX THE FAMILY CAR.
- PAINT A PICTURE.
- WASH THE DISHES

This amounts to a total of $272,000 (with the 1000x inflation).

Some role-playing will be required as follows: Team #1 is a Christian team. It should play the game making all its decisions from a Christian point of view. Team 2 is a non-Christian team. It can do anything it likes. Team 3 is also a Christian team. Team 4 is a non-Christian team.

As play proceeds, each team should play out its role according to its resources and assigned religious/moral persuasion. Teams 3 and 4 will probably get bored pretty fast. The non-Christians may lie and cheat and steal. The bored players may drift away and refuse to play. These developments are all part of the game.

Play for as long as the group wants to. It can end when one or more groups are out of money or they are at each others' throats. Each team should have a leader/spokesperson who handles the team's money, rolls the dice, and so on. If the leadership is good, the game will be lively and lots of fun as kids try to outwit or take advantage of each other. Following the game you will need to debrief the group and talk about what happened. This is the most important part. Discuss the decisions that were made and how close to reality they really were. Compare the game to the current world situation. The discussion possibilities are great. *Steve Yamaguchi*

PATHWAY OF PRAYER

Here's a good way to help your kids learn a lot about prayer while playing a game. It can be played by individuals or by teams. You'll need to create a game board similar to the diagram below. It can be small if you play the game in small groups, or it can be large—if you play the game with the entire group divided up into teams. If you have a big blackboard, you could just draw a reasonable facsimile up on the board, and each player could keep track of his or her position with different colored chalk. An overhead projector could be used in the same way. You can make the pathway as long or as short as you want, depending on the size of the group and how much time you have.

If you choose, you can get a little more creative with the game board and have a few obstacles along the way ("You fell asleep during prayer—go back two spaces."), or you could make some chutes and ladders similar to the other board games. It's all up to you. Players start out on one end of the path and end up at the throne of grace (see Heb.4:16) or whatever you prefer as a goal.

Also needed for this game are Scripture cards. There are seven different categories that a verse might touch on. They are:

1. Prayer Promises (results of prayer)
2. Prayer Petitions (what to pray for)
3. Prerequisites to Prayer (conditions)
4. Places to Pray
5. Prayer Periods (when to pray)
6. Pathetic Prayer (not pleasing to God)
7. Prayer Positions (bodily positions for prayer)

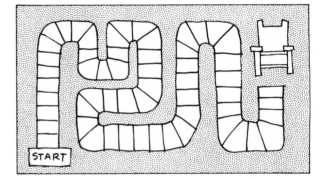

As the game progresses each player or team will select a card on his or her turn. They should read out loud the verse on the card, and then note which categories the verse deals with. These categories determine the number of spaces on the game board that the player gets to move:

1. Promises—Move ahead 1
2. Petitions—Move ahead 1
3. Prerequisites—Move ahead 1
4. Places—Move ahead 3
5. Periods—Move ahead 2
6. Pathetic—Move back 1
7. Positions—Move ahead 3

So, if the selected verse deals with Places, Petitions, and Promises, the player gets to move ahead a total of five spaces on the game board.

To maximize learning along with the game, be sure that the kids understand the verses as they are being read. Have them locate in each verse the details of the category that is being discussed. Exactly what is the promise in that verse? What are the prerequisites to prayer in this verse? And so on. This game should be used as a springboard to further thinking and learning about the role of prayer in their lives. It can be a very effective tool.

Listed below are 75 verses that you can use for your "Scripture cards." Also listed are the categories that go with each verse:

Scripture Cards should be made this way: one side of the card should have the verse printed on it. The other side of the card should have the prayer categories listed that the verse specifically deals with (either "prerequisites," "promise," "position," etc.)

•2 Chronicles 7:14 Prerequisites (humble, turn, seek, pray)Promises (hear and heal land)

•Nehemiah 8:6 Positions (hands lifted, head bowed, face to ground)

•Psalm 5:3 Periods (in the morning)

•Psalm 32:6 Periods (while there's still time, while you may be found)

•Psalm 50:15 Prerequisites (call) Periods (day of trouble) Promises (deliverance)

•Psalm 55:17 Periods (evening and morning, noon) Promises (He shall hear)

•Psalm 66:18 Pathetic Prayer (cherish sin in hearts)

•Psalm 88:13 Periods (morning)

•Psalm 122:6 Petitions (peace in Jerusalem) Promises (love, Jerusalem shall prosper)

•Psalm 145:18 Prerequisites (call in truth) Promises (Lord is near)

•Proverbs 15:29 Prerequisites (righteous) Promises (He hears)

•Proverbs 28:9 Pathetic Prayer (refuses to obey the law)

•Isaiah 26:16 Pathetic (only in distress)

•Isaiah 56:6-7 Prerequisites (keep sabbath) Promises (make joyful)

•Jeremiah 33:3 Prerequisites (call) Promises (will answer)

•Jeremiah 42:3 Petitions (where to go)

•Lamentations 3:24-25 Prerequisites (wait and seek him) Promises (Lord is good)

•Matthew 5:44 Petitions (those who use you, your enemies)

•Matthew 6:5 Pathetic Prayer (seen by men)

•Matthew 6:6 Prerequisites (in secret) Promises (rewards)

•Matthew 6:7 Pathetic (repeating over and over)

•Matthew 6:10 Petitions (his kingdom come)

•Matthew 6:11 Petitions (daily bread)

•Matthew 6:12 Petitions (forgive our sins) Prerequisites (as we forgive others)

•Matthew 7:7-8 Prerequisites (ask, seek, knock)Promises (receives)

•Matthew 9:38 Petitions (Lord will send laborers)

•Matthew 18:19-20 Prerequisites (two agree)Promises (done for them)

•Matthew 21:22 Prerequisites (believe) Promises (receive)

•Matthew 26:41 Petitions (enter not into temptation)

•Mark 1:35a Periods (before day)

•Mark 1:35b Places (solitary place)

•Mark 11:24 Prerequisites (believe) Promises (it will be yours)

•Mark 11:25 Positions (stand) Prerequisites (forgive) Promises (be forgiven)

•Luke 2:37 Periods (day and night)

•Luke 6:12 Periods (all night) Places (to a mountain)

•Luke 11:13 Prerequisites (ask) Petitions (for Holy Spirit) Promises (give Holy Spirit)

•Luke 18:1 Periods (always)

•Luke 20:47 Pathetic (long showy prayers)

•Luke 21:36 Petitions (counted worthy) Periods (always)

•Luke 22:41 Places (away) Positions (knelt down)

•John 9:31 Prerequisites (does his will) Promises (He will hear)

•John 14:14 Prerequisites (in Jesus' name) Promises (God will do it)

•John 15:7 Prerequisites (abide in me) Petition (ask what you will) Promises (it shall be done)

- Acts 8:15 Petitions (receive Holy Spirit)

- Acts 8:22 Petitions (forgiveness) Prerequisites (repent)

- Acts 16:25 Periods (midnight)

- Acts 21:5 Positions (knelt down) Places (seashore)

- Romans 8:26 Promises (Spirit intercedes)

- Romans 10:1 Petitions (others saved)

- Romans 10:13 Prerequisites (call) Promises (be saved)

- 1 Corinthians 14:13 Petition (interpretation)

- Ephesians 6:18 Periods (always) Petitions (for all saints)

- Philippians 1:9-11 Petitions (have fruit of righteousness)

- Philippians 4:6-7 Petitions (in everything) Promises (peace)

- Colossians 1:3 Periods (always)

- Colossians 1:9 Periods (don't cease) Petitions (filled with knowledge, etc.)

- 1 Thessalonians 5:17 Periods (without ceasing)

- 2 Thessalonians 1:11 Petition (counted worthy and fulfill purposes)

- 2 Thessalonians 1:12 Petition (Jesus be glorified and you in him)

- 2 Thessalonians 3:1 Petition (message be spread)

- 1 Timothy 2:1-2 Petitions (for all men)Promise (live peacefully)

- 1 Timothy 2:8 Positions (lifting up hands) Prerequisites (without anger)

- James 1:5 Prerequisites (ask) Promises (gives) Petitions (for wisdom)

- James 1:6a Prerequisites (ask in faith nothing doubting)

- James 1:6b, 7 Pathetic (doubter)

- James 4:2-3 Pathetic (wrong motives)

- James 5:15 Prerequisites (faith) Promises (save the sick)

- James 5:16a Prerequisites (confess faults) Petitions (for each other) Promise (be healed)

- James 5:16b Prerequisites (earnest, righteous) Promise (effective)

- 1 Peter 3:7 Prerequisites (honor wife) Promises (prayers not hindered)

- 1 Peter 3:12 Prerequisites (righteous) Promise (he hears)

- 1 John 1:9 Prerequisites (confess) Promises (forgive and cleanse) Petition (forgiveness)

- 1 John 3:22 Prerequisites (keep his commands) Promises (receive)

- 1 John 5:14 Prerequisites (ask according to his will) Promises (he hears us)

- 1 John 5:16 Pathetic (sin that leads to death)

Sheila Dudney

MONEY MANAGEMENT GAME

Try this game to help your young people learn a little more about money management. It allows players to decide how they will spend their "salary" on certain items which are worth points. The object is to accumulate the most points by making wise purchases.

Divide into pairs, with one player in each pair designated player "A" and one as "B." Give each pair a playing board (page 161). Every pair should also have a die and a pencil.

To begin, player A rolls the die. The number on the die represents A's salary for that turn, which is recorded in the first middle block labeled DOLLAR CREDITS. Then player B rolls the die and records the salary for his or her turn in the first dollar credit box of the B section on the playing board.

When it's A's turn again, he can choose to buy any item shown at the bottom of the board for which he has sufficient dollar credits. For example, if A's dollar credit total is 6, a camera can be bought for 5 dollar credits, leaving 1 credit. For this purchase, a -5 would be recorded in the second of the upper boxes labeled ITEM COST. This will help players maintain a record of purchases.

According to the "Cost-Point Schedule" at the bottom of the board, the camera is worth 20 points, so now A writes "20" in the second of the lower boxes (labeled POINTS) where the cumulative point total is kept. Then the die is rolled again, and the new dollar credit total is figured by adding the new salary to the credits remaining after the purchase was made. For example, if the new salary shown on the die is 4, then the new cumulative dollar credit total will be: 6 (salary from turn 1) minus 5 (cost of the camera) plus 4 (new salary), which equals 5. So "5" will be recorded in the second dollar credit (middle) box. Then it's B's turn.

If at the beginning of his turn, A had insufficient dollar credits to make a purchase, or had chosen not to do so, A would simply have rolled the die for a new salary and recorded the new total of dollar credits in the second dollar credit box. Then B would take a turn.

B follows the same procedure for her turns, and the game continues this way. On turn 3, players graduate from high school; after that turn their salary is doubled. Players will receive twice the amount shown on the die for the turn.

On turn 7, players have a choice to go to "college" or to continue in their present "career." Players who choose college must lose 1 turn. After that turn, however, salary will be figured by throwing the die twice and adding the total of the 2 throws (then doubling as for all plays after finishing high school). Players who choose to continue in their present career lose no turns but continue on their current salary schedule.

Play continues until one of the players reaches box 24. At that point play stops immediately—no other plays can be made. Total dollar credits for each player are transferred into points according to the Transfer Schedule at the bottom of the playing board. Then add the total of these points plus the cumulative total from the Points box. Player with the highest number of points in each pair wins. You may also want to have playoffs between winners and losers of different pairs.

Be sure to combine this game with some discussion of biblical principles of financial management. Some appropriate verses to read together would be Colossians 3:23-24, Ephesians 4:28, and Mark 12:41-44. *Phil Blackwell*

MONEY MANAGEMENT GAME

A

	1	2	3	4	5	6	7	8	9	10	11	12
Item Cost												
Dollar Credit												
Points												

	13	14	15	16	17	18	19	20	21	22	23	24
Item Cost												
Dollar Credit												
Points												

B

	1	2	3	4	5	6	7	8	9	10	11	12
Item Cost												
Dollar Credit												
Points												

	13	14	15	16	17	18	19	20	21	22	23	24
Item Cost												
Dollar Credit												
Points												

COST–POINT SCHEDULE:

Cost	Points	Cost	Points	Cost	Points
5	20	40	300	50	500
10	30	15	40	30	150
30	100	30	60	25	120

TRANSFER SCHEDULE:

Credits		Points
0–9	=	0
10–49	=	8
50–99	=	15
100–149	=	30
150 and up	=	40

SPECIAL GUESTS

Your students may love you and your teaching, but there's still nothing like a new voice in the youth room. Special guests can provide a spark every now and then—or, better yet, every month. On these pages you'll see how Christian professionals, visitors from another youth group, a married couple, a shepherd (of sheep, not of people), and even your pastor can contribute to your group.

ON THE JOB—AS A CHRISTIAN

Young people of today will find it extremely helpful to hear from caring adults about how to select a career, find employment—and then do their job with a Christian mindset. One good way to do this is to invite a variety of persons—from within your congregation or from without—to come and share about their occupations with the youth group. You might want to invite a factory worker, a social worker, an accountant, a school teacher, a business person, and your pastor. Just try to get a good cross-section of occupations. Start the ball rolling by asking how the adults came to do their jobs.

Then focus on how their businesses or occupations are affected by their Christian beliefs. Panel members can share from their own personal experiences, offering suggestions to the young people on pitfalls to avoid and so on. Allow kids to quiz them about on-the-job ethics, whether or not their goals are any different as a Christian, etc.

With such input by adults, students gain insight about their own future vocations and college plans—and how it all fits with their Christianity. *Kathy Lincks and David Markle*

UNWANTED GUEST

One problem most church youth groups confront is making new people feel welcome. The following project has been proved and tested several times.

Arrange for a kid from another youth group (far away enough so as not to be recognized) to come and spend a Sunday at your church—preferably more than one meeting, like Sunday school, church, maybe a softball game that afternoon, and a get-together after church that night.

Your guest should be dressed normally but not stylishly. He or she should be friendly but quiet and should speak only when spoken to. (This may take a little bit of acting.)

That night at the get-together, have your mystery guest report to the crowd how he was received and treated. If you want to get really heavy, have the person even share with the group how individuals went out of their way to accept or ignore him. Before the visitor begins, take the pressure off by introducing him to the group and letting them know that the person was a "plant." Some will want to crawl under the tables. Others will feel as if they have finally done something right. Either way it's a great learning experience for everyone. *Marty Edwards*

GRILL THE PASTOR

This idea is designed to help your young people become better acquainted with your church's pastor and see him or her as a person—not just a pulpit personality who preaches and officiates at worship services.

Have the pastor visit the youth group (in casual attire) and let the kids ask questions like those below. It's a good idea to have some questions prepared beforehand because some of the kids may feel a little shy about asking personal questions. Print them on index cards, distribute them to the kids, and let them ask these or their own questions.

• What are some of the things you like to do in your spare time?

• What are a few of your favorite movies or TV shows?

• If you weren't a pastor, what would be your second choice for a career?

• What do you say to a person whose family member just died?

• How many marriages and funerals do you conduct during a year?

• What do you especially enjoy about being a pastor?

• What kind of books do you enjoy reading?

• Where did you grow up? What was it like there?

• How do you go about putting together a sermon?

• What is one of your favorite parts of the Bible?

• What kind of music do you like?

• What kinds of things did kids do when you were our age?

• What advice can you give us about our youth?

• Who would you consider to be your personal heroes?

• How did you become a Christian?

Before the meeting is over, you might let the pastor ask a few questions of the group as well. You'll find that this type of meeting encourages positive feelings between the pastor and the kids, especially when the pastor is new. *Michael Bell*

SHEPHERD SHOW-UP

Here's a great way to enhance a study of John 10—the story of the Good Shepherd. Invite a real shepherd (someone local who raises sheep) to come to your meeting and bring along a couple of sheep or lambs. Then interview the shepherd:

• How long have you been raising sheep?

• Describe their unusual mannerisms and behavior for us.

• Do they know who you are? How do you know for sure?

• Will they listen to my commands as well as yours? Allow the kids to ask questions of their own, too.

Then ask the kids these questions:

• Now that you see these sheep, can you see what it was about them that prompted Jesus to compare us to them?

• In what ways do we behave like sheep?

• Why did Jesus refer to himself as a shepherd instead of a general or a manager? *Robert Crosby*

THE SWORD OF THE LORD

If you are doing a series or a message on the Word of God, you might consider focusing on Hebrews 4:12 and entitling it "Swordsmanship." A great way to illustrate the theme is to invite two people who are skilled in fencing. Have them fence a match at the beginning of your meeting. The kids will love it.

After the demonstration sit down with the guest fencers and interview them about their sport. Draw from the following questions if you want, and come up with some of your own.

• What essential principles have to be learned and developed to become skillful at this sport?

• In what way is balance important?

• How essential is concentration to fencing?

• What does fencing do for your body and mind?

• In what ways does technique affect your swordsmanship?

Relate the answers to handling the Sword of the Lord—the Bible. You will be amazed at the correlation. Fencing is considered an ideal relaxation because it exercises every part of the body and requires a high degree of concentration. However tired or worried one may be, a bout of fencing will restore freshness of mind and a sense of physical well-being. It requires skill, finesse, balance, poise, and self-discipline.

To locate a fencing team, you may want to call your local YMCA, community sports center, college athletics department, or TV station sports desk. *Robert Crosby*

MARRIAGE PANEL

Next time you teach love and marriage (or maybe as part of a Valentine's party or banquet), seat a panel of three or four long-married couples (whom you asked ahead of time, of course—and make sure they're couples with expertise at marriage, and not just longevity) and let the kids ask them questions about love and marriage. Chances are good that this will be your students' first time in one room with several successful, long-term marriages. Questions that you could ask that would get the ball rolling include these:

• How (and where and when) did you meet him?

• How did you know that she was the one for you?

• What dreams for your marriage have you realized?

• What was the hardest season of your marriage?

• How has being part of this church affected your marriage?

• Did you ever feel like giving up?

Then be prepared for the panel to take over—for older people with something to say are seldom quiet once you get them primed. Leave time, too, for kids to ask questions. If you ask a closing question, like "What one piece of advice would you leave with the teenagers of this church?" be ready for poignant reminiscing, poetry, Valentine cards—and, of course, some old-fashioned advice. *Steven Mabry*

LIFESAVER NIGHT

In advance arrange at least four people to be special guests at your Lifesaver Night. Be sure they represent different age groups—college, young married, the 30-to-50 age group, and 50 or older. (Include a married couple to share together as one of the four.) Ask these people to talk from their hearts about a time in their lives when a Christian made their lives sweeter in some way—led them to Christ, helped them in a time of critical need, or modeled for them a quality of Christ that they in turn adopted into their lives. If you have a time limit or want to conclude with questions from the kids, let your guests know ahead of time.

On Lifesaver Night explain the format of the evening and introduce the speakers as they take their turns before the kids. Then close the meeting by bringing out a pack of Lifesavers. Explain that the package unit is made up of many different flavors and colors of Lifesavers, but they are all part of the same roll. Christians also come in many different flavors and colors, but we are part of the same body—Christ's body—and we all have the same purpose—to grow up to be like Christ. When we tell others about Jesus or others see Jesus in us, our particular flavor makes their lives sweeter.

Then pass around six-inch pieces of string (one per student) and packs of Lifesavers. The student can choose three to five of their favorite flavors and place the Lifesavers on the string. Challenge the youths to go out and be lifesavers. Each time they tell someone about Jesus or reach out to help someone in Jesus' name, they can bite a Lifesaver off the string and eat it. Tell them you trust them not to eat any of the Lifesavers unless they have met the requirements. Follow up by asking at the next meeting how long it took them to eat their whole string of Lifesavers. *Danny Balint*

SPECIAL
PROJECTS

These out-of-the-ordinary meetings aren't for every week or for every group. But take a chance on some of these unusual teaching projects, like toe painting, create-a-devotional, and filling a time capsule—they just may hold valuable lessons for your group.

TOE PAINTING

Here is an idea that will allow youths to creatively express themselves in an unusual way. Prior to the meeting, the participants should be instructed that they are to come with extra-clean feet. In addition, it will be helpful if they bring a towel. These instructions generally arouse questions and generate a good response because the group wants to know why such weird orders. They soon find out. When the youths have gathered, they are instructed to take off all shoes and socks and to roll up their pant legs several inches. The reason why is they are going to toe paint. And all that is is finger painting, only you stand up and let your toes do the work.

All painting materials have been gathered together ahead of time and have been placed in an area where water is handy and where no damage will occur should a few painted footprints touch the floor.

The toe paintings can be done individually or the group can combine toe talents and paint a mural.

First, here is what could happen when you do it on an individual basis. Select a general theme such as "Show What God Means to You Today," and have the young people express their feelings about this theme by toe painting. After the group has fin-ished painting, form a circle in some other part of the church and allow each person to share her painting with the group by telling in words what feelings she painted.

To paint a mural, sheets of finger painting paper are taped together prior to the meeting. Again a general theme is selected, such as Christmas. The mural can then be divided into three parts and the young people can select the section they wish to paint in. One third of the mural might show the wise men and their camels heading toward Bethlehem. The middle section could show the stable with the Christ child in a manger. The last section would show the shepherds watching over their flocks. After the mural is finished (and dried, of course) it is hung so that it can be appreciated by all.

No matter which way you choose to use toe painting, it is helpful and fun to have a polaroid camera ready to take pictures of your toe painting process. These pictures are also displayed along with the finished paintings. Some people will find it hard to believe that your group really painted with toes because the quality of art is really pretty good. The pictures of the process bear witness that you really put your foot into it. *Earl H. Estill*

YOUTH GROUP DEVOTIONALS

Daily devotional guides (like *Our Daily Bread*) don't have to bore your students. They can write their own! This gives the young people a chance to express their ideas about the Christian faith. Most importantly, the kids will want to read the devotionals because they know the authors and they can relate to their own peers better. Of course, you could follow any format you want. These are examples of how you might do it.

WEDNESDAY—Matthew 7:1-2 (Living Bible)

"Don't criticize, and then you won't be criticized. For others will treat you as you treat them."

This is another one of those verses that I feel everyone should follow. Before I read this verse, I never realized that one reason people used to criticize me so much was because I criticized them! And I did. I found myself telling people they had bad tempers, etc., but it never even crossed my mind to think I had a bad temper! So next time you go to criticize someone, stop and think, are you really perfect enough to criticize another person? —Kim Francis

Thought: We really need one another as we walk in our everyday life. We can add so much to one another as we share our love and importance with each other. Today, tell someone in person, or on the phone, how much you need them, and how thankful you are that they are part of your world.

TUESDAY—Ephesians 6:2

"Honor your father and mother."

Even though parent-child relationships are not always the best, each one of us owe a lot to our mothers and fathers. From the time we were born, our parents have loved and cared for us. My parents have done a lot for me and they are both very special. Often though, I take them for granted, and I don't take time to tell them I love them.

I could do many small things to show them I care. What keeps me from showing them that I need and cherish them? I really don't know. I do know that I love them, need them, owe a lot to them, and should not take them for granted. To honor my parents would mean simply to love and respect them. Today and everyday, I want to show them just how special they are to me and how much I care. —Anita Cassie

Thought: For a few minutes think about all your parents have done for you, given you, and cared for you. Today show them how special they are to you. Show them love, and thank God if they are still alive, that you have this day to live with them.

Or if you want to create a devotional for the entire year with shorter individual entries, give everyone a small stack of 3x5 index cards. The number will be determined by how many kids you have. If you have 30 kids or so, then everyone will need about a dozen cards each.

Instruct the kids to spend some time in the Bible and to write down a favorite meaningful verse or passage of Scripture on each of the cards. If they want they can also add a few words of commentary with the Scripture like: "This verse gives me real hope for the future!"

When everyone has finished collect the cards and organize them into a daily devotional guide for an entire year (365 days). If you prefer, you could shorten this time by making it a devotional guide for only nine months of the school year. You will need to remove any duplicates, add any others that you choose, and then assign each card a date, beginning with the first day of the first month.

Now the cards can be duplicated and distributed to each young person. You might want to have a meeting in which the kids create their own "card files" out of balsa wood (or whatever) to keep the card in.

Instruct the kids to pull out the card for each day and to meditate on it before heading off to school, before going to bed, or whenever they choose. The fact that all the kids in the group are studying the same Scripture passages each day can add considerably to a spirit of unity. This idea can also be used as a fundraiser by making these devotional cards available for sale to others, or as a gift-making idea at Christmas.
David Washburn and Mike Slater

THOUGHT FOR THE WEEK

Here's a ministry of encouragement your group can have in the church. Have kids search the Scriptures for verses that are especially meaningful. Then have them write one thoughtful sentence to accompany the verse.

Have kids write the verse and thought on sheets of colorful paper; cut the papers into strips. Roll up or fold the strips and place them in baskets, which are situated near the sanctuary doors after regular weekly worship services. Ask your pastor to remind people in the congregation to grab a verse or to pick up a thought for the week on their way out, courtesy of the youth group. These strips can be used as bookmarks, hung on the refrigerator door, or just read and thrown away.

If you do this regularly, people will look forward to their special verses each week and really take them to heart! *David Washburn*

"I can do everything through him who gives me strength" (Phil. 4:13)

Tackle together a job that is especially hard.

"When you give to the needy, do not let your left hand know what your right hand is doing." (Matt. 6:3)

Give secretly to the poor.

GOSPEL NEWSPAPER

This activity involves everyone and allows kids to think through and express what they consider to be the important tenets of the Christian faith.

If possible visit the publishing offices of a local newspaper, to get the feel for newspaper publishing and journalism. Then challenge your group to publish at least one issue of its own newspaper. Include editorials, articles, poems, song lyrics, cartoons, photos, interviews, drawings, verses of Scripture, etc., to communicate some of the most important aspects of Christianity to a person who knows nothing about it. Discuss how to become a Christian and what it means to live a Christian life and how to communicate these ideas to non-Christians.

The easiest way to create the newspaper is on computer. Perhaps you or some of your kids have access to a computer and know some of the programs. The length of the project can vary with the complexity of the design and the interest of the group. Encourage kids to work in areas that interest them; they can be reporters, photographers, illustrators, poets, editors, designers, theologians, distributors of the paper, etc. To help pay for the project, you could invite local religious organizations to buy advertising space and you could offer to create simple ads for them. Actually having to define Christianity on paper can be a faith-building and enlightening experience. *Deborah Harris*

PARADOXES OF SCRIPTURE

This program idea can be used to involve a number of students with Scripture. Plan a debate or series of debates using the paradoxes found in the Bible. Issues can include law versus license, God's mercy versus God's justice, forgiveness versus judgment, strength versus weakness, boldness versus gentleness, Old Covenant versus New Covenant, etc. The debates should involve lots of research and should be conducted using a debate format. It is an exciting way for teens to develop their communication skills and sharpen their reasoning abilities. *Robert Crosby*

CHRISTIAN MISSIONARY MAGAZINE

"CM Magazine" is a good way to give kids a better understanding of the missions program of your church or denomination. It's patterned after television magazine shows like "60 Minutes."

Put together a list of the missionaries your church or mission board supports. Present the list to the youth group and have the kids select a few of these missionaries for the "show."

Next, divide into groups and give each group one of the missionaries to do a story on. They must create an interesting presentation which can include such things as a taped interview (done on the telephone or in person), slides (which can usually be obtained by request), photos, articles from publications, interviews with people who know the missionary or who have been to the foreign country they're serving in, and so on.

Obviously, this is a project which will take some time. Allow four to six months for the kids to gather all their information and develop their presentations. Then the program "CM Magazine" can be presented to the entire church. *Larry Stoffel*

DEBATE TEAMS

At school kids often participate in structured debates. Why not try one in your youth group? Form debate teams and give each team a subject and a syllabus for study on the topic. Allow the kids a couple of weeks to do their research and to develop their arguments. Have one team argue for a specific proposition ("Abortion is ethical") and the other against it for a specified amount of time. If you want you can use standard debate procedures. You might even want to invite the high school debate teacher to judge.

Choose topics which will stir up plenty of controversy. *Stan Lindstadt*

Here are some examples:

Abortion	Church attendance
Drinking	R-rated movies
Biblical inerrancy	Divorce
Rock music	The second coming of Christ
Eternal security	Faith vs. good works
(of the believer)	Sex before marriage

TIME CAPSULE

Have your group send a "mission" to their children or their children's children by putting together an authentic time capsule. The kids must first decide how large they want it to be, and when they want it opened (in their own lifetime or in a later generation). Then give them a week to consider what kinds of items they want to consider including in it, and why.

To make the capsule itself, buy a length of plastic PVC Pipe (2½ feet of 4-inch pipe is a good size) and two end caps. Attach one cap with PVC solvent glue. You'll need envelopes for the small items, a black permanent marker, and a small packet of silicone gel to remove unwanted humidity (silicone is available in hobby or craft stores).

A number of items could be selected for inclusion in the capsule to reflect your group's faith as well as common or significant aspects of their daily lives. The kids will have to narrow their choices, however, to items that will fit the size capsule you choose. Some suggestions:
- A video tape of the community, with views of the church, people, streets, stores, and surrounding countryside.
- An instant photo of the group that made the capsule, with a list of their names, ages, and addresses.
- A small, recent translation of the Bible (NIV, for example).
- A sermon of the current pastor.
- A history of the local church to date.
- A local newspaper.
- A current news magazine.
- A current local phone directory.
- A cheap digital watch.
- A current issue of TV Guide.
- A can of Coke.
- Any small, common items in daily use—a mechanical pencil, can opener, light bulb, or whatever.
- Brief thoughts written down by group members about the problems of the day, and how they predict these problems will be resolved in the future.

If you plan to bury the capsule somewhere, make sure it's well marked in permanent ink or paint, and that records of its existence and whereabouts are left in other places. Don't include liquids unless the capsule is so far underground (such as in the subbasement of the church building) that the ground temperature is a constant in the low 50s. Items that might leak (ink pens) should be placed in separate envelopes. Mark one end of the pipe outside as the bottom, and place lighter items on top of heavier ones.

After you've put all your items inside, seal the top cap with PVC solvent glue and mark on the outside where it should be cut to open. Label it clearly, along with the intended date for opening, and put it in its resting place while the group looks on. You may even want to pray for the people who will open it, asking God to bless your "mission" to the future. *David S. Parke*

MISSION TIME CAPSULE — OPEN — TOP — BOTTOM — PVC SOLVENT GLUE — BLACK PERMANENT MAGIC MARKER — SILICONE GEL PACKET (CAN BE PURCHASED AT HOBBY-CRAFT STORES)

Some of these are informal, others take a liturgical turn—yet they're all creative, designed to make worship even more meaningful for your young people. You'll find ideas for Communion, confession, music, prayer, and Scripture reading.

WORSHIP SERVICES

SILENT WORSHIP SERVICE

This creative service can be a totally different approach to the worship experience. It is completely silent, that is, no one speaks, sings, or makes any verbal utterances during any part of the service. The congregation should be aware ahead of time of what will happen and how they are to respond (distribute the explanation provided on page 178 or reprint it in your program). The youths can be in charge of conducting the service and preparing the church for the worship experience.

The order of worship may include the following kinds of things:

- **Meditative prayer while waiting.** No organ prelude, etc.
- **Greeting.** Two or more youths come out, shake hands, wave to congregation, get the congregation involved in shaking hands also.
- **Call to worship.** Youths light candles, open Bible, dramatize the coming of the Spirit to the service.
- **Hymns.** Congregation is instructed in the bulletin or program to turn to this hymn, read and meditate on its message. Give them plenty of time for this.
- **Meditation on current events.** A slide presentation can be used to show areas of concern for the church in today's world, followed by silent prayer.
- **The Lord's prayer.** The words may also be creatively shown on a screen with other slides to illustrate and give added meaning to the prayer.
- **Scripture reading.** Provide Bibles. Read silently.
- **Sermon.** The sermon can take many forms. It can be a printed article that everyone can read. It can be a dramatic presentation done by the youths using only actions, not words. It can be painted signs held up by the youths combined with a slide presentation, etc.
- **Communion.** The youths can feed each other and motion to the congregation to do likewise with elements provided.
- **Doxology.** This can be used at the conclusion to break the silence with everyone singing together a capella.

Steve Burgener

Silent Worship Service

Are you afraid of silence? Do you become uneasy when all the talk stops in a group and people only sit and look away or at each other? Yes silence can be frustrating in this world of noise and mass media, but it also can be a meaningful time. Silence gives us the chance to digest ideas and analyze feelings. It can be a time of struggle or relaxation.

Our silence today does not approximate deafness, but muteness. Even without anyone speaking, listen to all the other sounds you hear. Have you been aware of all of them? The deaf person cannot even hear these "background" sounds.

This is why we are having a silent service:

• There is more to worship than listening to the words of a sermon.

• We should be aware of all sounds.

• Maybe we do not realize the value of speech and singing.

• Maybe we don't realize the value of silence as an equal to sound.

• It's a real chance to talk and listen to God.

• Communication is possible in silence

PROGRESSIVE WORSHIP SERVICE

Here's an interesting way to involve young people in worship. It can be done in a church, in homes, or on a weekend retreat. There really is no limit to its possibilities. It works just like a progressive dinner.

A worship service has a variety of elements, just like a dinner does. By taking each element of worship separately and in a different location, it provides a good opportunity to teach young people about these elements of worship. Acts 2:42 and Colossians 3:16 provide a good scriptural base. Here's one way to do it:

• **Fellowship.** Begin with some kind of group interaction or sharing that provides a chance for the kids to get to know one another better. Something that would put the kids in a celebrative—but not rowdy—mood would be appropriate.

• **Spiritual songs.** At the next location, have someone lead the group in a variety of well-known hymns and favorite songs of worship.

• **Prayer.** Move to another location that provides a good atmosphere for prayer. If outside, a garden would be nice, as Jesus often chose a garden for prayer. Have the kids offer prayer requests, thanksgivings, etc. and have several kids lead in prayer.

• **Scripture reading.** At the next location, have several kids read a lesson from the Old Testament, the New Testament, and perhaps the Psalms. Use a modern English translation.

• **Teaching.** The next stop can be where the sermon is preached. If you prefer, you could accomplish the same thing without being preachy by substituting a dialogue sermon, a film, or something of that nature.

• **Communion.** The last stop can be around the Lord's table, with a Communion service. Conduct this however you choose, but it should be a time of celebration and joy.

There are other ingredients that go into worship (like the offering), which you can incorporate into the others or take separately. Design your own progressive worship service, and you can be sure that your group will never forget it. *Al Michael*

QUAKER WORSHIP SERVICE

The Quaker Worship Service (or you may call it Spontaneous Worship) may be used in any setting. It works well on retreats as climax of the weekend. The service eliminates the anxiety of one individual making or breaking the service, and allows total participation from the group. It places the responsibility for worship where it should be: on the worshippers rather than on those up front. Here are some guidelines for leading such a service.

Assemble together. A small chapel or a room with chairs in rows or in a horseshoe works well. Stand before the group and give the introduction supplied on page 180.

Allow as much time as necessary, but count on at least 45 minutes to an hour. When you see a good place to lead into Communion, do so either with Scripture or a song. Have the elements already prepared on a table at the front of your worship room. Encourage them to partake individually when they are ready.

When all are finished, stand before the group for the closing. Share your own thoughts, or say something like, "When Jesus and his disciples finished the Passover meal, the Bible says they sang a hymn and went out to the Mount of Olives. Let's stand and sing..." *Gary Black*

ROCK WORSHIP

This idea uses rock music as a way to help your young people worship God. It's especially effective on retreats, lock-ins, and special youth services. Preparation takes a little time, but the result is usually worth it.

To put this worship experience together, purchase cassette tapes or CDs of eight to 10 popular songs that your kids are familiar with. Choose songs about themes with biblical applications—love, friendship, rebellion, sin, forgiveness, loneliness, etc. You can use either secular music or, if you prefer, Christian music. A mixture of the two also works well.

Decide on the order of the songs, and then record them onto a cassette tape or CD, with perhaps 15 to 20 seconds of silence between songs.

Next, write an "Order of Worship" that includes the title of each song and a short meditation for each song to be read while the song is being played. Each meditation should consist of a question and a Scripture. If the subject of the song is loneliness, the meditation might include a question like, "How is it possible to be lonely when you are surrounded by so many people?" as well as an

Quaker Worship Service

Today we're going to share in an old-fashioned Quaker service. We could have planned an order of service as we have on other occasions. But instead we want the Spirit to lead each of us today. The early Quakers believed in sitting quietly until someone was moved by the Holy Spirit to sing or speak or testify, and then they would do it.

Worship must be more than someone preforming to our satisfaction. In fact, in worship we are the performers and God is the audience. So let's take our directions for worship from the Bible. (Read Ephesians 5:19, Colossians 3:16, Hebrews 10:24-25)

Today no one will tell you what to do or when to do it. Each one is responsible to respond to the leading of God's Spirit. You may want to read a Scripture for us all to hear, you may think of a song to sing, you may want to provoke or encourage us in some way with an exhortation, or give a testimony of God's work in your life. It's up to you. If you think of a song, either start it or say, "Let's sing so-and-so" or "Someone start so-and-so." The only rule is that the same person should not share twice in a row. After someone else has had a chance, then you may share again.

There will be times during the service when we are all silent. Let the silence happen. Use it to worship God individually rather than being uncomfortable with it. After we have shared, when it seems appropriate I will lead into our Communion service.

accompanying, relevant Scripture.

Before the service begins, pass out the Order of Worship to each person. Explain to the kids what will happen: They will listen to the music, one song at a time. As each song is played, the kids read the meditation and discuss the question with a partner. Between songs, during the silence, the kids are to move to another location so that they have a new partner for the next song.

Use a good cassette or CD player for a quality sound. The kids will be talking, so it will need to be louder than they are.

You'll find this to be effective with your kids—depending, of course, on the music you choose, the setting, and other variables. One benefit is the help it gives kids to connect the music they hear on the radio with biblical truth. *Michael McKnight*

SANCTUARY CAMPFIRE SERVICE

Have a campfire service right inside your church sanctuary by constructing a mock camp setting. You can invite the whole congregation and let the kids lead the service.

Set up artificial trees and maybe even a pup tent in the front of the sanctuary, and build an artificial fire in the middle using the diagram provided. The kids can be seated on the floor around the fire, in front of the congregation.

Invite everyone to wear jeans, flannel shirts, or other outdoor attire, and to bring flashlights. Use food gear made for camping to share Communion, sing camp songs accompanied by guitar, and make sure the lights are out so you have to do everything by flashlight. You may even want to give out marshmallows! *Dave Seely*

How to Make an Artificial Campfire

1. Cut several clothes hangers here.

2. Bend them out.

3. Tape them together.
4. Tape them to a fan.

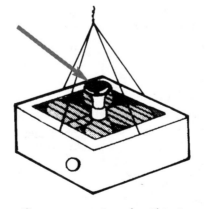

5. Fix a red or yellow floodlight here.

6. Tape orange and yellow crepe paper on alternate sides of the wire, cut in the shape of flames.
7. Place logs around in teepee fashion to complete the effect.

8. Turn on the fan and light, and get out the marshmallows!

DEDICATION SERVICE

Adapt the script on page 183 to suit your own needs when you plan a service devoted to recognizing Sunday school teachers, department superintendents, youth sponsors, etc. *Denny Finnegan*

WALLS

This experience has been designed to illustrate how walls are often erected between man and God and between members of the body of Christ. It is best with smaller groups (25 or so) but can be adapted for larger ones. It is described here for use in a typical church sanctuary, but it can be done in any room with theater-style seating and a middle aisle.

The auditorium should be prepared with a butcher-paper wall running down the middle of the center aisle. Perhaps the simplest way to do this is to string some cord from the front (the pulpit, if in a church) to another object (like a coat rack) toward the back of the aisle. Then drape two long sheets of butcher paper, which have been taped together at the top, over the line. The result should be a sort of paper volleyball net that is at least six feet high and as long as half the number of rows as you have participants. Thus, if you have 20 people, the wall needs to run the length of the front 10 rows of seats. In the songbook racks (if you have them) closest to the center aisle, hide a pair of labeled scissors in each. Write on each label a different Christian attribute such as the fruit of the Spirit in Galatians 5 or the characteristics of love from 1 Corinthians 13. Then in the foyer (or at the entry to the building you are meeting in) place chairs for everyone, spacing them as far apart as possible. On the door to the auditorium tape a large piece of butcher paper. Now you are ready to begin.

Have the participants sit in the chairs provided and then explain that the foyer (or the area outside the auditorium where they are seated) represents the world with its cold alienation. (This could be even more graphic if they are seated outside in cold weather.) The paper on the door leading into the auditorium represents the wall between the sinful world and God. Have a discussion on what kind of bricks a wall like that is made of. Write their answers on the paper with a large felt pen. If no one volunteers it, lead them to finally say that all

these add up to one thing: sin. Then ask them how the wall can be removed. The answer should eventually be given as the "Cross of Christ," "the blood of Christ," etc. Draw a large red cross on the paper and then pull the wall down and discard it. Now you are ready to take the group inside.

Before opening the door say something like this, "But before we enter into the presence of God, I must ask if you REALLY want to. The only way you can enter is to admit your own spiritual bankruptcy, die to self, and trust only in Christ to bring you in...so...count the cost, then when you are ready, come in."

Have them enter one at a time alternating sides of the paper wall they go on. (Some will probably hesitate for some time: if possible a helper might stay back with them in case they need to talk about it.) Have each one sit on the end of a pew alone so that when everyone is in, you have people paired off on opposite sides of the wall.

At this point, if your line is tied to the pulpit, walk up there and give the following explanation: "From where I am, I can see all of you but you can't see each other. Now the view from up here is kind of like God's, but the view from down there is what it's still like between a lot of brothers and sisters. Now maybe that's you; if so, tell us about it. What are the bricks of YOUR wall made of?" Have each one think of one thing, fear, pride, whatever, that is part of his wall. Beginning with the two people on the front pews, give them markers and have each write down what his brick is and tell the rest about it, then pass the marker back, again, alternating sides. When they've done this, say something like, "Now that wall doesn't have to stay there, but some of us feel more secure walled in...some church people are content to just sit in their pew and wait for someone else to reach out first. But if you really want that wall down, God's got a gift for you in—of all places—that songbook rack in front of you! See if you can find it."

After everyone has discovered the scissors, start at the front again asking each one to tell why his particular pair (trust, patience, etc.) is important in the task of tearing down the wall. "How can THAT help?" Then, before you call on them to destroy the wall with their scissors, point out that it can go down only by God's power—the fruit of the Spirit—but at the same time, we have to cooperate.

Then allow them to attack the wall with all the joyous abandon they deserve to express after all

Dedication Service

ADDRESS

This morning in both of these worship services we want to do more than just recognize and applaud the efforts of our Sunday school teachers, department superintendents, and youth advisors—we want to dedicate and commission their efforts to the Lord. As the apostle Paul wrote in 1 Corinthians 3:6, "I planted the seed, Apollos watered it, but God made it grow."

CHARGE TO THE TEACHERS AND YOUTH ADVISORS

To the teachers and youth advisors, here is your charge:

• James 3:1 says, "Not many of you should presume to be teachers, my brothers, because you know that we who teach will be judged more strictly." James wants us to take seriously our role and our responsibility. If you will take your role and responsibility seriously, say "I will."

• Philippians 3:14 says, "I press on toward the goal to win the prize for which God has called me heavenward in Christ Jesus." The apostle Paul knew how important it was for us to personally keep growing in Christ. You can't give what you don't have. If you will seek to keep growing in your relationship with Jesus Christ, say "I will."

• John 10:12-13 says, "The hired hand is not the shepherd who owns the sheep. So when he sees the wolf coming, he abandons the sheep and runs away. Then the wolf attacks the flock and scatters it. The man runs away because he is a hired hand and cares nothing for the sheep." Jesus calls us to be his shepherds, not his hired hands. If you will take care of and love these sheep entrusted to you, say, "I will."

CHARGE TO THE CONGREGATION

To you who are under the care of these shepherds, here is your charge:

• Hebrews 13:17 says, "Obey your leaders and submit to their authority. They keep watch over you as men who must give an account. Obey them so that their work will be a joy, not a burden, for that would be of no advantage to you." Submit is an unpopular word today. But unless the sheep submit to the love and care of the shepherd, the sheep can easily be harmed. If you will seek as best you can in God's grace and power to submit to these leaders, say "I will."

• Ephesians 4:13 says that teachers are given to the body of Christ so that it may be built up "until we all reach unity in the faith and in the knowledge of the Son of God and become mature, attaining to the whole measure of the fullness of Christ." As the teachers and youth advisors are to seek their growth, so are you to seek your growth. If you will seek to become mature in Christ Jesus, by God's grace and God's power, say, "I will."

CHARGE TO ALL

The final charge is to us who recognize that it truly is God who causes the growth.

• Ephesians 6:18 says, "Pray in the spirit on all occasions with all kinds of prayers and requests. With this in mind, be alert and always keep on praying for all the saints." It is vital that we continually and earnestly lift one another up before God in prayer. No one's prayer is unimportant. And so my charge to each one of us is: If you will seek to pray regularly and sincerely for each other—teacher and advisors for their students, the students for their teachers and advisors—say, "I will."

PRAYER OF THE COMMISSIONING AND DEDICATION

It is God who causes the growth. Let us pray...

that. But when they're through, close with remarks something like these: "Now...there's one more wall to tear down, but we can't illustrate it so easily. You see, it's the wall inside you—between you and the real you—between where you are now and where Jesus is calling you to be. And, after all, aren't all the walls really inside? God wants that wall—all the walls *down*. He wants you to know peace, with him, with your brothers and sisters, and even with yourself." Here you may wish to encourage everyone to inwardly make that commitment; you may even afford them the opportunity to do so publicly, especially if there are some non-Christians there. In any case, a song would be a most appropriate ending. *Larry Hall*

SECRET MEETING OF THE SAINTS

This is a very simple idea which can be an extremely effective means of strengthening the faith of your youth group. It works best with high school kids rather than junior high, but will work with mixed groups (part junior high, part high school, part college, etc.).

The idea is to set up a situation in which everyone is to imagine that our country has been taken over by a foreign power and to worship God or to have church is now a crime, punishable by death or torture or both. Bibles, religious literature, hymnbooks, etc., have all been confiscated, and all ministers and preachers have been imprisoned.

The group must then plan a "secret meeting" similar to those of the early Christians. It is best to schedule it for a time that requires a great deal of effort to make, like about 3:00 a.m., while it is still dark. It cannot be held in a church, since all the churches have been burned down, so it is best to meet in a home or basement. The kids cannot travel to the meeting in groups larger than two or three, or else it might arouse suspicion of the authorities, etc.

The meeting itself consists of prayer, sharing Bible verses from memory, soft singing of gospel songs everyone knows, and the sharing of testimonies and thoughts to strengthen each other. The group should sit in a circle, using only one candle for light. The windows are covered to help create the atmosphere. Sometimes the taking of Communion is a good idea for this meeting as well. A feeling of unity and love is encouraged in this atmosphere of persecution. Perhaps a short taped message from the pastor (in prison) can be played, offering encouragement and a thought or two.

The success of such a meeting is dependant upon the attitude of the kids involved. It should not be presented as a game, but as a serious attempt to experience a new appreciation for the freedoms which we possess in America and the faith which many before us have died for. Repeating this meeting periodically usually encourages Bible memorization and a greater involvement of the kids in other church activities as well. *Avery Powers*

COMMUNION

HOMEMADE COMMUNION

Here's a meaningful way to involve your young people in Communion. It's especially effective with junior highers. After a time of prayer and a few songs, move the group into the kitchen and allow them to make their own unleavened bread. Give each person a job to do, from cracking the eggs to taking turns rolling the dough out paper-thin. Here's the recipe:

Cream together:
   ¼ c. sugar
   ¾ c. shortening
Mix in:
   1 t. salt
   1 ½ c. buttermilk (milk soured
   with 1 T. vinegar may be substituted)
   ½ t. baking soda
Add:
   4-5 c. flour
Divide the dough into four balls.
Roll out on floured surface until wafer-thin.
Place on greased cookie sheet.
Fork the dough to prevent shrinkage.
Bake at 450 degrees until light brown,
approximately 15-20 minutes.

While the bread is baking, have the kids make the "wine" (grape juice). Provide a large quantity of whole, seedless grapes and let the kids crush them in a bowl using a crushing stick. This last act can symbolize the fact that because we've sinned, we all had a part in the crucifixion of Christ. When the grapes are all crushed, pour the juice into glasses.

Now, serve Communion as you normally would, using these homemade elements. It will add a great deal to this important sacrament of the church. *Jon Adams*

TIE ONE ON COMMUNION

Make Communion more meaningful with the use of visual symbols.

Using an 18-inch-long rope, tie two people together with one loop around the wrists. Let the people share Communion by twos. After the Communion, separate the two by cutting the rope two or three inches from the knot. The rope forms the shape of the cross and becomes "the tie that binds." Have the two discuss what the cross means to them and let them decide who will keep it.

Or after Communion, place the wrists and rope over a block of wood. Separate the two with a pair of scissors. (With one stroke, God wiped out man's sin.) Let the people wear the rope bracelets as a reminder that they have been tied to Christ through another person. *Dietrich Schleef*

COMMUNION ON CANVAS

For a truly unique approach to the Communion service, hang a giant canvas (butcher paper will do) in front of your meeting room, large enough for everyone participating to draw a small "painting" upon. Set up a table with the wine and bread on one end, and paints, paste, pictures, etc. on the other. After some singing, read appropriate Scripture from a modern translation. Without further words, the leader then goes to the canvas and draws a picture, then partakes of the Communion elements. (The leader's picture may be anything she wishes, perhaps only words.) The second person does the same and then the leader serves the second person with the elements saying, "This is the blood of the Lord which was shed for you, Mike. This is the body of the Lord, broken for you, Amanda. The second person serves the third, and so on. The result will in all probability be a magnificent painting depicting the group's beliefs and hopes, and an unusually beautiful worship experience. *Glen Warner*

UPPER ROOM COMMUNION

To add an extra dimension to a youth Communion service, use an upstairs room (if you have one available), with a long table and chairs arrangement similar to the upper room description in the New Testament. There should be 13 chairs (one left vacant to symbolize Christ's presence in the room). Kids should be brought in 12 at a time, to pass the common cup and loaf of bread. Use candlelight and allow time for individual prayer and meditation. *Joe Conarroe*

WORLD COMMUNION BREAD

In many churches "World Communion Sunday" is the first Sunday in October. If your church observes this day on the church calendar, here is a good way to involve the young people in a meaningful way.

Have the students get together on the Saturday before World Communion Sunday and bake bread of different types, symbolic of various cultures around the world. It's relatively easy to make good recipes for all kids of bread: black bread, rye bread, whole wheat bread, middle eastern flat bread, cornbread, rice bread, and so on. You would probably only need about five different kinds. Have the students decide which breads they'd like to make. Then have each person bring two or three ingredients with them to either the church kitchen or to some other place where there would be ample oven space.

Have the youths mix the ingredients for each dough, do the necessary kneading, and so on. Bake the loaves in a variety of loaf pans, pie pans, or no pans at all. It's easy to explain that bread doesn't always come in neat loaves. While the bread is rising, you can play some games, eat lunch, participate in some learning games, or just take it easy. While the bread bakes, the students plan how to present their bread for Communion on Sunday morning.

Since a bread recipe usually makes a couple of loaves, you might plan to enjoy the extra loaves with the group while they're still warm. Just have some butter and jam on hand. Of course you would want to save the best loaves for the Communion service.

During the service on Sunday, the students who baked the bread should bring forward their loaves and place them on the Communion table. They can also explain the particular loaf of bread they are bringing. They should tell what kind it is, what the ingredients are, where it is most common, etc. They might also say something to the effect that while there are many people around the world, symbolized by the various kinds of bread, it is Christ, remembered here in the bread and wine, who unites us all. This experience can be very meaningful for the young people as well as for the congregation. *Sue Ann Looft*

FEEDING AT THE MASTER'S TABLE

Here is a Bible study you can use to celebrate Communion. Have the group sit in a circle in preparation for the meal. Before taking part in it together, share the following insights from John 6.

1. Who prepared the meal? (6:32-35, 50-51)
• Every meal has to be prepared by someone. Jesus said that God had prepared a kind of bread even better than the manna he gave the Israelites in the desert.
• If God prepares a feast, you know that he'll serve the very best.
• God himself has made the preparations and provisions for the Lord's Supper.

2. What is the food being served? (6:48, 51, 55)
• Jesus said that the food found at the Master's table is his own flesh and blood (the sacrifice of these on the cross).
• Jesus himself is the bread God sent down from heaven.
• Jesus described his sacrifice as true food and drink (v. 55). This means that it was food and drink in the highest sense—an eternal food and drink that would satisfy the soul forever.
• God offers us an opportunity to eat this food at the Master's table—the Lord's Supper.

3. How do we eat the food? (6:53-56)
• The best way to understand what Jesus meant by eating the food is to remember what the food is: Christ's work of salvation on the cross. To "eat" his sacrifice is to receive it through faith, by trusting that what he did on the cross he did for you.
• The utensils we eat with are our hearts and minds.

4. What is the nutritional value of the food? (6:53-58)
• Jesus explained these benefits of eating his meal: eternal life, hope of the resurrection in the last day, unity with Christ—(you are what you eat), and his help to live every day.
• The spiritual nutrients found in this meal can't be found in any other food.

5. Who can take part in this meal? (6:51, 54, 56)
• Jesus said that this bread was given to the whole world.
• The table is open to anyone who willingly comes

to feed by faith at the Master's table.
• We should confess our sins and cleanse our hearts as we approach the meal (1 Cor. 11:28).

6. Three things to remember about this meal:
1. We cannot have eternal life without eating and drinking this meal.
2. Feeding by faith on this meal unites us with Christ and provides us with its benefits.
3. Feeding is a personal act. No one can make you eat or eat in your place. Only you can eat for yourself.
Brian Fullerton

CHORAL READINGS

REACH OUT AND TOUCH SOMEONE— MARK 5:24-34

A choral reading that is quite simple but very dramatic is on page 187. Even if your church does not use readings or liturgy, you will find this very effective. *Elaine Lidholm*

RICHER THAN YOU THINK— PROVERBS 3:9-10

There's a reading on page 188 that's somewhere between liturgical and humorous—yet it makes its point about giving. Your students can perform it during the worship service immediately before the offering. Assign the individual parts to the same three kids, or give several kids a line or two. *Mike Heinz*

BUILT TO CODE—PARABLE OF THE HOUSE BUILDERS, MATTHEW 7 & LUKE 6

You will find a dramatic reading on page 189 of the parable of the wise man and the foolish man (Matthew 7; Luke 6) who both built houses. It would be especially effective in a youth-led worship service. *Bob Stebe*

Reach Out and Touch Someone

MARK 5:24-34

NARRATOR: A great crowd followed Jesus and thronged about him. In the crowd was a woman.

VOICE 1: A sick woman,

VOICE 2: a woman in need,

VOICE 3: a woman who believed!

NARRATOR: Though she had suffered much under many physicians and was no better, but rather worse,

VOICE 3: Still she believed!

WOMAN: If I could only touch his robe, just a touch, I shall be made well.

VOICE 2: Just a touch?

VOICE 1: Of his robe?!

VOICES 1 & 2: Foolish woman!!!

WOMAN: If I could just touch him! *(pause)*

JESUS: Who touched me?

VOICE 3: Touched you? Lord, hundreds touch you—even now.

VOICE 2: Look around, Lord.

VOICE 1: Be sensible, Lord.

JESUS: Someone touched me, took the power from me. *(gently)* Who touched me?

VOICE 2: *(quick to accuse)* She did it! I saw her!

VOICE 1: Yes, she did it.

VOICE 2: Confess.

VOICE 3: Tell him it was you.

VOICES 1,2,3: Confess!! *(silence)*

WOMAN: *(very quietly, a bit fearfully)* It was I, Lord. I touched you— to be made well.

VOICE 3: She wants to be made well.

VOICES 1 & 2: We told you, Jesus. She did it—

VOICE 2: *(scornfully)* To be made well.

JESUS: Daughter, your faith has made you whole. Go in peace now. Be healed.

VOICE 1: *(with awe)* She...she touched him...

VOICE 2: ...to be made well.

VOICE 3: She believed!

Richer Than You Think
PROVERBS 3:9-10

ALL: Honor the Lord with your wealth!

1: Well, that leaves me out.

2: Me, too. I'm sure not wealthy.

3: *(tongue-in-cheek)* Oh, poor little _____ *(name speaker 2)*. Could barely afford _____ (that new pickup, those Nikes, those jeans, that new Jars of Clay CD, etc.).

ALL: Honor the Lord with the first fruits of all your crops.

1: I ain't no farmer. I ain't got no crops.

2: You ain't got no good grammar, neither.

3: But you do have more food than you need. When was the last time you went to bed hungry?

ALL: Then your barns will be filled to overflowing.

2: Sounds good to me!

1: But I ain't got no barns 'cuz I ain't got no crops.

3: But you do have a garage that's so full of stuff you can't park your car in it.

ALL: And your vats will brim over with new wine.

1: Hmpf. That's obviously not written for me.

2: Yeah. We're not even legal age yet.

3: You don't get it yet, do you? This proverb isn't about crops or barns or wine—it about us. We are wealthy.

1: Huh?...Oh, I think I'm beginning to understand.

2: Yeah, we have all that we need and more.

3: Now you got it! And more than that, we have Christ, who gives us ultimate meaning through eternal life.

ALL: By George, we think they've got it!

Built to Code

Matthew 7, Luke 6

READER: Hey, everybody—come on down here! I've got a story to tell! *(all come running from every corner of the sanctuary and sit at the feet of the storyteller)*

READER: Everyone who hears the words of Jesus, everyone who see the example of Jesus and does the same, is like a wise man...*(wise man stands up from the crowd, looks very wise, and steps off to stage right, facing the congregation)*

READER:...who built his house upon the rock.

(Wise man begins the building process: Stomps ground showing that it's firm and hard—stomps so hard, in fact, that he hurts his foot. Then he goes to one person at a time from the crowd at the storyteller's feet and uses them as pillars for his house. He places each one in place by "pounding" them into the ground—the "pillars" gradually sink to kneeling positions as they're pounded—and nailing them together. Wise man builds a complete "house" around himself and stands proudly in his new home.)

READER: And the rains fell *(some in the crowd with squirt guns shoot water up and onto the house so that the congregation can see the water)* and the floods came *(two people with blue streamers enter the sanctuary running down the aisle and around the house)* and the winds blew and beat upon that house *(the crowd blows on the house)*—but it did not fall apart *(house sways a little from all these things, but stands firm)* because it had been built upon the rock. *(pillars and wise man smile proudly)*

READER: *(with emphasis)* BUT everyone who hears the words of Jesus, everyone who sees the example of Jesus, and does NOT do the same...*(crowd's pride disappears with these words, and they respond with a "Huh?," then slowly gather back around storyteller's feet)*...everyone who does NOT do the same as Jesus is like the foolish man...*(foolish man stands up from the crowd and walks to stage left, facing the congregation)*

READER:...who built his house upon the sand. *(foolish man walks to gather his pillars from the crowd, walking as if walking in sand. He puts the pillars into the sand—they go in easily, but are unsteady, crooked, wobbly.)*

READER: *(same actions as before during this line...)* And the rains fell and the floods came and the winds blew and beat upon that house—*(...but this time the pillars and foolish man are roughly tossed about and look terrified)* and it FELL, *(house crashes down)* and great was the fall of it. *(everyone quietly slips back to sit at the storyteller's feet to hear the rest of his words)*

READER: And when Jesus had finished telling this same story, the crowds were astonished at his teaching, for he taught them as one who had authority, and not as their other leaders.

THE END

  189

THE APOSTLES CREED

When recited by young people, the Apostles Creed is often meaningless. The version on page 191 is good for use with youths or adults in a creative worship experience. One group reads the part in bold type, another group reads the responses that follow. *Larry Houseman*

PEACE, LOVE, AND JOY WORSHIP

This is an excellent creative worship idea, which is simple, yet effective. As each person enters the room, give him a "peace" flower, a "love" flower, or a "joy" flower. Balloons may be substituted for flowers if you choose, with *peace*, *love*, or *joy* written on them. Regardless, the purpose is to divide the group into three groups so the reading on page 192 can be read by the appropriate groups, as a responsive reading. The verse in each section may be read by the leader and the response (the bold type portion) by the group, or the group can read the entire segment, or the boys in the group can read the verse with the girls answering with the response, or any other way you want. However you feel the most meaning can be read into it is the best way.

Close with a round of prayer, passing the peace, batting the balloons, or however you wish. *Cindy Baw*

RESPONSIVE LORD'S PRAYER

The Lord's Prayer is repeated so many times during church service that its meaning is often overlooked or lost altogether. The responsive reading on page 193 is designed to cause people to think more about the meaning of the Lord's Prayer as it is being recited in worship. *Donald M. Topp*

OTHER WORSHIP IDEAS

CANDLELIGHT SERVICE

At the end of a youth program or worship service, give each one present a small candle. From the light of a candle at the altar, light each person's candle. As the candles are being lighted, sing some very worshipful songs or have complete silence.

When all of the candles are lighted, slowly leave the building to a designated place outside. At the vacant spot, you have formed a cross on the ground with adding machine tape. (This should be done before the group comes out.) Explain to the group that the candles they are holding represent their lives. Have them place their candles on the paper cross. When each candle has been placed, you have a burning cross. The group then forms a circle around the cross and sings. A short devotion may be given and should be ended with a prayer. The group should leave quietly allowing others to remain as long as they wish. *Clifford Lee*

THE COVERING BLOOD OF JESUS

Symbols are very meaningful to young people. On the beach for a service let sand represent sin (dirty and more than you can count). Have everyone make a footprint in the sand and put some of the sand out of the footprint into a container that can be closed. As part of the service, pour wine over the sand in the container until it is full and close it, the personal sin. Just as the wine covers all the sand, so the blood of Christ covers all my sin. Let the people take their containers home and put them in a prominent place to be constantly reminded of the forgiveness of sin. Baby food jars as containers may symbolize the faith of an infant. Medicine vials as containers may symbolize the "cure" for all of us. Use your own imagination. *Dietrich Schleef*

BODY OF CHRIST WORSHIP

This activity is good for a youth worship service, emphasizing the body of Christ—not only relationships between believers, but also the relationship between a corporate body of believers and its head.

Prior to the service or time of use, have an artist in your group or church make a life-size (between five and six feet) human silhouette out of colored poster board. (You many need to use a number of pieces of poster board.) Select a different color for the legs and arms of the body; the head, neck, and shoulders; and the main part of the body. Next, cut the body into a puzzle—the exact number of pieces that you have teens and adults participating. But do not cut the head into any parts. In bold print with a magic marker, write across the head: "Jesus Christ."

The Apostles' Creed

I believe in God the Father Almighty, maker of heaven and earth

and maker of black, brown, red, yellow, and white persons,

And in Jesus Christ—his only son

our Lord, conceived by the Holy Spirit

To live in eternity

Born of the Virgin Mary,

To live on earth.

Suffered under Pontius Pilate,

And you and me

was crucified, dead, and buried.

The third day he arose from the dead

and ascended into heaven and sitteth

on the right hand of God the Father

Almighty. From thence he shall come

to judge the quick and dead—

And that's you and me.

I believe in the Holy Spirit;

Present in five o'clock traffic

present in family discussions

present in mixed marriages

present in the lives of those on welfare

present in the people of China, America, Russia, and Africa.

present in this congregation and present in myself.

I believe in the holy catholic church

Which includes Baptists, Episcopalians, Lutherans, Roman Catholics, United Methodists, Presbyterians, and a lot of others.

I believe in the communion of saints

And the communion of all people around one universal table.

I believe in the forgiveness of sin

For community leaders apprehended by the law

for people who spread rumors

for those who slam down phones

for people who transfer when they are mad

for proud professors—for bullies—

for murderers—for prostitutes

for priests and pastors, for me.

I believe in the resurrection of the body—

For people I can't stand

for those who criticize my work

for beauty queens

for my father and mother

for myself,

And the life everlasting,

I am trying Lord. Am I a believer? (all) AMEN

Peace, Love, and Joy

LOVE: Love is very patient and kind, never jealous or envious, never boastful or proud. (1 Corinthians 13:4)

> I asked God for love.
>
> Instead he showed me
>
> How he could love through me.

JOY: He is my strength, my shield from every danger. I trusted in him and he helped me. Joy rises in my heart. (Psalm 28:7)

> I asked God for joy.
>
> Instead he let me fully trust
>
> From whence my joy came.

PEACE: Since we have been made right in God's sight by faith in his promises, we can have real peace with him. (Romans 5:1)

> I asked God for peace.
>
> Instead I was confessing everything.
>
> Then my peace came.

LOVE: Love does not demand its own way; it is not irritable or touchy, nor does it hold grudges. (1 Corinthians 13:5)

> I asked God to give me my own way.
>
> Instead he let me give to my family—
>
> Yes, mother, father, brother, and sister.

JOY: We confidently and joyfully look forward to becoming all that God has had in mind for us to be. (Romans 5:2)

> I asked God to make me successful.

> Instead he gave me humility.
>
> Joyfully, I followed his will for my life.

PEACE: His peace will keep your thoughts and hearts quiet and at rest as you trust in Christ Jesus. (Philippians 4:7)

> I asked God that I might worry less.
>
> Instead he took all the worry from me
>
> And peace was mine.

LOVE: If you love someone you will always believe in him, always expect the best of him and always stand your ground defending him. (1 Corinthians 13:7)

> I asked and expected too much, God.
>
> Instead I learned to love my family,
>
> And all around me in a positive way.

JOY: O God, in mercy bless us. Let your face beam with joy as you look down on us. (Psalm 67:1)

> I asked God for discipline in
>
> church attendance.
>
> Instead he showed me what worship
>
> Is all about.
>
> O joy in his worship!

PEACE: He will give his people strength, he will bless them with peace. (Psalm 29:11)

> I asked God for peace in all the world.
>
> Instead he showed me his timing
>
> In my life and for mankind.

Responsive Lord's Prayer

LEADER: Our Father

PEOPLE: a real person, who cares for and loves me

LEADER: Who art in heaven

PEOPLE: living higher than I am, understanding more than I

LEADER: Hallowed be thy name

PEOPLE: we honor and praise your holy name

LEADER: Thy kingdom come

PEOPLE: yes, come quickly Lord Jesus, live in our lives

LEADER: Thy will be done

PEOPLE: you always know what is best for us

LEADER: On earth as it is in heaven

PEOPLE: as you always have and always will

LEADER: Give us this day our daily bread

PEOPLE: you have always supplied our needs

LEADER: And forgive us our debts

PEOPLE: in the name of Christ

LEADER: As we forgive our debtors

PEOPLE: seventy times seven, Lord

LEADER: And lead us not into temptation

PEOPLE: give us the strength to resist

LEADER: But deliver us from evil

PEOPLE: when we fail, you come through

LEADER: For thine is the kingdom

PEOPLE: in which we share

LEADER: and the power

PEOPLE: greater than anything we have ever known

LEADER: And the glory forever

ALL: Amen!

At this part of your service, direct each teen and adult (including yourself) to pick up one piece of the puzzle and sign in ink his or her name on the puzzle part. Next, direct all with the same color to gather into a group to fit their pieces together before the whole group puts the entire puzzle together. While fitting their pieces together, someone should tape the head of the body to the wall (or whatever way you choose to mount the puzzle).

After each group has worked out its part of the puzzle, all three groups should get together to put the puzzle into a complete form. First, direct the group with the neck and shoulders to attach its parts under the head, followed by the group with the body parts, followed by the legs and arms.

This activity should be used as part of the worship time, not for the entire service. Reading certain portions of Scripture (1 Corinthians 12), singing appropriate hymns or choruses, taking Communion, sharing, and prayer as well as this activity make for an effective and meaningful time of worship.

This activity vividly demonstrates what Paul was talking about in terms of Christians being parts of the body of Christ. It gives teens and adults an opportunity to work together in building a symbol of the body of Christ. Variations of this basic pattern are possible to illustrate other truths—for example, what the body is like when certain parts are sick, broken, or missing. *Douglas Swank*

DEATH DRUM

This idea works well in a worship service stressing hunger and starvation in the world. According to statistics (which you may need to update) someone dies of starvation every eight seconds. During the worship service, have someone beat a drum every eight seconds to symbolize another death taking place. The drum interrupting the normal course of the service very dramatically illustrates how we often try to ignore the problem of hunger in the world, but it just won't go away unless we do something about it. *Nancy Lee Head*

NAILING OUR SINS TO THE CROSS

As a symbolic representation of how Christ took our sins with him to the cross, have students write their sins down on pieces of paper and one at a time nail them to a wooden cross. After a time of individual silent prayer, the sins can be removed from the cross and destroyed, symbolizing how our sins have been erased from God's memory forever. *Lanny Bruner*

TWO-DIMENSIONAL PRAYER

Most prayer is somewhat one-sided, that is, we do all the talking. We rarely listen to what God has to say to us. In an effort to do something about this in a symbolic way, one youth group composed a dialogue with God at a retreat by asking God questions they wanted some answers to. They then wrote what they thought God's answers might be based on Scripture and their understanding of the nature of God. The finished product was then presented to the church in a contemporary worship service. Each young person would step forward and pray one question, which was then answered by a tape recording of the responses, recorded with much echo and played back to have a mysterious, awesome quality. Perhaps your group can compose a similar prayer as a worship experience A sample is below.. *Bruce Brigden*

A Dialogue With God

God, are you really there? I need to talk to someone who knows the truth about life and can give me some real answers.

I AM HERE AND I AM THE ANSWER TO ALL QUESTIONS. THE WORDS YOU HEAR COME FROM YOUR OWN HEART. I SPEAK NOT WORDS BUT THE WORD.

Where are you, God? Are you in Heaven or everywhere? Am I talking to you "long distance" or are you right here?

I AM WHERE YOU ARE AND THERE IS NO PLACE THAT I AM NOT. THERE IS NO DISTANCE! I AM BESIDE YOU, ABOVE YOU, AROUND YOU AND WITHIN YOU.

Do you always hear us when we pray? Or is this time a special deal?

I HEAR ALL YOU SAY OR THINK OR DREAM OR IMAGINE, AND I CARE.

While I'm hearing you in words, there are lots of things I've always wondered about. Would you tell me what I want to know?

I AM WHAT YOU WANT TO KNOW. ASK AND LISTEN AND HEAR!

God, why did you make man, anyway?

I MADE YOU FOR MYSELF AND FOR YOURSELF. YOU WERE MADE TO BELONG TO ME. APART FROM ME, YOU HAVE NO MEANING, LIKE A SHIP WITHOUT A SEA.

Were we created by evolution, from cells in the ocean or did you make us from the dust of the earth, personally, like Genesis says?

YOU, AND THE DUST, AND THE SEA, I MADE FROM NOTHING AND THEY STILL ARE NOTHING, APART FROM ME. ALL THINGS YOU KNOW ARE BUT AN ECHO OF MY WORD.

Now, God, I don't understand that, just answer simply, How did you create me?

I CREATED YOU ETERNALLY, ABOVE AND BEYOND ALL YOU KNOW OF SPACE AND TIME. ON EARTH, YOU ARE NOT YET CREATED. I AM STILL BUILDING WHAT YOU SHALL BE.

Lord, will there ever be peace on earth? When will it be?

THE WORLD CAN NEVER BE AT PEACE. I MADE THE EARTH FOR CHANGE AND UNREST AND TRIAL.

You mean that there's no cure for the world's problems and troubles?

FEAR NOT: TIME CURES MOST PROBLEMS AND ETERNITY CURES THEM ALL!

Why do you let men sin? Why don't you make men live as you planned?

SIN IS PART OF MY PLAN. TO CHOOSE FREELY, A MAN MUST BE ABLE TO CHOOSE AGAINST ME.

Is the church doing what you want it to?

ALL THINGS DO MY WILL. THE CHURCH IS THOSE WHO SERVE ME BECAUSE THEY KNOW ME AND LOVE ME. THE REST OF THE WORLD SERVES ME IN SPITE OF THEMSELVES.

Do people really still respond to your call today, like in bible times?

I AM IRRESISTIBLE. ALL MEN OBEY MY COMMANDS. SOME MEN ALSO CHOOSE TO OBEY MY LOVE.

God, what does it mean—to love?

I AM ONENESS. I AM LOVE. TO LOVE IS TO BECOME A PART OF ME.

So there really are some true christians in the world today?

THERE ARE MANY IN THIS PLACE WHO LOVE ME MORE THAN LIFE AND WHO SHALL GIVE ME THEIR LIVES WHEN I ASK.

Is the Judgment Day near?

JUDGMENT DAY IS ALWAYS NEAR: IT IS TODAY!

So be it, then, Lord, we'll be seeing you! God be with us!

I AM...(echoing off into the distance.)

SINGING WORSHIP SERVICE

This is an attempt to put more meaning into the songs we sing in church. Have the kids (one at a time) request favorite songs. The only condition to singing it is that the kid must give a personally meaningful reason for requesting that particular song. *Ron Wilburn*

WORSHIP DIARY

This is an idea designed to enrich your group's worship experience and at the same time receive some constructive feedback on this most important area in the church's life. Have each member in your group begin a worship diary in which they write their response to the worship service.

They should be writing their responses to questions like these: How did I feel? Was I bored, happy, moved? What was the response of the people around me? What was most helpful? Least helpful? Did I learn anything? If so, what? Did I feel restricted or inhibited? Did the sermon help me at all? Have the group keep the diary for about four weeks and then have a meeting where everyone compares notes. The discussion following could be quite enlightening. *Vernon Edington*

LET THERE BE LIGHT

This is a good discussion experience that would also be effective during a time of worship. It should be done at night (or in a room that can be darkened), and it works best with smaller groups. You will need candles and Bibles.

The group sits on the floor in a circle. Explain at the beginning that they will be doing the teaching themselves. The subject is "light." Ask them to spend a few minutes looking up passages of Scripture that deal with light. They may help each other, or they can use Bible concordances, etc. to help them find Scripture that talks about light in some way. (Take as long as you need for this.) Tell the group that they will need to memorize the passage, or at least the thought, as they may not have enough light to read.

Now turn out the lights, making it as dark as possible. Give each person an unlit candle. Have each person go around the circle and say something about darkness. This can be a definition of darkness or just a statement about what darkness reminds them about.

Next, light one candle, telling the group that they will pass the flame around the circle from candle to candle. As the flame is passed around, each person is to share what they have discovered that the Bible says about light. They can quote their passage or comment on the meaning of the passage. They then light the candle of the next person, who also shares. Do this until everyone's candle is lit. You as the leader can then wrap up any way you want. The result is usually very meaningful. *Jerry Martin*

PARAPHRASING THE HYMNAL

Here's a great learning strategy that everyone will enjoy. Have the students in your group take some old familiar hymns and paraphrase them. They should read the hymns and try to restate the message of the hymn in common, everyday language. Do this with a number of hymns from your church's hymnbook, and then have the youth read them to the adults in your congregation at one of your services, and see if they can identify the hymn that has been paraphrased.

This exercise can accomplish three things: First, it helps students to look for the meaning in the hymns that they sing in church. Second, it shows the value of the poetry in the song. Usually students will discover that even though their paraphrased versions are easy to understand and conceptually correct, they still lack the impact of the original hymn. Third, the exercise is fun and gets everybody involved.

Here are some sample hymn paraphrases (first verses only), written by one group of young people. *Jerry Daniel*

I NEED THEE EVERY HOUR

There's no time of day or night, Lord, when I'm self sufficient. The calming influence of your words keeps me going. I hope you will help me, since I'm so lost without you.

"Joy to the World"
Since Jesus came in royal power, the whole earth can be glad, if we will only allow him to be our master. To do this we must each one individually get our hearts ready for him; but when we do this we'll rejoice just like the natural and supernatural world does.

"All Hail the Power of Jesus' Name"
Everyone, including the angles, should lie down in homage to the greatness of the Savior of the world. In fact, we should be willing to let him be our boss all the time, even our King.

196

ASH WORSHIP

This idea is not really a new one, but rather a recovery of a church worship practice that is easily used in a youth group setting. This is based on a service for Ash Wednesday, but is appropriate for use at other times of the year.

In a group setting have the leader talk about sin and grace. After the talk have students privately write down on a piece of paper something they wish to be forgiven for (or they can draw a symbol). Collect the papers and set them on fire over a nonflammable trash can or wok (have a fire extinguisher on hand for an emergency).

Collect the ashes and after they have cooled, invite each student to place her finger in the ashes and turn to the person on her right and make the sign of the cross on that person's forehead. The leader can then explain that in our repentance, Christ has forgiven us and is with us. This can be a powerful way to understand sin, grace, and forgiveness. *Malcolm McQueen*

ARMOR OF GOD

This idea is a visual translation of Ephesians 6:10-18 that's especially appropriate for a youth service. You'll need a cast of seven or eight: a reader, a catcher, two or three people planted in the audience who can throw a baseball well, a base stealer, a second baseman, and an ump. The script is on page 198.

The reader can stand on stage, a little off center; the catcher, a few feet away from her, a pile of catcher's equipment at his feet. Off to one side is second base, by which the second baseman and ump stand.

The catcher dresses and performs according to the following script during the reading of the Scripture passage. As the reader begins, the catcher is sitting in a chair. *Steve Swope*

BAND-AID BURDEN BEARERS

All you need for this close to a service or study about bearing each other's burdens (Galatians 6:2) is a box of Band-Aids and a pencil for each student. Distribute the Band-Aids and pencils, instructing the kids to anonymously write on the Band-Aid wrapper a big problem or frustration they are facing. Students should have enough privacy to write their problem without it being seen by others. As they finish writing instruct them to come to the front (to the altar, to a cross fabricated from two-by-fours or from cardboard, to the steps, to a kneeling rail, etc.) and lay down their "burdens" (their Band-Aids) in a pile.

When all Band-Aids are at the front, ask the students to pair up with each other (preferably with someone besides a best friend), come to the front together, choose two Band-Aids at random, then find some corner in the room where the pair can pray for the problems on the two Band-Aids.

Then, to symbolically bear each other's burden (and this is a practical way to remember to pray for each other), the students should come to the front again, carefully remove the Band-Aids from their wrappers, and attach the Band-Aids themselves to their shoulders (where burdens are carried). The wrappers (with the anonymous problems jotted on them) should be saved to use as a bookmark, to tape to a mirror—to put wherever the burden-bearing students will see them often and remember to pray.

Depending on the mood of the meeting, you may urge the kids to keep the Band-Aids on for the remainder of the day or evening, whether they go to work, out to eat, or to home, and be ready to explain its significance to anyone who asks. *Michael Capps*

KINGDOM CROSS

When kids gain an insight or make a decision, creating an item for display—a modern memorial of sorts—can be a powerful reminder of the event.

Before the session build a wooden form for a modest-sized cross (see diagram). Just prior to the meeting,

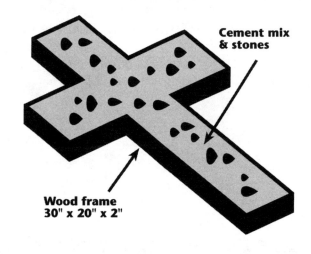

Cement mix & stones

Wood frame 30" x 20" x 2"

Armor of God

Reader

Finally, be strong in the Lord and in his mighty power. Put on the full armor of God so that you can take your stand against the devil's schemes. For our struggle is not against flesh and blood, but against the rulers, against the authorities, against the powers of this dark world and against the spiritual forces of evil in the heavenly realms.

Therefore put on the full armor of God, so that when the day of evil comes, you may be able to stand your ground, and after you have done everything, to stand.

Stand firm then, with the belt of truth buckled around your waist, with the breastplate of righteousness in place, and with your feet fitted with the readiness that comes from the gospel of peace.

In addition to all this, take up the shield of faith,

with which you can extinguish all the flaming arrows of the evil one.

Take the helmet of salvation

and the sword of the Spirit, which is the word of God.

And pray in the Spirit on all occasions with all kinds of prayers and requests. With this in mind, be alert

and always keep on praying for all the saints.

Catcher

(Walks over to the equipment)

(Puts on his chest protector then puts on baseball shoes and shin guards)

(Slips his hand into his catcher's glove and pounds it two or three times)

(A couple people in the audience aggressively throw baseballs or tennis balls at him—which he catches deftly)

(Puts on catcher's mask)

(Picks up baseball)

(Someone else in the audience tries to "steal" second base. The catcher sees him and rifles the ball to the second baseperson, who tags the would-be stealer. The ump gestures dramatically and yells, "You're out!")

pour cement into the form. (A small amount of calcium chloride will make it harden quickly.) The cross should be somewhat mobile, so don't make it too large. Also have on hand two baskets of small stones—one basket containing common rocks, the second containing polished stones (you can pick them up inexpensively at rock and gem shops). At the session discuss with your students how we experience the reign of God now in the ordinary joys and struggles of life, yet we look forward to the unveiling of the full glory of the kingdom. Then pass around the two baskets of rocks, allowing the teens to select one stone from each basket. Ask them to reflect on how the two stones represent their own experience of the now and the not yet. Prompt them to focus on one or two specific examples of the struggle and joy they're experiencing right now, represented by the common stone. Then give them time to handle the polished stone as they consider their hopes for the kingdom to come.

After a few minutes of reflection, roll the cement cross up to the front as you explain how believers experience the kingdom of God through the cross. As music plays invite the teens to come and set their stones in the wet cement in such a way that they are visible. You may want to read 1 Peter 2:4ff about being living stones in the temple of God. Once the cross hardens, it can be used as a centerpiece for future worship times. *Bill Swedberg*

Youth Ministry Programming

Camps, Retreats, Missions, & Service Ideas (Ideas Library)

Compassionate Kids: Practical Ways to Involve Your Students in Mission and Service

Creative Bible Lessons from the Old Testament

Creative Bible Lessons in 1 & 2 Corinthians

Creative Bible Lessons in John: Encounters with Jesus

Creative Bible Lessons in Romans: Faith on Fire!

Creative Bible Lessons on the Life of Christ

Creative Bible Lessons in Psalms

Creative Junior High Programs from A to Z, Vol. 1 (A-M)

Creative Junior High Programs from A to Z, Vol. 2 (N-Z)

Creative Meetings, Bible Lessons, & Worship Ideas (Ideas Library)

Crowd Breakers & Mixers (Ideas Library)

Downloading the Bible Leader's Guide

Drama, Skits, & Sketches (Ideas Library)

Drama, Skits, & Sketches 2 (Ideas Library)

Dramatic Pauses

Everyday Object Lessons

Games (Ideas Library)

Games 2 (Ideas Library)

Good Sex: A Whole-Person Approach to Teenage Sexuality and God

Great Fundraising Ideas for Youth Groups

More Great Fundraising Ideas for Youth Groups

Great Retreats for Youth Groups

Holiday Ideas (Ideas Library)

Hot Illustrations for Youth Talks

More Hot Illustrations for Youth Talks

Still More Hot Illustrations for Youth Talks

Ideas Library on CD-ROM

Incredible Questionnaires for Youth Ministry

Junior High Game Nights

More Junior High Game Nights

Kickstarters: 101 Ingenious Intros to Just about Any Bible Lesson

Live the Life! Student Evangelism Training Kit

Memory Makers

The Next Level Leader's Guide

Play It! Over 150 Great Games for Youth Groups

Roaring Lambs

Special Events (Ideas Library)

Spontaneous Melodramas

Student Leadership Training Manual

Student Underground: An Event Curriculum on the Persecuted Church

Super Sketches for Youth Ministry

Talking the Walk

Teaching the Bible Creatively

Videos That Teach

What Would Jesus Do? Youth Leader's Kit

Wild Truth Bible Lessons

Wild Truth Bible Lessons 2

Wild Truth Bible Lessons—Pictures of God

Worship Services for Youth Groups

Professional Resources

Administration, Publicity, & Fundraising (Ideas Library)

Equipped to Serve: Volunteer Youth Worker Training Course

Help! I'm a Junior High Youth Worker!

Help! I'm a Small-Group Leader!

Help! I'm a Sunday School Teacher!

Help! I'm a Volunteer Youth Worker!

How to Expand Your Youth Ministry

How to Speak to Youth...and Keep Them Awake at the Same Time

Junior High Ministry (Updated & Expanded)

The Ministry of Nurture: A Youth Worker's Guide to Discipling Teenagers

Purpose-Driven Youth Ministry

Purpose-Driven Youth Ministry Training Kit

So That's Why I Keep Doing This! 52 Devotional Stories for Youth Workers

A Youth Ministry Crash Course

The Youth Worker's Handbook to Family Ministry

Discussion Starter Resources

Discussion & Lesson Starters (Ideas Library)

Discussion & Lesson Starters 2 (Ideas Library)

EdgeTV

Get 'Em Talking

Keep 'Em Talking!

High School TalkSheets

More High School TalkSheets

High School TalkSheets: Psalms and Proverbs

Junior High TalkSheets

More Junior High TalkSheets

Junior High TalkSheets: Psalms and Proverbs

Real Kids: Short Cuts

Real Kids: The Real Deal—on Friendship, Loneliness, Racism, & Suicide

Real Kids: The Real Deal—on Sexual Choices, Family Matters, & Loss

Real Kids: The Real Deal—on Stressing Out, Addictive Behavior, Great Comebacks, & Violence

Real Kids: Word on the Street

Have You Ever...? 450 Intriguing Questions Guaranteed to Get Teenagers Talking

Unfinished Sentences: 450 Tantalizing Statement-Starters to Get Teenagers Talking & Thinking

What If...? 450 Thought-Provoking Questions to Get Teenagers Talking, Laughing, and Thinking

Would You Rather...? 465 Provocative Questions to Get Teenagers Talking

Art Source Clip Art

Stark Raving Clip Art (print)

Youth Group Activities (print)

Clip Art Library Version 2.0 (CD-ROM)

Digital Resources

Clip Art Library Version 2.0 (CD-ROM)

Ideas Library on CD-ROM

Videos & Video Curricula

EdgeTV

Equipped to Serve: Volunteer Youth Worker Training Course

The Heart of Youth Ministry: A Morning with Mike Yaconelli

Good Sex: A Whole-Person Approach to Teenage Sexuality and God

Live the Life! Student Evangelism Training Kit

Purpose-Driven Youth Ministry Training Kit

Real Kids: Short Cuts

Real Kids: The Real Deal—on Friendship, Loneliness, Racism, & Suicide

Real Kids: The Real Deal—on Sexual Choices, Family Matters, & Loss

Real Kids: The Real Deal—on Stressing Out, Addictive Behavior, Great Comebacks, & Violence

Real Kids: Word on the Street

Student Underground: An Event Curriculum on the Persecuted Church

Understanding Your Teenager Video Curriculum

Student Books

Downloading the Bible: A Rough Guide to the New Testament

Downloading the Bible: A Rough Guide to the Old Testament

Grow For It Journal

Grow For It Journal through the Scriptures

Spiritual Challenge Journal: The Next Level

Teen Devotional Bible

What Would Jesus Do? Spiritual Challenge Journal

What Almost Nobody Will Tell You About Sex

Wild Truth Journal for Junior Highers

Wild Truth Journal—Pictures of God